"THE AMBER GODS"
and Other Stories

AMERICAN WOMEN WRITERS SERIES

Joanne Dobson, Judith Fetterley, and Elaine Showalter, series editors

ALTERNATIVE ALCOTT
Louisa May Alcott
Elaine Showalter, editor

STORIES FROM THE COUNTRY OF
LOST BORDERS
Mary Austin
Marjorie Pryse, editor

CLOVERNOOK SKETCHES AND
OTHER STORIES
Alice Cary
Judith Fetterley, editor

HOBOMOK AND OTHER WRITINGS
ON INDIANS
Lydia Maria Child
Carolyn L. Karcher, editor

"HOW CELIA CHANGED HER MIND"
AND SELECTED STORIES
Rose Terry Cooke
Elizabeth Ammons, editor

THE LAMPLIGHTER
Maria Susanna Cummins
Nina Baym, editor

RUTH HALL AND OTHER
WRITINGS
Fanny Fern
Joyce Warren, editor

QUICKSAND AND PASSING
Nella Larsen
Deborah E. McDowell, editor

OLDTOWN FOLKS
Harriet Beecher Stowe
Dorothy Berkson, editor

HOPE LESLIE
Catharine Maria Sedgwick
Mary Kelley, editor

THE HIDDEN HAND
E.D.E.N. Southworth
Joanne Dobson, editor

"THE AMBER GODS" AND
OTHER STORIES
Harriet Prescott Spofford
Alfred Bendixen, editor

WOMEN ARTISTS, WOMEN
EXILES
"Miss Grief" and Other Stories
Constance Fenimore Woolson
Joan Myers Weimer, editor

"THE AMBER GODS"
and Other Stories

HARRIET PRESCOTT SPOFFORD

Edited and with an Introduction by

ALFRED BENDIXEN

RUTGERS UNIVERSITY PRESS

New Brunswick and London

Library of Congress Cataloging-in-Publication Data

Spofford, Harriet Elizabeth Prescott, 1835–1921.
The amber gods, and other stories / Harriet Prescott Spofford
edited and with an introduction by Alfred Bendixen.
p.   cm.—(American women writers series)
Bibliography: p.
Contents: In a cellar—The amber gods—Circumstance—In the
Maguerriwock—The moonstone mass—The black Bess—Her story—
Miss Susan's love affair—Old Madame—The godmothers.
ISBN 0-8135-1400-2   ISBN 0-8135-1401-0 (pbk.)
I. Bendixen, Alfred.   II.   Title.   III.   Series.
PS2896.B46 1989   88-28299
813'.4—dc19   CIP

British Cataloging-in-Publication information available

CONTENTS

Acknowledgments vii

Introduction ix

Selected Bibliography xxxv

A Note on the Text xxxviii

In a Cellar 1

The Amber Gods 37

Circumstance 84

In the Maguerriwock 97

The Moonstone Mass 115

The Black Bess 129

Her Story 148

Miss Susan's Love Affair 167

Old Madame 181

The Godmothers 206

Explanatory Notes 217

ACKNOWLEDGMENTS

I am grateful to the librarians and libraries that provided access to Spofford's unpublished letters as well as valuable information, especially Natalie Sonevytsky and Tatiana Keis, Barnard College; Charles W. Mann, Penn State University; Ruth Mortimer, Smith College; Sidney Ives, University of Florida; Prudence Backman, Essex Institute; Sara S. Hodson, Huntington Library; Jean F. Preston, Princeton University; Fred Bauman, Library of Congress; and the library staffs of the New York Public Library, American Antiquarian Society, Historical Society of Pennsylvania, and the University of Virginia. Quotations from unpublished letters are printed with the permission of the repositories. I also owe special thanks to four students at Barnard College who read Spofford's tales with care and enthusiasm and shared their impressions with me: Elizabeth Larsen, Jacqueline Shea Murphy, Victoria Pesce, and Beth Wightman. Jane Dieckmann generously offered advice and information that made the preparation of the notes much easier. My greatest debts are to Leslie Mitchner and Judith Fetterley, who provided perceptive critiques of earlier versions of the introduction.

INTRODUCTION

In 1858 James Russell Lowell faced a peculiar problem. He was serving as editor of the recently established *Atlantic Monthly,* and a "demure little Yankee girl" had submitted a story of such power and ingenuity that he seriously doubted her authorship of the piece (Higginson, *Letters* 103). Here was a vivid tale of mystery and political intrigue with picturesque descriptions of Parisian society, brilliant flashes of dialogue, and a wickedly cosmopolitan tone. The carefully wrought series of dramatic confrontations through which the plot unfolded seemed to reveal an intimate knowledge of European diplomacy and foreign mores as well as the sure hand of an experienced author. No American writer had ever done anything like it. How could this shy young woman from a sheltered New England background have produced such a work? Lowell suspected that it was really a translation from the French. His doubts were relieved only when Thomas Wentworth Higginson, who now is remembered mostly as Emily Dickinson's "dear perceptor," assured him and the rest of the *Atlantic*'s editorial staff that Harriet E. Prescott was indeed the author of "In a Cellar."

The story's appearance in the February 1859 issue of the *Atlantic Monthly* created a sensation. Rose Terry Cooke, who was herself one of the most important contributors of fiction to the *Atlantic,* later said that "this new and brilliant contribution dazzled us all with the splendors, the manners, the political intrigues, the sin-spiced witchery of Parisian life" (531).

Spofford confirmed her ability to dazzle readers with her second contribution to the *Atlantic,* "The Amber Gods" (Jan. and Feb. 1860), a long story that seemed to challenge the conventional boundaries of both language and morality. It featured a completely self-centered female narrator who indulged in lavish descriptions and pagan speculations as she proceeded to defy all the pieties of nineteenth-century America. This romantic tale culminated in the revelation that the narrator was actually dead and speaking from beyond the grave. Elizabeth Stuart Phelps singled out the story in her 1910 essay on "Stories That Stay," asserting that though she could no longer remember a single detail of the plot, "The Amber Gods" "took a grip upon something deeper than taste or imagination in me" and that she could never forget the "alien chill" that ran through her fifty years earlier as she read the final sentence.

Other works by this new writer also attracted attention. "Circumstance" (*Atlantic,* May 1860), a tale of a pioneer woman menaced by a ferocious animal that is kept at bay only by the woman's songs, earned the admiration of writers as different as Emily Dickinson and William Dean Howells. Dickinson wrote to her sister-in-law, Susan Huntington Dickinson, praising the story as "the only thing that I ever saw in my life that I did not think I could have written myself" and asking her to send "everything she writes." Dickinson paid a very different kind of tribute to the terrifying nature of the story when she wrote to Higginson that "I read Miss Prescott's 'Circumstance,' but it followed me, in the Dark—so I avoided her—" (St. Armand, *Emily Dickinson* 173). Howells, proclaiming the story "still unsurpassed of its kind," spoke warmly of the thrill it evoked in its first readers and reprinted it in his important anthology, *The Great Modern American Stories* (1920).

In the early 1860s Harriet Prescott was perceived as one of the most important, exciting, and promising young writers in the nation. Her first novel, *Sir Rohan's Ghost,* received extraordinary praise from several reviewers. In the February 1860 issue of the *Atlantic,* Lowell noted the book's weaknesses, but insisted that no American writer had ever produced a first book "showing more undoubtful symptoms of genuine poetic power." His assertion that the author was "destined for great things" seemed corroborated by the appearance of her first collection of tales, *The Amber Gods and Other Stories,* in 1863. The volume even earned praise from the young Henry

James, who in the *North American Review* (Oct. 1863) objected strongly to her "morbid and unhealthful" fascination with the "diseased side of human nature," but admired the "united strength and brilliancy of her descriptions." Even when they voiced reservations about some aspect of her art, the reviewers made it clear that they were dealing with a major talent, with a writer who showed promise of being able, as James put it, "to assume a foremost place" in American literature.

Today Harriet Prescott Spofford is almost completely forgotten. During a career that spanned more than six decades and resulted in hundreds of stories, poems, and essays, she produced only a relatively small number of works of genuine power and imagination. She was sometimes willing to sacrifice literary quality to the demands of an eager audience, and she had some difficulty in adapting her romantic inclinations to an age that demanded literary realism. Nevertheless, Harriet Prescott Spofford merits rediscovery as a writer who challenged and enlarged the boundaries of American fiction. She endowed the symbolic romance with a feminine and sometimes feminist sensibility, and she played an important role in the development of certain popular genres, including the detective story and the supernatural tale. Her best work represents not only the final flowering of the romantic impulse in nineteenth-century New England, but also the most significant female counterpart to the essentially male tradition of American romantic fiction.

AT THE HEART of Harriet Prescott Spofford's best writing is a love of poetic language, of richly sensuous description, of striking phrases and extravagant images. A fascination with the exotic and the strange touches almost every aspect of her fictional art; it influences diction and shapes plot. One of the best descriptions of Spofford appears in an essay by Rose Terry Cooke:

> Under her quiet aspect, wistful regard, and shy manner, lay a soul full of imagination and passion, and a nature that revelled in the use of words to express this fire and force. In her hands the English language became sonorous, gorgeous, and burning. She poured out such luxury of image, such abundant and splendid epithet, such derivative stress, and such lavish color and life, that the stiff old mother-tongue

seemed to have been molten and fused in some magic crucible, and
turned to liquid gold and gems. (531)

As Cooke realized, Spofford's daring experiments with sound and image
represented nothing less than an attempt to revitalize language itself, an
attempt to transform the literary word into a force capable of challenging
and enlarging the reader's perception of reality.

Cooke also compares Spofford's prose to a gorgeous fire-lily blazing
forth against the pale and drab landscape of New England (530–31), an
image that accurately identifies Spofford's fiction as both a product of and
a reaction against certain aspects of New England life. In some respects,
Spofford's passionately sensual appreciation of the physical world is a rebuke to the stern moralizing and fondness for abstract speculation that
characterize the New England mind from Puritanism to Transcenden-
talism. But the portrait of the ardent romantic rebelling against a repressive culture needs to be balanced by a recognition of the ways her New
England upbringing nourished her imagination.

During Harriet Prescott Spofford's childhood and adolescence, her
family was never free of financial worries, but all the available evidence
suggests that her intellectual gifts were recognized and nurtured by her
parents, her grandmother, and her aunts, two of whom apparently taught
school for a while. The Prescotts were an old and distinguished family, but
the War of 1812 created economic havoc for the shipping trade and financial ruin for William Pepperell Prescott, Spofford's grandfather. Her father, Joseph Newmarch Prescott, struggled to rebuild the family fortunes
but never with much success. At first he was a merchant engaged primarily
in the lumber business, but he went on to study and practice law, serve as
postmaster and justice of the peace, and take an active part in local politics.
After his father's death in 1831, he assumed the responsibility of supporting his mother and his four sisters. In 1833, he married Sarah Bridges, who
has been described by Cooke as "a beautiful, proud, and intellectual girl."
Harriet Elizabeth Prescott, the first of their seven children (two of whom
died in infancy), was born on 3 April 1835 in Calais, Maine. She was
originally named Elizabeth Josephine Prescott, but the name was changed,
apparently to please her grandmother, Harriet Delesdernier Prescott, a
vibrant, intelligent, and articulate woman who probably had a large influ-

ence on the child's development. Spofford herself never cared for the name Harriet; close friends and family members called her Hal or Hallie.

The family anecdotes, as recorded by Cooke, portray the future author as a bright, adventurous child with a deep devotion to her family and a vivid imagination. Her first exposure to poetic language seems to have come from hearing the Bible read to her each evening by one of her aunts. If the family legends are true, then Spofford's fascination with sound and image dates back to the time when she was four years old and expressed a special delight at those passages in which God says "Let there be light!" and "The heavens declare the glory of God, and the firmament showeth His handiwork." But she was also deeply troubled by the story of Abraham and Isaac and its portrayal of a God who demands human sacrifice. She is said to have burst into tears and exclaimed: "Oh! I hope God won't ask me to offer up my little sister, for I am afraid I shouldn't want to do it!" When she was ten, she responded to the death of her younger brother with intense grief and poignant symbolism. At her first sight of the dead child, she fainted, but the next day she was found in the room containing the child's body, "covering the couch with pale primroses from the garden, and bitter leaves of wormwood." That gesture suggests much about the development of her imagination, but it failed to assuage her grief, which was so strong that her family feared she would be afflicted with "congestion of the brain" (Cook 525, 526).

For the most part, however, Cooke's biographical sketch describes Harriet Spofford as a healthy and "active child, full of quaint wit and keen questioning." Besides the Bible, the family's reading included the novels of Sir Walter Scott and the works of the major English poets. She probably started writing poetry, and perhaps fiction, at an unusually early age. One anecdote portrays the young child astounding her teacher and classmates by producing a long poem tracing the shifting nature of "Hope" from infancy to old age and devoting a separate canto to each period.

Nevertheless, financial constraints made it difficult for the Prescott family to afford even the limited schooling opportunities available in Calais. In 1849, when she was about fourteen, Spofford moved with her grandmother and one of her aunts to Newburyport, Massachusetts, where another aunt, Elizabeth Betton, kept a boarding house. The move enabled the precocious teenager to take advantage of the superb education offered by the Putnam Free School, and it eased the Prescott family's financial burdens. At some point (probably in 1850), Joseph Newmarch Prescott decided to seek his fortune in the West and settled for a number of years in Oregon. His wife moved to another town in Maine where she cared for the younger children and where the youngest child was born in October 1850. Shortly thereafter, she and the children moved to Derry, New Hampshire, where they remained for the next few years.

Harriet Spofford's separation from her parents and younger siblings must have been difficult, but Newburyport opened up a new world for her. Newburyport, a substantial country town on the Merrimack river about thirty-five miles northeast of Boston, brought her closer to the literary center of New England and provided her with rich cultural resources. The Putnam Free School seemed designed especially for the aspiring young writer. There she met others who shared and fostered her love of literature; in her 1916 memoir, *A Little Book of Friends,* she remembered walking the halls with her friend, Louisa Stone, "at recess, reading Tennyson and Shelley and Milton from the same book" (132). Besides providing courses in rhetoric emphasizing the analysis of poetry, the school also encouraged original composition in a variety of forms. Spofford contributed regularly to the school paper and took a leading role in the annual anniversary exercises, for which she wrote essays, hymns, and long dramatic dialogues in blank verse. When she was sixteen, she won a prize for "a very daring and original essay on Hamlet" (Higginson, *Cheerful Yesterdays* 130) and attracted the attention of one prize-giver, Thomas Wentworth Higginson. Higginson's reformist zeal for such causes as abolitionism and woman's suffrage had cost him his position as pastor of a local Unitarian church, but he continued to devote much of his enormous energy to improving Newburyport's cultural life. Spofford took part in one of his poetry groups and also taught in the evening classes for working people which he established. Higginson provided her with advice and encouragement, and the two remained lifelong friends. The early years at Newburyport played a crucial role in forming her literary tastes and values, providing her with confidence in her ability as a writer, and shaping the direction of her future life. During this period she also met and fell in love with Richard S. Spofford, her future husband.

Upon her graduation in 1852, she joined her family in Derry and attended Pinkerton Academy when it began readmitting women students in 1853. In 1855 or 1856 the entire family was reunited and settled in Newburyport, but here their financial difficulties intensified. Either in Oregon or shortly after his return, Spofford's father fell victim to a "lingering paralysis" which rendered him a helpless invalid until his death in 1881. Her mother's health also collapsed, and she found herself desperately in need of a way to support herself, her parents, and her younger siblings. She turned to the rapid production of cheap, sensationalistic fiction as the only mode of earning a living available to her. Her chief market was the Boston "story papers," which featured melodramatic fiction. Our knowledge of her contributions to these journals is sketchy, largely because publication was anonymous, and she never cared to collect or acknowledge these early productions. Her career as a professional author apparently began when one of these story papers offered her $5 for her first tale and encouraged her to submit more. We don't know how many other papers published her work or how many stories she dashed off during this time, but, according to her biographer, Elizabeth K. Halbeisen, she wrote about a hundred stories for this one periodical alone over the next three years, even though the rate of payment eventually dropped to $2.50 per tale. During these difficult times, she often worked for fifteen hours each day. Once she wrote frantically for an entire night in the hopes of winning the prize in a story competition; she not only failed to win but found her hand and arm "swollen and inflamed from incessant use" (Halbeisen 50). We have to appreciate the mixture of desperation and heroic effort that led Spofford to write this kind of fiction at such a furious pace and with so little reward. The experience resulted in her mastery of the conventions of popular fiction, but it also taught her that she could write quickly and that she could sell bad work.

The *Atlantic*'s publication of "In a Cellar" in 1859 transformed Spofford almost immediately from an obscure, miserably paid hack writer to a highly acclaimed author of remarkably original fiction. Although she was indignant when she heard the editors had suspected her of trying to foist a translation on them, she was thrilled to learn she would receive the enormous sum of $105 for her story. For the first time in her life, both

Introduction

financial security and literary fame seemed within her grasp. In both unpublished letters and public interviews, Spofford consistently valued her
poetry more highly than her fiction. Although she probably would have
preferred to devote her talent to verse, the constant need for money and
the nature of the literary marketplace compelled her to turn to more
profitable genres, and that led her inevitably to the novel.

Sir Rohan's Ghost apparently appeared at the beginning of 1860 though
the book's copyright date is 1859. This Gothic romance focuses on an artist
who is haunted by the ghost of the woman he has wronged and eventually
discovers that he has fallen in love with his own daughter. The publication
of her first and best collection of stories, The Amber Gods and Other Stories
(1863), provided more convincing evidence of Spofford's abilities. Of the
seven stories in this volume, only one had not already appeared in the
Atlantic. "Desert Sands," originally published in the Cosmopolitan Art Journal
(Dec. 1860), concerns a selfish artist who finds himself torn between his
virtuous wife, Eos, and the wild adventuress, Vespasia. Although insuffi-
ciently developed, the tale exemplifies Spofford's fascination with art and
artists, illicit passion and romantic triangles, egoism and the desire for
power, and the conflicts between "good" and "bad" women. These
themes received their fullest and most impressive development in the
remarkable long narrative, "The Amber Gods." The volume also contained
the racy detective story, "In a Cellar," the frightening tale of frontier
adventure, "Circumstance," and three other stories apparently chosen to
demonstrate the range of the young writer's talents. "Knitting Sale-Socks"
foreshadows the author's ability to be a competent writer of local color;
"The South Breaker" is typical of the sea stories she wrote throughout her
career; "Midsummer and May," the longest and weakest tale in the volume, focuses on the romantic triangle of mother and daughter in competition over the same man.

Unfortunately, we know relatively little about Spofford's life during
the 1860s when she was regarded as one of the most promising writers in
America. It seems clear, however, that any pleasure she might have experienced from her literary success was marred by desperate financial need.
She continued to be the primary support for her parents, and she also
aided her younger brother and sisters, one of whom, Mary N. Prescott,
also became a successful writer of magazine fiction. Her correspondence

with the energetic and shrewd editor of the *New York Ledger,* Robert Bonner, reveals the pressures under which she labored. Although she eventually agreed to write stories for his paper, she responded to his initial request for material with a reluctance to take on any "more transient labor":

> I am in receipt of as many orders as I should well know how to fill if I accepted them, having them for the current month from nearly every magazine in the country,—Harper's, Atlantic, Galaxy, Peterson, Northern Monthly, Lippincott's,—but I may frankly say to you that I find magazine writing onerous, and—although I am among the best-paid of such contributors,—not sufficiently remunerative to meet my necessities; and that I have wished to establish a relation with some newspaper which should allow me to furnish a certain number of columns per week, stories, sketches, or special subjects when desired, or else to write exclusively for one single publisher, or to furnish a serial, at a rate of compensation which should be satisfactory . . .   (unpublished letter, 30 Dec. 1867, Barnard College)

The haste with which she wrote is often apparent in the uncollected tales of the early and mid-1860s, but the most important of these works also reveal an ambitious attempt to experiment with literary form and language: "The Strathsays" (*Atlantic,* Jan. 1863), "Dark Ways" (*Atlantic,* May 1863), "Fiery Colliery of Fiennes" (*Harper's,* Oct. 1863), "Ray" (*Atlantic,* Jan. 1864), "The Rim" (*Atlantic,* May and June 1864), "Poor Isabel" (*Harper's,* Mar. 1865), "An Hour at Sea" (*Harper's,* July 1866), and "D'Outre Mort" (*Galaxy,* Nov. 1866). Moreover, a story like "Down the River" (*Atlantic,* Oct. 1865), which explores the developing consciousness of a female slave as she gradually reaches her decision to run away from the plantation, testifies to her continued power as a writer of romantic fiction. Though marred by racial stereotyping, "Down the River" illustrates the sentiments of Spofford's later declaration to William Hayes Ward, the editor of *The Independent:* "I was an ardent antislavery person, and woman suffragette from my fourteenth year" (unpublished letter, 31 Oct. 1896, U of FL).

Nevertheless, critics became increasingly impatient of her failure to fulfill her promise as an unusually gifted writer. While Henry James's first review treated her with respect even when he objected to the lack of originality in her plotting and the moral danger posed by her treatment of "illicit love," his review of her second novel, *Azarian* (1864), is almost uniformly negative and occasionally even savage in its criticism. Unfortunately, for the most part, his review is also quite fair. Spofford's desire to indulge in a highly wrought poetic language—often at the expense of plot and characterization—weakens most of her longer narratives and reaches an unfortunate climax in *Azarian*. Indeed, most of her longer narratives appear to be the work of a descriptive poet trapped in an uncongenial form.

In 1863, an acquaintance declared that Harriet Prescott "is as good as gold, but believes in nothing, past or future, man or woman, but is desperately in love with Dick Spofford" (quoted in Halbeisen 7). After a long engagement, Prescott married Richard S. Spofford on 19 December 1865. Both public accounts and unpublished private letters suggest that they had an almost ideal marriage. A successful lawyer and politician (associated for a time with the influential Caleb Cushing), Richard Spofford admired and encouraged his wife's literary work and also occasionally tried his own hand at verse. His business often led them to divide their time between Newburyport and Washington. Undoubtedly the most important event early in their marriage was the birth and death of their only child, Richard, who was born on January 30 in 1867 and died on September 10 of the same year.

For reasons not fully clear, the quality of Spofford's short fiction showed a marked improvement in 1868. Although the 1868 stories do not have the richness of the three earliest *Atlantic* works, they often reveal a strong authorial control over plot, character, and theme. The prose still aspires toward the poetic, but it maintains a high level of clarity and avoids the florid excesses often found in her earlier work. These works include an effective detective story, "In the Maguerriwock" (*Harper's,* Aug. 1868); an intriguing symbolic romance, "The Moonstone Mass" (*Harper's* Oct. 1868); and two of her strongest supernatural tales, "The Strange Passengers" (*Lippincott's,* June 1868) and "The Black Bess" (*Galaxy,* May 1868). The 1868 stories are marked by a fascination with the male mind and with the capacity of men to harm women or fear women. They also exemplify Spofford's ability to work in and transform genres generally regarded as primarily male.

By 1874 the financial crises that plagued her in the 1850s and 1860s had passed, and in that year the Spoffords were able to purchase Deer

Introduction

Island, a five-acre island in the Merrimack River connected by bridges to Newburyport and Amesbury. The property included a large house, once an inn, which the Spoffords were able to adapt to their own needs. Deer Island enabled them to provided a lifelong home for members of both their families, including her parents and his widowed mother as well as his sister, Frances, her sister Mary, and her brother, Otis. In 1885 the Spoffords became the legal guardians of Thomas and Marion Pierce, the orphaned children of close friends. Other relatives and friends (including important writers and editors) often visited, sometimes for extended periods. Servants handled most of the household tasks, allowing Spofford to entertain frequently while continuing to write prolifically. She developed a reputation as an excellent hostess and was even occasionally held up as a model for other female authors, because of her ability to maintain both a literary career and a gracious household.

By the 1870s financial pressures no longer determined the shape of Spofford's career, but other equally determinant forces were at work. In a late letter to scholar and literary critic Fred Lewis Pattee, she explained that "war had made the violent and dramatic seem natural" (unpublished letter, 19 Oct. 1914, Penn State). Nevertheless, in post–Civil War America, Spofford's romantic imagination seemed out of step with a nation already moving toward realism. James's review of *Azarian* in fact constitutes one of the important early manifestos of American critical realism. While she eventually took James's advice to abandon "the ideal descriptive style" and to "study the canons of the so-called realist school" (269–72), explaining to Pattee that she changed because "the public taste changed," she nevertheless insisted on her penchant for the romantic. Referring to the tales later collected in *The Elder's People* (1920), she wrote: "But although I like to write realistic stories like these last, yet I cannot say that I am entirely in sympathy with any realism that excludes the poetic and romantic" (unpublished letter to Pattee, 19 Oct. 1914, Penn State). And indeed her strongest later works manage to reconcile romantic subject matter with realism's preference for a clear and simple style.

Nevertheless, Spofford deserves some attention as an able practitioner of the realistic sketch—the literary mode that attracted the talents of many of the finest women writers in America during the last half of the nineteenth century. Her best realistic pieces show considerable interest and skill in the delineation of character. The strongest of these stories focus on the lives of elderly women in a New England village, and their handling is marked by both sympathy and humor. Moreover, these stories avoid or minimize the use of regional dialect. If she had written more works as good as "Aunt Pen's Funeral," "Miss Susan's Love Affair," or "Three Quiet Ladies of the Name of Luce" (*Harper's,* June 1872 and 1876, Nov. 1884), Spofford would have earned a distinguished place in the history of New England local color. In addition, Marshall P. Wilder's ten-volume collection, *The Wit and Humor of America* (1911), includes two stories by Spofford that provide further testimony to her ability to handle realism skillfully: "Our Very Wishes" (9:1637–53) and "Tom's Money" (10:1955–64). The bibliography in Halbeisen's book does not list them, and their original dates and places of publication remain unknown. Other effective stories in this mode may still be buried in unindexed nineteenth-century periodicals.

Many of Spofford's most interesting literary experiments never made it into book form, and most of the books that did appear under her name probably damaged her reputation. She never mastered the form of the novel, and her collections of fiction rarely represented her best work. *A Scarlet Poppy and Other Stories* (1894) gathered a number of decent but unexciting realistic stories, while *Old Madame and Other Tragedies* (1900) included two of her best stories, "Old Madame" (originally in the *Century,* Jan. 1882) and "Her Story" (*Lippincott's,* Dec. 1872), and three of her worst. Spofford was almost always interesting when she turned to the supernatural tale as in "The Godmothers" (*Cosmopolitan,* Mar. 1896), which deals with history and the power of women; "The Conquering Will" (*The Smart Set,* June 1901), which tells of a ghost who prevents his wife from remarrying; and "The Mad Lady" (*Scribner's,* Feb. 1916), which features a haunted automobile. Unfortunately, publishers were more receptive to collections based on gimmicks, such as the local colorist's focus on a single location. *Old Washington* (1906) contains five sentimental stories based on life in that city in the decades following the Civil War. Local color provided a better medium for Spofford in the fourteen stories of New England village life gathered in *The Elder's People* (1920). Spofford's most important models clearly were the stories about Old Chester and Dr. Lavendar written by Margaret Deland, but one can also detect traces of Rose Terry Cooke and Mary Wilkins Freeman in their most optimistic modes.

Introduction

As she grew older, Spofford's life was marked by an increased interest in religious principles and a deepening faith in Christianity, some of
which may have been the consequence of her husband's death in August
1888. She wrote to John Greenleaf Whittier about the comfort she tried to
derive from "the uplifting and rarefying power of *faith*,—faith the *evidence*
of things unseen," and explained: "While I had Dick I cared nothing about
the future,—I *felt* immortal. If I were going to die tonight,—as I wish I
were,—I would not care, possibly, either for this evidence or this knowledge;—but if I have to live,—as seems too probable,—I must feel that
Dick is living, too, somewhere, somehow, or else go beside myself,—
which after all does not always seem so hapless a fate" (unpublished letter,
29 Jan. 1889, Essex Institute). The poems, essays, and fiction she wrote in
the last three decades of her long life often reflect this increased belief in
religious faith.

After her husband's death, Spofford relied heavily on the companionship of her niece, Katherine Prescott Moseley, and of Marion Pierce,
both of whom became surrogate daughters to her. She usually spent the
winters in Washington and in Boston, where she became a welcomed
member of the group of women writers associated with Annie Fields.
Although she always felt uncomfortable at large public gatherings and
formal occasions, Spofford cherished these friendships and paid tribute to
many of these writers in *A Little Book of Friends*. She also won the affection of
almost every important woman writer in New England. Sarah Orne Jewett
once wrote to her: "What any 'sister authoress' would really love to do
would be to hold the pen that was equal to writing *you!*" (Halbeisen 209).

During the final years, Spofford seems to have accepted her position
as a popular writer of magazine fiction, whose early romantic tales had
once been acclaimed. To Pattee, she wrote that she had enjoyed writing
her fiction and verse, but said with her usual diffidence, "You asked what I
think I have accomplished. I don't think I have accomplished *anything*,
except to have made some hours pass pleasantly perhaps to some readers,—not very many" (unpublished letter, 19 Oct. 1914, Penn State). By
the time of her death on 14 August 1921, Spofford's reputation as a serious
writer of fiction was almost completely gone, and her work seemed
doomed to oblivion. The early tales occasionally received some praise,
most notably from Pattee in *The Development of the American Short Story* and

Arthur Hobson Quinn in *American Fiction,* but most literary scholars ignored her work. Even those who argued that the romantic mode was the dominant force in the shaping of American fiction have failed to acknowledge Spofford's place in our literary history. Although her importance rests on a relatively small number of tales, these works have added significantly to our literary heritage, enlarging our views of both the nature of American romantic fiction and the achievements of American women writers.

LIKE POE, HAWTHORNE, AND MELVILLE, Spofford expects readers to accept extravagant plots and exotic settings, extraordinary characters in unusual situations, a prose style that rejects the plain simplicity of ordinary speech in favor of an elaborately wrought literary language, and a process of symbolism in whch the natural merges with the supernatural. The American tradition of romantic fiction is also characterized by a deep fascination with aberrational psychology that often reveals an underlying skepticism about both human nature and human society. Emerson may have preached the gospel of self-reliance, but our best fiction writers have been more concerned with the corrosive effects of egoism, morbid obsessions sometimes leading to monomania, masochism, and the urge to self-destruction. Harriet Prescott Spofford merits attention as the major female practitioner of a mode of symbolic romance which many have asserted to be the mainstream of American fiction. Her major achievements stem from an ability to work in genres generally assumed to be traditionally male; her most interesting works transform these genres substantially.

Spofford's first major success, "In a Cellar," is one of the best detective stories produced by an American during the nineteenth century; it is rivaled only by Poe's best tales of ratiocination. Spofford's account focuses on the efforts of the narrator, an English diplomat in Paris, to recover a stolen diamond and to arrange an appropriate marriage for the intriguing young woman, Delphine de St. Cyr. The story shows only limited interest in detection: the resolution of the mystery depends less on the detective's analytical skill than on a series of coincidences and the misinterpretation of a single word. Some moments of dialogue show a dramatic flair (particularly the encounter between the narrator and Baron Stahl that leads to

Delphine's marriage), and the story offers a rich abundance of vivid description. Although some scenes are rendered in elaborate detail (especially the shop of the *marchand des armures*), the impression of the author's familiarity with the nuances of Parisian manners and diplomatic intrigue rests largely on a process of suggestiveness, in which the narrator's worldly and often witty cynicism implies more than is actually said. The missing details are filled in partly by the reader's imagination and partly by American prejudices concerning foreign mores.

The story's effectiveness depends largely on a vividness of style, a fascination with language which reveals both verbal magnificence and artistic control. In the long passage describing the narrator's first sight of the diamond, Spofford's descriptive genius brings an inanimate object to life and endows it with symbolic attributes. The quest to recover the gem assumes special significance, because it is "the female of diamonds, the queen herself, the principle of life, the rejoicing receptive force." The equation of the diamond and the female reinforces the explicit comparison of Delphine to a diamond in the early pages of the story, thus linking the narrator's search for the jewel with feminist issues. In its treatment of Delphine, the story explicitly raises the question of how a beautiful and talented woman can find fulfillment in a treacherous society. Delphine achieves a new vitality through her marriage, but she is aroused by power, not redeemed by love. The images used to describe her are drawn from classical or pagan sources, not Christian ones. Underlying the suggestive atmosphere of "In a Cellar" is an almost complete rejection of the moralistic tendencies of much nineteenth-century American fiction and an implicit rebellion against the moral heritage of New England culture.

Spofford's second *Atlantic* story was an even more daring experiment with fictional form, and a much more shocking challenge to the values of nineteenth-century America. In many respects, "The Amber Gods" is Spofford's masterpiece, but it is also a difficult and demanding tale. The long and intricate first part of the story, "Flower o' the Peach," focuses on Yone Willoughby, a passionately self-indulgent and self-centered woman who recounts in lush prose the way she enchants and marries a young artist, Vaughan Rose. She does this partly by convincing her chief rival, her virtuous cousin Louise, called Lu, to wear the amber beads that he finds repulsive. In the second part, "Astra Castra, Numen Lumen," Yone apparently becomes the victim of her own diseased sensibility, but any conventional moralizing is undercut at the end by the revelation that she is actually speaking from beyond the grave.

The only major study of "The Amber Gods" is a perceptive essay by Barton Levi St. Armand, who expresses doubts about the tale's literary merits, but argues for its historical importance: "Not only did it inspire Emily Dickinson to dare the technique of describing the moment of death from the dying person's point of view in such poems as 'I heard a Fly buzz when I died,' 'Because I could not stop for Death,' and 'I felt a Funeral in my Brain,' but it startled the American public into a confrontation with, if not a tolerance for, the erotic nature of woman" (*Haunted Dusk* 115). Later portrayals of exotic or unconventional women also show traces of Yone. In fact, Spofford's story may explain the appearance of amber beads around the necks of several important female characters in other American novels, most notably Verena Tarrant in *The Bostonians* by Henry James and Ellen Olenska in *The Age of Innocence* by Edith Wharton.

"The Amber Gods" merits attention on several different levels. It is a brilliant study in egoism, a stylistic tour de force, an exploration of the artistic imagination, and a radical inquiry into the position of women in a repressive society. The power of the story lies in Spofford's brave decision to make Yone the narrator as well as the central character. Yone's voice is the heart and soul of the story, but the story suggests that Yone possesses neither heart nor soul. The completely self-centered Yone lacks any moral sense, any real capacity to sympathize with or even comprehend the suffering of others. She is vain and selfish, sensual and seductive, devious and even demonic. Her long monologues provide a curious blend of childlike egotism, pagan vitality, and amoral erotism—qualities Spofford captures through a prose style so luxuriant that it sometimes threatens the boundaries of language itself. In fashioning the perversely fascinating Yone Willoughby, Spofford has given voice to a woman that her own culture would have labeled "unspeakable."

In a letter to Elizabeth Stuart Phelps, Spofford said of "The Amber Gods": "I recall the perfect rapture in which I wrote it. I never enjoyed writing anything so much in all my life!" (unpublished letter, 22 June 1910, U of FL). That sense of rapture emerges in the prose style and in the creation of Yone, the most significant embodiment in New England fiction of what Freud later called the pleasure principle. Yone affirms a sensuous enjoyment of the physical world and of the human body. She takes enormous delight in her luxurious blonde hair and even manages to find erotic pleasure in sunlight: "Sunbeams like to follow me, I think. Now, when I stand in one before this glass, infiltrated with the rich tinge, don't I look like the spirit of it just stepped out for inspection? I seem to myself like the complete incarnation of light, full, bounteous, overflowing, and I wonder at and adore anything so beautiful; and the reflection grows finer and deeper while I gaze, till I dare not do so any longer." In her erotic self-absorption, Yone poses a defiant challenge to a culture that feared the body and often tried to relegate women to a spiritual sphere.

To fully appreciate the degree of Yone's rebellion, one has to remember that nineteenth-century America would have been shocked simply by the idea of a woman talking about herself for so long. Yone's bold egocentricity reveals an almost pathological narcissism, but it is also a powerful rebuke to a society that regarded self-reliance as a manly virtue and preferred that women be quiet, passive, and unassuming. Yone's virtuous cousin, Lu, exemplifies the conventional feminine values that New England cherished and Yone rejects with scorn; Lu is pure, kind, submissive, self-effacing, and self-sacrificing. Yone's rebellion, to a large extent, takes a linguistic form: her attempt to enlarge the boundaries of conventional language reflects a larger desire to revolt from the constrictions of society. Yone herself recognizes the degree to which her vivid language is a response to a repressive society, a society that seems unable to distinguish between poetry and slang: "Slang? No,—poetry. But if your nature had such a wild tendency as mine, and then were boxed up with proprieties and civilities from year's end to year's end, maybe you, too, would escape now and then in a bit of slang."

Yone identifies herself with a "tropical luxuriance" that must contend with the cold atmosphere of New England. The nature of New England society also emerges in its treatment of little Asian, the original owner of the amber beads. The depicton of her relies somewhat on racist stereotyping, a fault all too common in nineteenth-century American fiction, but it enables Spofford to connect New England culture with slavery, with a desire to enslave and tame all that is wild and free. All that New England can do is stunt her growth and distort her energy into violence and hatred. Little Asian in some respects is an ironic mirror of Yone (just as Pip is an ironic reflection of Ahab in *Moby-Dick*), but she is also an emblem of the damage all women suffer in a repressive society.

St. Armand has correctly described Yone as "a psychic vampire who feeds largely upon herself and the praise of others" (*Haunted Dusk* 104), but Yone also transforms Vaughan Rose into a superior artist. Like many other romantic works, "The Amber Gods" is partly a parable about the nature of art and the artist. Spofford's treatment of this theme depends on a number of allusions, some of which the modern reader is likely to miss. In the scene in which Rose first kisses Yone, for instance, the interweaving of lines from Robert Browning's "Pippa Passes" raises several intricate questions about the redemptive power of art. The most important allusion, however, is to the Venetian painter after whom Yone has been named, Giorgione. According to Giorgio Vasari's *Lives of the Artists,* Giorgione "displayed very amorous propensities" and died at the age of thirty-four from a plague he contracted from his lover. His personal life, however, is less important than his role as a transitional figure in the movement from medieval to Renaissance art. Vasari praises the artist's ability "to infuse his figures with spirit and to counterfeit the freshness of living flesh better than any painter" (168–69). Giorgione, whose students included Titian, embodies the shift from static art to liberation through color and thus aptly represents the effect Yone has on the artist, Vaughan Rose. Yone, who becomes both art object and artistic inspiration, often boasts of her ability to bring Rose's artistic genius to fruition. Nevertheless, Spofford ultimately concludes that the artist must first come to know and then transcend the world of sensuous experience represented by Yone. In this sense, the true hero of "The Amber Gods" is Vaughan Rose, whose relationship with Yone and Lu exemplifies the artist's need to confront and reconcile opposing qualities (physical and spiritual, sensual and moral, pagan and Christian). "The Amber Gods" is thus the work of a romantic rebel who ultimately manages to strike a compromise with the culture that has produced her.

It is easy to understand the nightmares "Circumstance" provoked in Emily Dickinson and other readers, for it is an effective tale of terror and can be read as a symbolic investigation of the agonies facing the creative woman in America. To some extent, the story probably expresses Spofford's own frustration as a poet forced to cater to the beast of the

American reading public. Apparently based on an experience of Spofford's maternal great-grandmother, "Circumstance" recounts the tribulations of a pioneer woman trapped by a wild beast known as the Indian Devil. The animal, presumably a panther, threatens to devour the woman, who discovers that her only means of preventing the beast's assault is to sing. But she also discovers that the creature refuses to be appeased or distracted with just a single tune; in order to save her life she must continually find new kinds of song to sing. Singing thus becomes both a life-saving, life-affirming act and an act of continual desperation, the woman's only defense against a brutal and savage world. As recent studies of the tale by Judith Fetterley and Anne Dalke have shown, Spofford makes full use of the rich resources of the symbolic romance, creating a work that paradoxically explores both the helplessness and power of women.

"Circumstance" can best be understood as a female counterpart to the more familiar stories of male initiation in which the protagonist journeys into a psychic wilderness, confronts his own fears through a series of symbolic adventures involving entrapment and escape, eventually comes to terms with his own sexual nature, accepts the reality of death, and finally emerges able to acknowledge his limitations and make full use of his potential in the face of a difficult and often hostile universe. Here the beast who entraps the woman is clearly shown to embody "the strength of our lower natures let loose," and the details used to describe his hold on her are filled with images of sexual violence: this "living lump of appetites," with his "hot, foetid breath," "fiery eyeballs," "foaming chops," and "savage caresses," insists on having complete control over the helpless woman, insists, in fact, that she either charm him or die. In the vivid depiction of the animal's savage force and of the woman's need to submit to his whims, "Circumstance" provides a harrowing portrait of the powerlessness of women. Even the act of singing, traditionally a form of celebration and self-expression, becomes a manifestation of helpless submission.

Nevertheless, "Circumstance" is also the tale of a strong woman who discovers the strengths and limits of her own voice; a woman who manages to confront and overcome the savagery of animal passion, the inevitability of death, and the indifference of nature; a woman who is finally able to transform—at least to some degree—the horror into a religious experience. When first captured, the woman had called upon her husband instead of God, but in her moment of deepest desolation and despair, she turns, almost unconsciously, to a special kind of religious music and sings "old Covenanting hymns." At this point, the woman is no longer singing to appease the beast, but to "renew" her communion with God. Her singing becomes an act of personal affirmation which leads her to a mystical transcendence of all pain and suffering. Significantly, the imagery shifts from the harsh, violent suggestion of sexual rape toward the expression of a divine and natural love: "'My beloved is mine, and I am his,' she sang over and over again, with all varied inflection and profuse tune. How gently all the winter-wrapt things bent toward her then! into what relation with her had they grown! how at one with Nature had she become!" Her music is "no longer despondency" and it is "neither prayer nor petition." Instead, it becomes both an acceptance of God's will and an assertion of personal salvation that she experiences "in her divine rapture."

"Circumstance" balances the graphic depiction of horror with a symbolic tale of learning and transcendence. In the midst of her greatest danger, the woman discovers that "she had learned the secret of sound at last." Moreover, the songs she sings take her through a realm of human experience that transcends the limits of gender—it is significant that she begins with the feminine cradle song, almost loses her life when she finds her thoughts fixated on her family, and then saves herself by singing sea songs (a distinctly masculine form of music). The pattern is repeated in a way that emphasizes that the conventional thoughts of family, husband, and child pose a threat to the woman on the frontier, whose salvation depends on her ability to experience and express a wider range of emotions. Thus, before finding the music that expresses and affirms her personal relationship to God, she must move through songs of wild joy and intense pain: from the "gayest reel" and "an Irish jig" to "wild, melancholy, forsaken songs." Once she has the transcendent experience, she finds herself psychologically protected from the horror the beast represents, but this mystical experience also isolates her from and makes her independent of husband and child. When her "mother instinct" makes her look down to see her husband who has appeared to rescue her, she returns to the world of "earthly hope," but loses "the fervent vision of God's peace." Before returning to the earth and to her normal role of wife and mother, she also loses her voice. In depicting the inherent conflict between the demands of "mother instinct" and the "divine rapture" of her songs, "Circumstance" assumes an important place in the long tradition of fictional works, including *The Story of Avis* (1877) by Elizabeth Stuart Phelps and *The Awakening* (1899) by Kate Chopin, exploring the conflicts and agonies facing the woman artist.

Edgar Allan Poe has justly been credited with inventing the modern tale of detection, but American women writers (including Spofford, Metta Victor, Anna Katherine Green, and Mary Roberts Rinehart) played an important role in its development. Spofford introduced a new detective in "Mr. Furbish" (*Harper's*, Apr. 1865), a competently handled murder mystery in which photography plays an important role. She may have had plans for a series of stories featuring this detective and may even have published other Mr. Furbish stories that have not yet been located and identified. The only other one presently known, however, is "In the Maguerriwock," which provides an intriguing contrast to the earlier and more impressive "In a Cellar." Instead of depicting the raciness of Paris life, Spofford now examines the depravity to be found in "an almost uncivilized region of the frontier forest" in America. Both stories, however, take the protagonist on a search below the surface of things (in cellars), and both connect the crime with the treatment of women. "In the Maguerriwock" links murder and wife abuse, clearly pointing to nineteenth-century America's legal indifference by having the sheriff respond to Mr. Furbish's desire to hang the culprit with: "I couldn't say of myself that he abused anybody but his wife; and a judge in Illinois decided lately that that was nothing—the wife must adopt more conciliating conduct." When Poe dealt with a similar subject, he almost always focused on the psychological state of the murderer. Instead, Spofford emphasizes the state of the murderer's wife, his other victim. The effectiveness of "In the Maguerriwock" stems less from the depiction of the powers of detection than from the graphic description of the woman driven mad, the woman driven into moaning: "Three men went down cellar, and only two came up!"

"The Moonstone Mass" owes a debt to Poe's tales of symbolic journeys and to some of the masterpieces of British romantic poetry, most notably Coleridge's "Kubla Khan" and "The Rime of the Ancient Mariner," but its detailed description of the caverns of ice and the moonstone mass bear the hallmarks of Spofford's earliest writing—a fascination with color and the symbolic treatment of gems. Once again, Spofford is working within a form normally associated with male writers—the adventure story—and adapting it so that it treats women's needs, frustrations, and aspirations. Ultimately, "The Moonstone Mass" is a rejection of the male quest for power (as expressed in the treasure hunt and other references to senseless greed) in favor of the world of feminine love and contentment (as represented by Eleanor). As the opening of the tale makes clear, "The Moonstone Mass" deals with a psychological journey. The nameless protagonist, torn between his greed and his love for Eleanor, follows the wishes of his uncle (who is significantly both a millionaire and a misogynist) and joins the quest for the Northwest Passage. When he is trapped on an ice floe, however, he finds himself changed; he even says: "I was no longer myself." His attempt to seize the moonstone is part of a complex symbolic and psychological process in which the narrator confronts both his love for Eleanor (whom he pictures in her "warm, sunny home") and his greedy desire for power (best represented in his words: "Should not I, a man, conquer this inanimate blind matter?"). The story ends by repudiating the values of his uncle and affirming those of Eleanor, but the last paragraph suggests the narrator has not fully learned the lesson.

Spofford's fascination with male psychology is also evident in "The Black Bess," which appears to draw from the tradition of the British ghost story, particularly as that form was used by some very talented (and now unjustly neglected) women writers, including Amelia Edwards, Rhoda Broughton, E. Nesbit. That British feminist tradition often uses a male narrator whose supernatural tale reveals an underlying fear of women and an inability to deal with sexuality. In some of these works, the narrator explains the way in which the ghost stole or killed his new bride, and his sexual anxieties are revealed through a strikingly Freudian use of phallic imagery (see, for example, Broughton's "Man with the Nose" and Nesbit's "Man-Size in Marble"). "The Black Bess" is a psychological study of the narrator, a railroad engineer who continually imagines that he sees his fiancée, Margaret, on the tracks ahead of him and his speeding train. The narrator's sexual confusion is evident throughout the story: from the disjointed comments on love in the opening paragraph to his expression of love for his train, the Black Bess (where he enjoys his "sense of mastery"), and the apparitions / hallucinations that delay his marriage. His problem is not relieved by the doctor who insists that his only means of dealing with the phantom is to run it / her down. Unfortunately, the ending of the story has been marred by editing over which Spofford had no control. In an unpublished letter to William Conant Church, the editor of the *Galaxy,* Spofford complained that "the concluding portion" had been "altered from the original and the best passages altogether omitted"; she was "exceedingly vexed" by the "ruinous mutilation" (unpublished letter, 25 Apr. 1868, NYPL). Even with the present mutilated ending, the work provides convincing evidence of Spofford's mastery of the supernatural tale.

In both "The Black Bess" and "The Moonstone Mass" the male narrator is not a voice of authority, but the author's means of exploring the male mind and its peculiar obsessions, which include a desire for power in conflict with the feminine values of love and family. Spofford's fascination with psychology extended to women as well and led eventually to "Her Story," one of her finest works. The narrator of "Her Story" is a woman in an insane asylum who is speaking to a female friend, trying to explain the reasons for her illness. She does not blame her unappreciative, egotistical husband, but concentrates almost all her anger and frustration on the woman who has stolen his love, even portraying her rival as a female vampire "swallowing the souls of men." In many respects, the rival, "a splendid tropical growth of the passionate heat and the slime," is a re-creation of Yone Willoughby; and "Her Story" is "The Amber Gods" retold from the point of view of the virtuous woman victim. This moving account of the narrator's descent into madness, however, demonstrates an artistic control and stylistic clarity lacking in even the best of Spofford's earlier works.

In its use of a mad narrator to depict feminist themes, "Her Story" is an important forerunner of Charlotte Perkins Gilman's classic story, "The Yellow Wallpaper" (1892) as well as a powerful tale in its own right. Significantly, neither of the two women in Spofford's romantic triangle possess names, but the name of the husband, Spencer, appears frequently throughout the story. The namelessness of the two chief female characters reflects the story's concern with the way women lose their identities, the way women often sacrifice their sense of selfhood to men. The narrator is a victim of her husband's callousness and her rival's schemes, but she is also a victim of her own willingness to surrender her entire sense of identity to

Introduction

her husband. Even her concept of religion and her views of heaven and hell
are distorted into a worship of her husband. The narrator's loss of selfhood
emerges clearly in her desperate assertion in the fourth paragraph to her
friend, Elizabeth, the woman (with a name!) who visits her in the asylum
and listens to her tale: "I am as much myself, I tell you, as you are." Those
words take on a wide range of implication, dramatizing the narrator's
confusion and extending her tale of suffering not only to Elizabeth, but to
the reader and, perhaps, to all women. In fact, the tale's power stems from
Spofford's ability to provide both a moving portrait of one woman's psychological state and a larger commentary on the relationships of women
with men and with other women. In its depiction of the rivalry between
the two women, the story points to the capacity of women to hurt other
women. Nevertheless, through its references to Elizabeth, "Her Story"
also insists that women have the potential to help one another—the potential to support and liberate one another.

    "Miss Susan's Love Affair" provides a good illustration of Spofford's
mastery of the realistic sketch. Its focus is on a single character, an old maid
whose entire life is based on a foolish fantasy—a completely imaginary
love affair with a man who is barely aware of her existence. The story
abandons the premises of romanticism completely; in fact, it partakes in
realism's characteristic depiction of all romanticized fancies and inclinations as dangerous and harmful. It also exemplifies realism's fascination
with the inner life of the apparently ordinary character, the forgotten and
neglected man or woman. Much of Spofford's best fiction shows us strong
women, women with a strong sense of identity and purpose. "Miss Susan's
Love Affair" on the other hand is a study in weakness, in folly, in failure. It
subtly and gracefully balances a genial satire of foolish illusions with a more
poignant and almost tragic portrayal of a wasted life.

    But the most important of Spofford's later stories are the romantic
tales, "Old Madame" and "The Godmothers." According to Halbeisen
(128), "Old Madame" is loosely based on historical fact; Spofford was
familiar with the history of Captain Francis Champernowne (1614–87),
but she chose to explore the decline of his descendents in the late eigh-
teenth and early nineteenth century. The tale traces the life of the beautiful
and proud Elizabeth Champernoune from her courtship and marriage to
Cousin Louis, through her confrontation with a long series of adversities

apparently stemming from a curse put on the family by Ben Benvoisie, to her death in virtual poverty at the age of eighty-five. "Old Madame" is Spofford's only effective treatment of the historical romance, a form she rarely attempted, but it reveals narrative power in its detailing of the succession of misfortunes that deprive the central character of both family and fortune. Moreover, it shows dramatic skill in the rendering of that character, a woman who is powerless against the curse and the course of events, but who maintains her pride, integrity, and force of will until the end. Like many of Spofford's best works, "Old Madame" draws its power from the vivid depiction of a strong woman's confrontation with a difficult world.

The power of women and the nature of history also play important roles in "The Godmothers," which originally appeared with five full-page illustrations by different artists in the *Cosmopolitan* (March 1896), and which Spofford tried in vain to reprint in book form as part of a collection of romantic tales (unpublished letter to Pattee, 19 Oct. 1914, Penn State). The story's strength comes from its revitalization of the familiar devices of the fairy tale and the Gothic novel, including supernatural beings, good and bad godmothers, and paintings that come alive. The central character, a wealthy American woman who has married an impoverished French nobleman, has just experienced the birth of her first child and now must come to terms with the child's hereditary past as it is manifested in the godmothers who appear to her. Spofford raises disturbing questions about the woman's American past as well as her husband's French heritage. Moreover, she once again draws a remarkable contrast between vibrant immoral women and bland virtuous ones:

> gentle ladies, quiet, timid, humble before heaven, ladies of placid lives, no opportunities, small emotions, narrow routine, praying by form, acting by precedent, without individuality, whose goodness was negative, whose doings were paltry, their poor drab beings swamped, and drowned, and extinguished in the purples and scarlets of these women of great passions, of scope, of daring and deed and electric force, mates of men of force, whose position had called crime to its aid, whose very crimes had enlarged, whose sins were things of power . . .

Introduction

Imbedded in the tale is Spofford's awareness that conventional social codes have often deprived women of full and rich lives, and that throughout history women could not experience passion or power without violating the moral boundaries. Nevertheless, "The Godmothers" ends by affirming the existence of a female principle both primitive and maternal, both savage and purifying.

Spofford has an important place in our literary history. The intense individualism, even narcissism of romantic literature, its pre-Freudian psychological investigation, and its stylistic complexity can now be more clearly seen not to have been strictly the preserve of male writers in nineteenth-century America. Like Hawthorne, Poe, and Melville, Spofford explored the passions that can lie beneath the staid exteriors of social life, forcing her readers to confront the reality of evil. Yet she offers a voice significantly different from that of her male counterparts within the same tradition. Underlying her love of a poetic language is a serious inquiry into the way women find or lose their voices. Indeed, her handling of theme and technique is marked by a concern with the frustrations women endure and the aspirations they share, by insights that add new dimensions to such traditionally male genres as the adventure story and the symbolic journey. Her tales of artists, detectives, and ghosts reveal a fascination with the way women assume power or are rendered powerless. Spofford's romantic tales of strong and weak women also provide an intriguing counterpart to the works of her female contemporaries, who usually did their best work in realistic modes. The ten stories collected in this volume will give us an opportunity to reassess Spofford's considerable literary importance.

The introduction is based on my examination of Spofford's unpublished letters, which are located in libraries throughout the United States, as well as on published sources. The most useful source for biographical information is still Elizabeth K. Halbeisen's biography, *Harriet Prescott Spofford* (1935). Rose Terry Cooke's essay in *Our Famous Women* (1884) is anecdotal and protective, but Spofford herself recommended it to correspondents who requested biographical information. The brief "Personals" that appeared frequently in *Harper's Bazaar* often provide useful insights.

SELECTED BIBLIOGRAPHY

ARCHIVAL MATERIAL

Unpublished letters have been cited from the following sources:

Barnard College	Overbury Collection, Barnard College Library, New York.
Essex Institute	Whittier Papers, Essex Institute, Salem, MA.
NYPL	William Conant Church Papers, Rare Books and Manuscripts Division, The New York Public Library, Astor, Lenox and Tilden Foundations, New York.
Penn State	Fred Lewis Pattee Papers, The Pennsylvania State University Libraries, University Park, PA.
U of FL	The Howe Library, Rare Books and Manuscripts, University of Florida Libraries, Gainesville, FL.

WORKS BY HARRIET PRESCOTT SPOFFORD

The Amber Gods and Other Stories. Boston: Ticknor and Fields, 1863.
Art Decoration Applied to Furniture. New York: Harper and Bros., 1878.
Azarian: An Episode. Boston: Ticknor and Fields, 1864.
The Elder's People. Boston: Houghton Mifflin, 1920.

Selected Bibliography

Hester Stanley at St. Marks. Boston: Roberts Brothers, 1882.
Hester Stanley's Friends. Boston: Little, Brown, 1898.
House and Hearth. New York: Dodd, Mead, 1891.
An Inheritance. New York: Charles Scribner's Sons, 1897.
In Titian's Garden and Other Poems. Boston: Copeland and Day, 1897.
A Little Book of Friends. Boston: Little Brown, 1916.
The Marquis of Carabas. Boston: Roberts Brothers, 1882.
The Maid He Married. Chicago: Herbert S. Stone, 1899.
The Making of a Fortune. A Romance. New York: Harper & Bros., 1911.
A Master Spirit. New York: Charles Scribners' Sons, 1896.
New-England Legends. Boston: James R. Osgood, 1871.
Old Madame and Other Tragedies. Boston: Richard G. Badger, 1900.
Old Washington. Boston: Little, Brown, 1906.
Poems. Boston: Houghton, Mifflin, 1882.
A Scarlet Poppy and Other Stories. New York: Harper & Bros., 1894.
The Servant Girl Question. Boston: Houghton, Mifflin, 1881.
Sir Rohan's Ghost: A Romance. Boston: J. E. Tilton, 1860.
The Thief in the Night. Boston: Roberts Brothers, 1872.

SOURCES AND FURTHER READING

Benardete, Jane, and Phyllis Moe, eds. *Companions of Our Youth: Stories by Women for Young People's Magazines, 1865–1900.* New York: Frederick Ungar, 1980.

Cooke, Rose Terry. "Harriet Prescott Spofford." *Our Famous Women.* Hartford: A. D. Worthington, 1884. 521–38.

Dalke, Anne. "'Circumstance' and the Creative Woman: Harriet Prescott Spofford." *Arizona Quarterly* 41/1 (Spring 1985): 71–85.

Fetterley, Judith. *Provisions: A Reader from 19th-Century American Women.* Bloomington: Indiana UP, 1985. 261–68.

Halbeisen, Elizabeth K. *Harriet Prescott Spofford: A Romantic Survival.* Philadelphia: U of Pennsylvania P, 1935.

Harper's Bazar. "Personals." 4 (25 Feb. 1871): 115; 5 (9 Mar. 1872): 171; 5 (27 Apr. 1872): 283; 15 (12 Aug. 1882): 499; 18 (21 Nov. 1885): 747;

22 (6 July 1889): 491; 22 (23 Nov. 1889): 835; 23 (6 Sept. 1890): 687; 25 (5 Nov. 1892): 891; 27 (24 Feb. 1894): 147; 29 (28 Mar. 1896): 275.

Higginson, Mary Thacher, ed. *Letters and Journals of Thomas Wentworth Higginson, 1846–1906.* New York: Da Capo, 1969.

Higginson, Thomas. *Cheerful Yesterdays.* Boston: Houghton, Mifflin, 1894.

Howells, W. D. *Literary Friends and Acquaintance.* 1900. rpt. Bloomington: Indiana UP, 1968.

————. "A Reminiscent Introduction." *The Great Modern American Stories.* New York: Boni and Liveright, 1920.

James, Henry. Rev. of *The Amber Gods. North American Review* (Oct. 1863): 568–70.

————. Rev. of *Azarian. North American Review* (Jan. 1865): 268–77.

Kelley, Mary. *Private Woman, Public Stage: Literary Domesticity in Nineteenth-Century America.* New York: Oxford UP, 1984.

Lowell, James Russell. Rev. of *Sir Rohan's Ghost. Atlantic Monthly* (Feb. 1860): 252–54.

Pattee, Fred Lewis. *The Development of the American Short Story.* New York: Harper, 1923.

Phelps, Elizabeth Stuart. "Stories That Stay." *The Century Magazine* N.S. 59: 118–23.

Quinn, Arthur Hobson. *American Fiction: An Historical and Critical Survey.* New York: Appleton, 1936.

St. Armand, Barton Levi. *Emily Dickinson and Her Culture.* Cambridge: Cambridge UP, 1984.

————. "'I Must Have Died at Ten Minutes Past One': Posthumous Reveries in Harriet Prescott Spofford's 'The Amber Gods.'" *The Haunted Dusk: American Supernatural Fiction, 1820–1920.* Eds. Howard Kerr, John W. Crowley, and Charles L. Crow. Athens: U of Georgia P, 1983. 101–19.

Vasari, Giorgio. "Giorgione da Castelfranco." *Lives of the Artists.* Trans. A. B. Hinds. New York: Dutton, Everyman's Library, 1963. 2:168–72.

A NOTE ON THE TEXT

The bibliography of Spofford's primary works in Elizabeth K. Halbeisen's biography lists some 275 stories; clearly it is incomplete. Spofford's unpublished letters sometimes refer to titles not listed there. Some of her fiction appeared anonymously and has never been identified. Some appeared in journals that have never been (and may never be) indexed. A good deal of this unknown fiction is likely to be ephemeral, but some impressive pieces may be buried away. Halbeisen's biography is still the fullest and most reliable guide to Spofford's life and works; it includes brief accounts of many of the stories that appeared in the major periodicals, attempting to single out those that possess merit. Although Halbeisen's judgment is usually sound, it is sometimes overly generous and rarely explains fully the strengths of Spofford's best work.

The ten stories selected from Spofford's six decades as a professional writer represent her most successful work and thus emphasize her attempt to extend the boundaries of American romantic fiction. For those stories collected in book form, the text is taken from first editions of *The Amber Gods* and *Old Madame;* a brief comparison with the original magazine versions reveals no major changes except for "The Amber Gods," which was divided slightly differently in its original publication in the *Atlantic*. The text of the original magazine version has been used for the five stories that Spofford never published in book form.

A Note on the Text

The publication history of the stories is as follows: "In a Cellar," *Atlantic* (Feb. 1859), "The Amber Gods," *Atlantic* (Jan. and Feb. 1860), "Circumstance," *Atlantic* (May 1860), all three rpt. in *The Amber Gods* (Boston, 1863); "In the Maguerriwock," *Harper's* (Aug. 1868); "The Moonstone Mass," *Harper's* (Oct. 1868); "The Black Bess," *Galaxy* (May 1868); "Her Story," *Lippincott's* (Dec. 1872), rpt. in *Old Madame* (Boston, 1900); "Miss Susan's Love Affair," *Harper's* (June 1876); "Old Madame," *Century* (Jan. 1882), rpt. in *Old Madame* (Boston, 1900); "The Godmothers," *Cosmopolitan* (Mar. 1896).

"*THE AMBER GODS*"
and Other Stories

IN A CELLAR

IT WAS THE DAY of Madame de St. Cyr's dinner, an event I never missed; for, the mistress of a mansion in the Faubourg St. Germain, there still lingered about her the exquisite grace and good-breeding peculiar to the old *régime,* that insensibly communicates itself to the guests till they move in an atmosphere of ease that constitutes the charm of home. One was always sure of meeting desirable and well-assorted people here, and a *contre-temps* was impossible. Moreover, the house was not at the command of all; and Madame de St. Cyr, with the daring strength which, when found in a woman at all, should, to be endurable, be combined with a sweet but firm restraint, rode rough-shod over the parvenus of the Empire, and was resolute enough to insulate herself even among the old *noblesse,* who, as all the world knows, insulate themselves from the rest of France. There were rare qualities in this woman, and were I to have selected one who with an even hand should carry a snuffy candle through a magazine of powder, my choice would have devolved upon her; and she would have done it.

I often looked, and not unsuccessfully, to discern what heritage her daughter had in these little affairs. Indeed, to one like myself, Delphine presented the worthier study. She wanted the airy charm of manner, the suavity and tenderness of her mother,—a deficiency easily to be pardoned in one of such delicate and extraordinary beauty. And perhaps her face was the truest index of her mind; not that it ever transparently displayed a genuine emotion,—Delphine was too well bred for that,—but the outline of her features had a keen regular precision, as if cut in a gem. Her exquisite color seldom varied, her eyes were like blue steel, she was statue-like and stony. But had one paused there, pronouncing her hard and impassive, he had committed an error. She had no great capability for passion, but she was not to be deceived; one metallic flash of her eye would cut like a sword through the whole mesh of entanglements with which you had surrounded her; and frequently, when alone with her, you perceived cool recesses in her nature, sparkling and pleasant, which jealously guarded themselves from a nearer approach. She was infinitely *spirituelle;*[1] compared to her, Madame herself was heavy.

At the first, I had seen that Delphine must be the wife of a diplomate. What diplomate? For a time asking myself the question seriously, I decided in the negative, which did not, however, prevent Delphine from fulfilling her destiny, since there were others. She was, after all, like a draught of rich old wine, all fire and sweetness. These things were not generally seen in her; I was more favored than many; and I looked at her with pitiless perspicacious eyes. Nevertheless, I had not the least advantage; it was, in fact, between us, diamond cut diamond,—which, oddly enough, brings me back to my story.

Some years previously, I had been sent on a special mission to the government at Paris, and having finally executed it, I resigned the post, and resolved to make my residence there, since it is the only place on earth where one can live. Every morning I half expect to see the country, beyond the city, white with an encampment of the nations, who, having peacefully flocked there over night, wait till the Rue St. Honoré shall run out and greet them. It surprises me, sometimes, that those pretending to civilization are content to remain at a distance. What experience have they of life,—not to mention gayety and pleasure, but of the great purpose of life,—society? Man evidently is gregarious; Fourier's fables[2] are founded on fact; we are nothing without our opposites, our fellows, our lights and shadows, colors, relations, combinations, our *point d'appui,*[3] and our angle of sight. An isolated man is immensurable; he is also unpicturesque, unnatural, untrue. He is no longer the lord of Nature, animal and vegetable,—but Nature is the lord of him; the trees, skies, flowers, predominate, and he is in as bad taste as green and blue, or as an oyster in a vase of roses. The race swings naturally to clusters. It being admitted, then, that society is our normal state, where is it to be obtained in such perfection as at Paris? Show me the urbanity, the generosity in trifles, better than sacrifice, the incuriousness and freedom, the grace, and wit, and honor, that will equal such as I find here. Morality,—we were not speaking of it,—the intrusion is unnecessary; must that word with Anglo-Saxon pertinacity dog us round the world? A hollow mask, which Vice now and then lifts for a breath of air, I grant you this state may be called; but since I find the vice elsewhere, countenance my preference for the accompanying mask. But even this is vanishing; such drawing-rooms as Mme. de St. Cyr's are less and less frequent. Yet, though the delightful spell of the last century daily dissipates itself, and we are not now what we were twenty years ago, still Paris is, and will be to the end of time, for a cosmopolitan, the pivot on which the world revolves.

It was, then, as I have said, the day of Mme. de St. Cyr's dinner. Punctually at the hour, I presented myself,—for I have always esteemed it the least courtesy which a guest can render, that he should not cool his hostess's dinner.

The usual choice company waited. There was the Marquis of G., the ambassador from home; Col. Leigh, an *attaché* of that embassy; the Spanish and Belgian ministers;—all of whom, with myself, completed a diplomatic circle. There were also wits and artists, but no ladies whose beauty exceeded that of the St. Cyrs. With nearly all of this assemblage I held certain relations, so that I was immediately at ease. G. was the only one whom, perhaps, I would rather not have met, although we were the best of friends. They awaited but one, the Baron Stahl. Meanwhile Delphine stood coolly taking the measurement of the Marquis of G., while her mother entertained one and another guest with a low-toned flattery, gentle interest, or lively narration, as the case might demand.

In a country where a *coup d'état* was as easily given as a box on the ear, we all attentively watched for the arrival of one who had been sent from a neighboring empire to negotiate a loan for the tottering throne of this. Nor was expectation kept long on guard. In a moment, "His Excellency, the Baron Stahl!" was announced.

The exaggeration of his low bow to Mme. de St. Cyr, the gleam

3

askance of his black eye, the absurd simplicity of his dress, did not particularly please me. A low forehead, straight black brows, a beardless
cheek with a fine color which give him a fictitiously youthful appearance,
were the most striking traits of his face; his person was not to be found
fault with; but he boldly evinced his admiration for Delphine, and with a
wicked eye.

As we were introduced, he assured me, in pure English, that he had
pleasure in making the acquaintance of a gentleman whose services were
so distinguished.

I, in turn, assured him of my pleasure in meeting a gentleman who
appreciated them.

I had arrived at the house of Mme. de St. Cyr with a load on my mind,
which for four weeks had weighed there; but before I thus spoke, it was
lifted and gone. I had seen the Baron Stahl before, although not previously
aware of it; and now, as he bowed, talked my native tongue so smoothly,
drew a glove over the handsome hand upon whose first finger shone the
only incongruity of his attire, a broad gold ring, holding a gaudy red
stone,—as he stood smiling and expectant before me, a sudden chain of
events flashed through my mind, an instantaneous heat, like lightning,
welded them into logic. A great problem was resolved. For a second, the
breath seemed snatched from my lips; the next, a lighter, freer man never
trod in diplomatic shoes.

I really beg your pardon,—but perhaps from long usage, it has become impossible for me to tell a straight story. It is absolutely necessary to
inform you of events already transpired.

In the first place, then, I, at this time, possessed a valet, the pink of
valets, an Englishman,—and not the less valuable to me in a foreign capital, that, notwithstanding his long residence, he was utterly unable to
speak one word of French intelligibly. Reading and writing it readily, his
thick tongue could master scarcely a syllable. The adroitness and perfection with which he performed the duties of his place were unsurpassable.
To a certain extent I was obliged to admit him into my confidence; I was
not at all in his. In dexterity and despatch he equalled the advertisements.
He never condescended to don my cast-off apparel, but, disposing of it,
always arrayed himself in plain but gentlemanly garments. These do not
complete the list of Hay's capabilities. He speculated. Respectable tene-

ments in London called him landlord; in the funds certain sums lay subject to his order; to a profitable farm in Hants he contemplated future retirement; and passing upon the Bourse, I have received a grave bow, and have left him in conversation with an eminent capitalist respecting consols, drafts, exchange, and other erudite mysteries, where I yet find myself in the A B C. Thus not only was my valet a free-born Briton, but a landed proprietor. If the Rothschilds blacked your boots or shaved your chin, your emotions might be akin to mine. When this man, who had an interest in the India traders, brought the hot water into my dressing-room, of a morning, the Antipodes were tributary to me. To what extent might any little irascibility of mine drive a depression in the market! and I knew, as he brushed my hat, whether stocks rose or fell. In one respect, I was essentially like our Saxon ancestors,—my servant was a villain. If I had been merely a civilian, in any purely private capacity, having leisure to attend to personal concerns in the midst of the delicate specialties intrusted to me from the cabinet at home, the possession of so inestimable a valet might have bullied me beyond endurance. As it was, I found it rather agreeable than otherwise. He was tacitly my secretary of finance.

Several years ago, a diamond of wonderful size and beauty, having wandered from the East, fell into certain imperial coffers among our Continental neighbors; and at the same time some extraordinary intelligence, essential to the existence, so to speak, of that government, reached a person there who fixed as its price this diamond. After a while he obtained it, but, judging that prudence lay in departure, took it to England, where it was purchased for an enormous sum by the Duke of —— as he will remain an unknown quantity, let us say X. There are probably not a dozen such diamonds in the world,—certainly not three in England. It rejoiced in such flowery appellatives as the Sea of Splendor, the Moon of Milk; and, of course, those who had but parted with it under protest, as it were, determined to obtain it again at all hazards;—they were never famous for scrupulosity. The Duke of X. was aware of this, and, for a time, the gem had lain idle, its glory muffled in a casket; but finally, on some grand occasion, a few months prior to the period of which I have spoken above, it was determined to set it in the Duchess's coronet. Accordingly, one day, it was given by her son, the Marquis of G., into the hands of their solicitor, who should deliver it to her Grace's jeweller. It lay in a small shagreen case, and before the Marquis left, the solicitor placed the case in a flat leathern box, where lay a chain of most singular workmanship, the clasp of which was deranged. This chain was very broad, of a style known as the brick-work, but every brick was a tiny gem, set in a delicate filagree linked with the next, and the whole rainbowed lustrousness moving at your will, like the scales of some gorgeous Egyptian serpent;—the solicitor was to take this also to the jeweller. Having laid the box in his private desk, Ulster, his confidential clerk, locked it, while he bowed the Marquis down. Returning immediately, the solicitor took the flat box and drove to the jeweller's. He found the latter so crowded with customers, it being the fashionable hour, as to be unable to attend to him; he, however, took the solicitor into his inner room, a dark fire-proof place, and there quickly deposited the box within a safe, which stood inside another, like a Japanese puzzle, and the solicitor, seeing the doors double-locked and secured, departed; the other promising to attend to the matter on the morrow.

Early the next morning, the jeweller entered his dark room, and proceeded to unlock the safe. This being concluded, and the inner one also thrown open, he found the box in a last and entirely, as he had always believed, secret compartment. Anxious to see this wonder, this Eye of Morning, and Heart of Day, he eagerly loosened the band and unclosed the box. It was empty. There was no chain there; the diamond was missing. The sweat streamed from his forehead, his clothes were saturated, he believed himself the victim of a delusion. Calling an assistant, every article and nook in the dark room was examined. At last, in an extremity of despair, he sent for the solicitor, who arrived in a breath. The jeweller's alarm hardly equalled that of the other. In his sudden dismay, he at first forgot the circumstances and dates relating to the affair; afterward was doubtful. The Marquis of G. was summoned, the police called in, the jeweller given into custody. Every breath the solicitor continued to draw only built up his ruin. He swallowed laudanum, but, by making it an overdose, frustrated his own design. He was assured, on his recovery, that no suspicion attached to him. The jeweller now asseverated that the diamond had never been given to him; but though the jeweller had committed perjury, this was, nevertheless, strictly true. Of course, whoever had the stone would not attempt to dispose of it at present, and, though communications were opened with the general European police, there was very little to work upon. But by means of this last step the former possessors became aware of its loss, and I make no doubt had their agents abroad immediately.

Meanwhile, the case hung here, complicated and tantalizing, when one morning I woke in London. No sooner had G. heard of my arrival than he called, and, relating the affair, requested my assistance. I confess myself to have been interested,—foolishly so, I thought afterward; but we all have our weaknesses, and diamonds were mine. In company with the Marquis, I waited upon the solicitor, who entered into the few details minutely, calling frequently upon Ulster, a young, fresh-looking man, for corroboration. We then drove to the jeweller's new quarters, took him, under charge of the officers, to his place of business, where he nervously showed me every point that could bear upon the subject, and ended by exclaiming, that he was ruined, and all for a stone he had never seen. I sat quietly for a few moments. It stood, then, thus:——G. had given the thing to the solicitor, seen it put into the box, seen the box put into the desk; but while the confidential clerk, Ulster, locked the desk, the solicitor waited on the Marquis to the door,—returning, took the box, without opening it again, to the jeweller, who, in the hurry, shut it up in his safe, also without opening it. The case was perfectly clear. These mysterious things are always so simple! You know now, as well as I, who took the diamond.

I did not choose to volunteer, but assented, on being desired. The police and I were old friends; they had so often assisted me, that I was not afraid to pay them in kind, and accordingly agreed to take charge of the case, still retaining their aid, should I require it. The jeweller was now restored to his occupation, although still subjected to a rigid surveillance, and I instituted inquiries into the recent movements of the young man Ulster. The case seemed to me to have been very blindly conducted. But, though all that was brought to light concerning him in London was perfectly fair and aboveboard, it was discovered that, not long since, he had visited Paris,—on the solicitor's business, of course, but gaining thereby an opportunity to transact any little affairs of his own. This was fortunate; for if any one could do anything in Paris, it was myself.

It is not often that I act as a detective. But one homogeneous to every situation could hardly play a pleasanter part for once. I have thought that our great masters in theory and practice, Machiavel and Talleyrand, were hardly more, on a large scale.

I was about to return to Paris, but resolved to call previously on the solicitor again. He welcomed me warmly, although my suspicions had not been imparted to him, and, with a more cheerful heart than had lately been habitual to him, entered into an animated conversation respecting the great case of Biter *v.* Bit, then absorbing so much of the public attention, frequently addressing Ulster, whose remarks were always pertinent, brief, and clear. As I sat actively discussing the topic, feeling no more interest in it than in the end of that cigar I just cut off, and noting exactly every look and motion of the unfortunate youth, I recollect the curious sentiment that filled me regarding him. What injury had he done me, that I should pursue him with punishment? Me? I am, and every individual is, integral with the commonwealth. It was the commonwealth he had injured. Yet, even then, why was I the one to administer justice? Why not continue with my coffee in the morning, my kings and cabinets and national chess at noon, my opera at night, and let the poor devil go? Why, but that justice is brought home to every member of society,—that naked duty requires no shirking of such responsibility,—that, had I failed here, the crime might, with reason, lie at my door and multiply, the criminal increase himself?

Very possibly you will not unite with me; but these little catechisms are, once in a while, indispensable, to vindicate one's course to one's self.

This Ulster was a handsome youth;—the rogues have generally all the good looks. There was nothing else remarkable about him but his quickness; he was perpetually on the alert; by constant activity, the rust was never allowed to collect on his faculties; his sharpness was distress-ing,—he appeared subject to a tense strain. Now his quill scratched over the paper unconcernedly, while he could join as easily in his master's conversation: nothing seemed to preoccupy him, or he held a mind open at every point. It is pitiful to remember him that morning, sitting quiet, unconscious, and free, utterly in the hands of that mighty Inquisition, the Metropolitan Police, with its countless arms, its cells and myrmidons in the remotest corners of the Continent,—at the mercy of so merciless a monster, and momently closer involved, like some poor prey round which a spider spins its bewildering web. It was also curious to observe the sudden suspicion that darkened his face at some innocent remark,—the quick shrinking and intrenched retirement, the manifest sting and rancor, as I touched his wound with a swift flash of my slender weapon and sheathed it again, and, after the thrust, the espionage, and the relief at believing it accidental. He had many threads to gather up and hold;—little electric warnings along them must have been constantly shocking him. He did that part well enough; it was a mistake, to begin with; he needed prudence. At that time I owed this Ulster nothing; now, however, I owe him a grudge, for some of the most harassing hours of my life were occasioned me by him. But I shall not cherish enmity on that account. With so promising a beginning, he will graduate and take his degree from the loftiest altitude in his line. Hemp is a narcotic; let it bring me forgetfulness.

In Paris I found it not difficult to trace such a person, since he was both foreign and unaccustomed. It was ascertained that he had posted several letters. A person of his description had been seen to drop a letter, the superscription of which had been read by one who picked it up for him. This superscription was the address of the very person who was likely to be the agent of the former possessors of the diamond, and had attracted attention. After all,—you know the Secret Force,—it was not so impossible to imagine what this letter contained, despite of its cipher. Such a person also had been met among the Jews, and at certain shops whose reputation was not of the clearest. He had called once or twice on Mme. de St. Cyr, on business relative to a vineyard adjoining her château in the Gironde,[4] which she had sold to a wine merchant of England. I found a zest in the affair, as I pursued it.

We were now fairly at sea, but before long I found we were likely to remain there; in fact, nothing of consequence eventuated. I began to regret having taken the affair from the hands in which I had found it, and one day, it being a gala or some insatiable saint's day, I was riding, perplexed with that and other matters, and paying small attention to the passing crowd. I was vexed and mortified, and had fully decided to throw up the whole,—on such hairs do things hang,—when, suddenly turning a corner, my bridle-reins became entangled in the snaffle of another rider. I loosened them abstractedly, and not till it was necessary to bow to my strange antagonist, on parting, did I glance up. The person before me was evidently not accustomed to play the dandy; he wore his clothes ill, sat his horse worse, and was uneasy in the saddle. The unmistakable air of the *gamin* was apparent beneath the superficies of the gentleman. Conspicuous on his costume, and wound like an order of merit upon his breast, glittered a chain, *the* chain,—each tiny brick-like gem spiked with a hundred sparks, and building a fabric of sturdy probabilities with the celerity of the genii in constructing Aladdin's palace. There, a cable to haul up the treasure, was the chain;—where was the diamond? I need not tell you how I followed this young friend, with what assiduity I kept him in sight, up and down, all day long, till, weary at last of his fine sport, as I certainly was of mine, he left his steed in stall and fared on his way a-foot. Still pursuing, now I threaded quay and square, street and alley, till he disappeared in a small shop, in one of those dark crowded lanes leading eastward from the Pont Neuf, in the city.[5] It was the sign of a *marchand des armures*,[6] and having provided myself with those persuasive arguments, a *sergent-de-ville* and a *gendarme,* I entered.

A place more characteristic it would be impossible to find. Here were piled bows of every material, ash, and horn, and tougher fibres, with slackened strings, and among them peered a rusty clarion and battle-axe, while the quivers that should have accompanied lay in a distant corner, their arrows serving to pin long, dusty, torn banners to the wall. Opposite the entrance, an archer in bronze hung on tiptoe, and levelled a steel bow, whose piercing *flèche*[7] seemed sparkling with impatience to spring from his finger and flesh itself in the heart of the intruder. The hauberk and halberd, lance and casque, arquebuse and sword, were suspended in friendly congeries; and fragments of costly stuff swept from ceiling to floor, crushed and soiled by the heaps of rusty firelocks, cutlasses, and gauntlets thrown upon them. In one place, a little antique bust was half hid in the folds of some pennon, still dyed with battle-stains; in another, scattered treasures of Dresden and Sèvres brought the drawing-room into the campaign; and all around bivouacked rifles, whose polished barrels glittered full of death,— pistols, variously mounted, for an insurgent at the barricades, or for a lost millionnaire at the gaming-table,—foils, with buttoned bluntness,—and rapiers whose even edges were viewless as if filed into air. Destruction lay everywhere, at the command of the owner of this place, and, had he possessed a particle of vivacity, it would have been hazardous to bow beneath his doorway. It did not, I must say, look like a place where I should find a diamond. As the owner came forward, I determined on my plan of action.

"You have, sir," I said, handing him a bit of paper, on which were scrawled some numbers, "a diamond in your possession, of such and so many carats, size, and value, belonging to the Duke of X., and left with you by an Englishman, Mr. Arthur Ulster. You will deliver it to me, if you please."

"Monsieur!" exclaimed the man, lifting his hands, and surveying me with the widest eyes I ever saw. "A diamond! In my possession! So immense a thing! It is impossible. I have not even seen one of the kind. It is a mistake. Jacques Noailles, the vender of jewels *en gros*,[8] second door below, must be the man. One should perceive that my business is with arms, not diamonds. I have it not; it would ruin me."

Here he paused for a reply, but, meeting none, resumed. "M. Arthur Ulster!—I have heard of no such person. I never spoke with an Englishman. Bah! I detest them! I have no dealings with them. I repeat, I have not your jewel. Do you wish anything more of me?"

His vehemence only convinced me of the truth of my suspicions.

"These heroics are out of place," I answered. "I demand the article in question."

"Monsieur doubts me?" he asked, with a rueful face,—"questions my word, which is incontrovertible?" Here he clapped his hand upon a *couteau-de-chasse*[9] lying near, but, appearing to think better of it, drew himself up, and, with a shower of nods flung at me, added, "I deny your accusation!" I had not accused him.

"You are at too much pains to convict yourself. I charge you with nothing," I said. "But this diamond must be surrendered."

"Monsieur is mad!" he exclaimed, "mad! he dreams! Do I look like one who possesses such a trophy? Does my shop resemble a mine? Look about! See! All that is here would not bring a hundredth part of its price. I beseech Monsieur to believe me; he has mistaken the number, or has been misinformed."

"We waste words. I know this diamond is here, as well as a costly chain—"

"On my soul, on my life, on my honor," he cried, clasping his hands and turning up his eyes, "there is here nothing of the kind. I do not deal in gems. A little silk, a few weapons, a curiosity, a nicknack, comprise my stock. I have not the diamond. I do not know the thing. I am poor. I am honest. Suspicion destroys me!"

"As you will find, should I be longer troubled by your denials."

He was inflexible, and, having exhausted every artifice of innocence, wiped the tears from his eyes,—oh, these French! life is their theatre,— and remained quiet. It was getting dark. There was no gas in the place; but in the pause a distant street-lamp swung its light dimly round.

"Unless one desires to purchase, allow me to say that it is my hour for closing," he remarked, blandly, rubbing his black-bearded chin.

"My time is valuable," I returned. "It is late and dark. When your shop-boy lights up—"

"Pardon,—we do not light."

"Permit me, then, to perform that office for you. In this blaze you may perceive my companions, whom you have not appeared to recognize."

So saying, I scratched a match upon the floor, and, as the *sergent-de-ville* and the *gendarme* advanced, threw the light of the blue spirt of sulphurous flame upon them. In a moment more the match went out, and we remained in the demi-twilight of the distant lantern. The *marchand des armures* stood petrified and aghast. Had he seen the imps of Satan in that instant, it could have had no greater effect.

"You have seen them?" I asked. "I regret to inconvenience you; but unless this diamond is produced at once, my friends will put their seal on your goods, your property will be confiscated, yourself in a dungeon. In other words, I allow you five minutes; at the close of that time you will have chosen between restitution and ruin."

He remained apparently lost in thought. He was a big, stout man, and with one blow his powerful fist could easily have settled me. It was the last thing in his mind. At length he lifted his head,—"Rosalie!" he called.

At the word, a light foot pattered along a stone floor within, and in a moment a little woman stood in an arch raised by two steps from our own level. Carrying a candle, she descended and tripped toward him. She was not pretty, but sprightly and keen, as the perpetual attrition of life must needs make her, and wore the everlasting grisette costume, which displays the neatest of ankles, and whose cap is more becoming than wreaths of garden millinery. I am too minute, I see, but it is second nature. The two commenced a vigorous whispering amid sundry gestures and glances. Suddenly the woman turned, and, laying the prettiest of little hands on my sleeve, said, with a winning smile,—

"Is it a crime of *lèse-majesté?*" [10]

This was a new idea, but might be useful.

"Not yet," I said; "two minutes more, and I will not answer for the consequence."

Other whispers ensued.

"Monsieur," said the man, leaning on one arm over the counter, and looking up in my face, with the most engaging frankness,—"it is true that I have such a disamond; but it is not mine. It is left with me to be delivered to the Baron Stahl, who comes as an agent from his court for its purchase."

"Yes,—I know."

"He was to have paid me half a million francs,—not half its worth,—in trust for the person who left it, who is not M. Arthur Ulster, but Mme. de St. Cyr."

Madame de St. Cyr! How under the sun—No,—it could not be possible. The case stood as it stood before. The rogue was in deeper water than I had thought; he had merely employed Mme. de St. Cyr. I ran this over in my mind, while I said, "Yes."

"Now, sir," I continued, "you will state the terms of this transaction."

"With pleasure. For my trouble I was myself to receive patronage and five thousand francs. The Baron is to be here directly, on other and public business. *Reine du ciel,* [11] Monsieur! how shall I meet him?"

"He is powerless in Paris; your fear is idle."

"True. There were no other terms."

"Nor papers?"

"The lady thought it safest to be without them. She took merely my receipt, which the Baron Stahl will bring to me from her before receiving this."

"I will trouble you for it now."

He bowed and shuffled away. At a glance from me, the *gendarme* slipped to the rear of the building, where three others were stationed at the two exits in that direction, to caution them of the critical moment, and returned. Ten minutes passed,—the merchant did not appear. If, after all, he had made off with it! There had been the click of a bolt, the half-stifled rattle of arms, as if a door had been opened and rapidly closed again, but nothing more.

"I will see what detains my friend," said Mademoiselle, the little woman.

We suffered her to withdraw. In a moment more a quick expostulation was to be heard.

"They are there, the *gendarmes,* my little one! I should have run, but they caught me, the villains! and replaced me in the house. *Oh, sacre!*"— and rolling this word between his teeth, he came down and laid a little box on the counter. I opened it. There was within a large, glittering, curiously-cut piece of glass. I threw it aside.

"The diamond!" I exclaimed.

"Monsieur had it," he replied, stooping to pick up the glass with every appearance of surprise and care.

"Do you mean to say you endeavored to escape with that bawble? Produce the diamond instantly, or you shall hang as high as Haman!" I roared.

Whether he knew the individual in question or not, the threat was efficient; he trembled and hesitated, and finally drew the identical shagreen [12] case from his bosom.

"I but jested," he said. "Monsieur will witness that I relinquish it with reluctance."

"I will witness that you receive stolen goods!" I cried, in wrath.

He placed it in my hands.

"Oh!" he groaned, from the bottom of his heart, hanging his head, and laying both hands on the counter before him,—"it pains, it grieves me to part with it!"

"and the chain," I said.

"Monsieur did not demand that!"

"I demand it now."

In a moment, the chain also was given me.

"And now will Monsieur do me a favor? Will he inform me by what means he ascertained these facts?"

I glanced at the *garçon,* who had probably supplied himself with his master's finery illicitly;—he was the means;—we have some generosity;—I thought I should prefer doing him the favor, and declined.

I unclasped the shagreen case; the *sergent-de-ville* and the *gendarme* stole up and looked over my shoulder; the *garçon* drew near with round eyes; the little woman peeped across; the merchant, with tears streaming over his face, gazed as if it had been a loadstone; finally, I looked myself. There it lay, the glowing, resplendent thing! flashing in affluence of splendor, throbbing and palpitant with life, drawing all the light from the little woman's candle, from the sparkling armor around, from the steel barbs, and the distant lantern, into its bosom. It was scarcely so large as I had expected to see it, but more brilliant than anything I could conceive of. I do not believe there is another such in the world. One saw clearly that the Oriental superstitition of the sex of stones was no fable; this was essentially the female of diamonds, the queen herself, the principle of life, the rejoicing receptive force. It was not radiant, as the term literally taken implies; it seemed rather to retain its wealth,—instead of emitting its glorious rays, to curl them back like the fringe of a madrepore, and lie there with redoubled quivering scintillations, a mass of white magnificence, not prismatic, but a vast milky lustre. I closed the case; on reopening it, I could scarcely believe that the beautiful sleepless eye would again flash upon me. I did not comprehend how it could afford such perpetual richness, such sheets of lustre.

At last we compelled ourselves to be satisfied. I left the shop, dismissed my attendants, and, fresh from the contemplation of this miracle, again trod the dirty, reeking streets, crossed the bridge, with its lights, its warehouses midway, its living torrents who poured on unconscious of the beauty within their reach. The thought of their ignorance of the treasure, not a dozen yards distant, has often made me question if we all are not equally unaware of other and greater processes of life, of more perfect, sublimed, and, as it were, spiritual crystallizations going on invisibly about us. But had these been told of the thing clutched in the hand of a passer, how many of them would have know where to turn? and we,—are we any better?

II

FOR a few days I carried the diamond about my person, and did not mention its recovery even to my valet, who knew that I sought it, but communicated only with the Marquis of G., who replied, that he would be in Paris on a certain day, when I could safely deliver it to him.

It was now generally rumored that the neighboring government was about to send us the Baron Stahl, ambassador concerning arrangements for a loan to maintain the sinking monarchy in supremacy at Paris, the usual synecdoche for France.

The weather being fine, I proceeded to call on Mme. de St. Cyr. She received me in her boudoir, and on my way thither I could not but observe the perfect quiet and cloistered seclusion that prevaded the whole house,—the house itself seeming only an adjunct of the still and sunny garden, of which one caught a glimpse through the long open hall-windows beyond. This boudoir did not differ from others to which I have been admitted: the same delicate shades; all the dainty appliances of Art for beauty; the lavish profusion of *bijouterie;* and the usual statuettes of innocence, to indicate, perhaps, the presence of that commodity which might not be guessed at otherwise; and burning in a silver cup, a rich perfume loaded the air with voluptuous sweetness. Through a half-open door an inner boudoir was to be seen, which must have been Delphine's; it looked like her; the prevailing hue was a soft purple, or gray; a *prie-dieu,* a book-shelf, and desk, of a dark West Indian wood, were just visible. There was but one picture,—a sad-eyed, beautiful Fate. It was the type of her nation. I think she worshipped it. And how apt is misfortune to degenerate into Fate!—not that the girl had ever experienced the former, but, dissatisfied with life, and seeing no outlet, she accepted it stoically and waited till it should be over. She needed to be aroused;—the station of an *ambassadrice,* which I desired for her, might kindle the spark. There were no flowers, no perfumes, no busts, in this ascetic place. Delphine herself, in some faint rosy gauze, her fair hair streaming round her, as she lay on a white-draped couch, half-risen on one arm, while she read the morning's *feuilleton,* was the most perfect statuary of which a room could boast,—illumined, as I saw her, by the gay beams that entered at the loftily-arched window, broken only by the flickering of the vine-leaves that clustered the curiously-latticed panes without. She resembled in kind a Nymph, just bursting from the sea; so Pallas might have posed for Aphrodite. Madame de St. Cyr received me with *empressement,* and, so doing, closed the door of this shrine. We spoke of various things,—of the court, the theatre, the weather, the world, —skating lightly round the slender edges of her secret, till finally she invited me to lunch with her in the garden. Here, on a rustic table, stood wine and a few delicacies,—while, by extending a hand, we could grasp the hanging pears and nectarines, still warm to the lip and luscious with sunshine, as we disputed possession with the envious wasp who had established a priority of claim.

"It is to be hoped," I said, sipping the *Haut-Brion,* whose fine and brittle smack contrasted rarely with the delicious juiciness of the fruit, "that you have laid in a supply of this treasure that neither moth nor rust doth corrupt, before parting with that little gem in the Gironde."

"Ah? You know, then, that I have sold it?"

"Yes," I replied. "I have the pleasure of Mr. Ulster's acquaintance."

"He arranged the terms for me," she said, with restraint,—adding, "I could almost wish now that it had not been."

This was probably true; for the sum which she hoped to receive from Ulster for standing sponsor to his jewel was possibly equal to the price of her vineyard.

"It was indispensable at the time, this sale; I thought best to hazard it on one more season.—If, after such advantages, Delphine will not marry, why—it remains to retire into the country and end our days with the barbarians!" she continued, shrugging her shoulders; "I have a house there."

"But you will not be obliged to throw us all into despair by such a step now," I replied.

She looked quickly, as if to see how nearly I had approached her citadel,—then, finding in my face no expression but a complimentary one, "No," she said, "I hope that my affairs have brightened a little. One never knows what is in store."

Before long I had assured myself that Mme. de St. Cyr was not a party to the theft, but had merely been hired by Ulster, who, discovering the state of her affairs, had not, therefore, revealed his own,—and this without in the least implying any knowledge on my part of the transaction. Ulster must have seen the necessity of leaving the business in the hands of a competent person, and Mme. de St. Cyr's financial talent was patent. There were few ladies in Paris who would have rejected the opportunity. Of these things I felt a tolerable certainty.

"We throng with foreigners," said Madame, archly, as I reached this point. "Diplomates, too. The Baron Stahl arrives in a day."

"I have heard," I responded. "You are acquainted?"

"Alas! no," she said. "I knew his father well, though he himself is not young. Indeed, the families thought once of intermarriage. But nothing has been said on the subject for many years. His Excellency, I hear, will strengthen himself at home by an alliance with the young Countess, the natural daughter of the Emperor."

"He surely will never be so imprudent as to rivet his chain by such a link!"

"It is impossible to compute the dice in those despotic countries," she rejoined,—which was pretty well, considering the freedom enjoyed by France at that period.

"It may be," I suggested, "that the Baron hopes to open this delicate subject with you yourself, Madame."

"It is unlikely," she said, sighing. "And for Delphine, should I tell her his Excellency preferred scarlet, she would infallibly wear blue. Imagine her, Monsieur, in fine scarlet, with a scarf of gold gauze, and rustling grasses in that unruly gold hair of hers! She would be divine!"

The maternal instinct as we have it here at Paris confounds me. I do not comprehend it. Here was a mother who did not particularly love her child, who would not be inconsolable at her loss, would not ruin her own complexion by care of her during illness, would send her through fire and water and every torture to secure or maintain a desirable rank, who yet would entangle herself deeply in intrigue, would not hesitate to tarnish her own reputation, and would, in fact, raise heaven and earth to—endow this child with a brilliant match. And Mme. de St. Cyr seemed to regard Delphine, still further, as a cool matter of Art.

These little confidences, moreover, are provoking. They put you yourself so entirely out of the question.

"Mlle. de St. Cyr's beauty is peerless," I said, slightly chagrined, and at a loss. "If hearts were trumps, instead of diamonds!"

"We are poor," resumed Madame, pathetically. "Delphine is not an heiress. Delphine is proud. She will not stoop to charm. Her coquetry is that of an Amazon. Her kisses are arrows. She is Medusa!" And Madame, her mother, shivered.

Here, with her hair knotted up and secured by a tiny dagger, her gauzy drapery gathered in her arm, Delphine floated down the green alley toward us, as if in a rosy cloud. But this soft aspect never could have been more widely contradicted than by the stony repose and cutting calm of her beautiful face.

"The Marquis of G.," said her mother, "he also arrives ambassador. Has he talent? Is he brilliant? Wealthy, of course,—but *gauche?*"

Therewith I sketched for them the Marquis and his surroundings.

"It is charming," said Madame. "Delphine, do you attend?"

"And why?" asked Delphine, half concealing a yawn with her dazzling hand. "It is wearisome; it matters not to me."

"But he will not go to marry himself in France," said her mother. "Oh, these English," she added, with a laugh, "yourself, Monsieur, being proof of it, will not mingle blood, lest the Channel should still flow between the little red globules! You will go? but to return shortly? You will dine with me soon? *Au revoir!*" and she gave me her hand graciously, while Delphine bowed as if I were already gone, threw herself into a garden-chair, and commenced pouring the wine on a stone for a little tame snake which came out and lapped it.

Such women as Mme. de St. Cyr have a species of magnetism about them. It is difficult to retain one's self-respect before them,—for no other reason than that one is, at the moment, absorbed into their individuality, and thinks and acts with them. Delphine must have had a strong will, and perpetual antagonism did not weaken it. As for me, Madame had, doubtless, reasons of her own for tearing aside these customary bands of reserve,—reasons which, if you do not perceive, I shall not enumerate.

"HAVE YOU MET WITH anything further in your search, sir?" asked my valet, next morning.

"Oh, yes, Hay," I returned, in a very good humor,—"with great success. You have assisted me so much, that I am sure I owe it to you to say that I have found the diamond."

"Indeed, sir, you are very kind. I have been interested, but my assistance is not worth mentioning. I thought likely it might be, you appeared so quiet."—The cunning dog!—"How did you find it, sir, may I ask?"

I briefly related the leading facts, since he had been aware of the progress of the case to that point,—without, however, mentioning Mme. de St. Cyr's name.

"And Monsieur did not inform us!" a French valet would have cried.

"You were prudent not to mention it, sir," said Hay. "These walls must have better ears than ordinary; for a family has moved in on the first floor recently, whose actions are extremely suspicious. But is this precious affair to be seen?"

I took it from an inner pocket and displayed it, having discarded the shagreen case as inconvenient.

"His Excellency must return as he came," said I.

Hay's eyes sparkled.

"And do you carry it there, sir?" he asked, with surprise, as I restored it to my waistcoat-pocket.

"I shall take it to the bank," I said. "I do not like the responsibility."

"It is very unsafe," was the warning of this cautious fellow. "Why, sir! any of these swells, these pickpockets, might meet you, run against you,—so!" said Hay, suiting the action to the word," and, with the little sharp knife concealed in just such a ring as this I wear, give a light tap, and there's a slit in your vest sir, but no diamond!"—and instantly resuming his former respectful deportment, Hay handed me my gloves and stick, and smoothed my hat.

"Nonsense!" I replied, drawing on the gloves, "I should like to see the man who could be too quick for me. Any news from India, Hay?"

"None of consequence, sir. The indigo crop is said to have failed, which advances the figure of that on hand, so that one or two fortunes will be made to-day. Your hat, sir?—your lunettes? Here they are, sir."

"Good morning, Hay."

"Good morning, sir."

I descended the stairs, buttoning my gloves, paused a moment at the door to look about, and proceeded down the street, which was not more than usually thronged. At the bank I paused to assure myself that the diamond was safe. My fingers caught in a singular slit. I started. As Hay had prophesied, there was a fine longitudinal cut in my waistcoat, but the pocket was empty. My God! the thing was gone. I never can forget the blank nihility of all existence that dreadful moment when I stood fumbling for what was not. Calm as I sit here and tell of it, I vow to you a shiver courses through me at the very thought. I had circumvented Stahl only to destroy myself. The diamond was lost again. My mind flew like lightning over every chance, and a thousand started up like steel spikes to snatch the bolt. For a moment I was stunned, but, never being very subject to despair, on my recovery, which was almost at once, took every measure that could be devised. Who had touched me? Whom had I met? Through what streets had I come? In ten minutes the Prefect had the matter in hand. My injunctions were strict privacy. I sincerely hoped the mishap would not reach England; and if the diamond were not recovered before the Marquis of G. arrived,—why, there was the Seine. It is all very well to talk,—yet suicide is so French an affair, that an Englishman does not take to it naturally, and, except in November, the Seine is too cold and damp for comfort, but during that month I suppose it does not greatly differ in these respects from our own atmosphere.

A preternatural activity now possessed me. I slept none, ate little, worked immoderately. I spared no efforts, for everything was at stake. In the midst of all, G. arrived. Hay also exerted himself to the utmost; I promised him a hundred pounds, if I found it. He never told me that he said how it would be, never intruded the state of the market, never resented my irritating conduct, but watched me with narrow yet kind solicitude, and frequently offered valuable suggestions, which, however, as everything else did, led to nothing. I did not call on G., but in a week or so his card was brought up one morning to me. "Deny me," I groaned. It yet wanted a week of the day on which I had promised to deliver him the diamond. Meanwhile the Baron Stahl had reached Paris, but he still remained in private,—few had seen him.

The police were forever on the wrong track. Today they stopped the old Comptesse du Quesne and her jewels, at the Barriere; to-morrow, with their long needles, they riddled a package of lace destined for the Duchess of X. herself; the Secret Service was doubled; and to crown all, a splendid new star of the testy Prince de Ligne was examined and proclaimed to be paste,—the Prince swearing vengeance, if he could discover the cause,—while half Paris must have been under arrest. My own hotel was ransacked thoroughly,—Hay begging that his traps might be included,—but nothing resulted, and I expected nothing, for, of course, I could swear that the stone was in my pocket when I stepped into the street. I confess I never was nearer madness,—every word and gesture stung me like asps,—I walked on burning coals. Enduring all this torment, I must yet meet my daily comrades, eat ices at Tortoni's, stroll on the Boulevards, call on my acquaintance, with the same equanimity as before. I believe I was equal to it. Only by contrast with that blessed time when Ulster and diamonds were unknown, could I imagine my past happiness, my present wretchedness. Rather than suffer it again, I would be stretched on the rack till every bone in my skin were broken. I cursed Mr. Arthur Ulster every hour in the day; myself, as well; and even now the word diamond sends a cold blast to my heart. I often met my friend the *marchand des armures.* It was his turn to triumph; I fancied there must be a hang-dog kind of air about me, as about every sharp man who has been outwitted. It wanted finally but two days of that on which I was to deliver the diamond.

One midnight, armed with a dark lantern and a cloak, I was traversing the streets alone,—unsuccessful, as usual, just now solitary, and almost in despair. As I turned a corner, two men were but scarcely visible a step before me. It was a badly-lighted part of the town. Unseen and noiseless I followed. They spoke in low tones,—almost whispers; or rather, one spoke,—the other seemed to nod assent.

"On the day but one after to-morrow," I heard spoken in English. Great Heavens! was it possible? had I arrived at a clew? That was the day of days for me. "You have given it, you say, in this billet,—I wish to be exact, you see," continued the voice,—"to prevent detection, you gave it, ten minutes after it came into your hands, to the butler of Madame——," (here the speaker stumbled on the rough pavement, and I lost the name,) "who," he continued, "will put it in the——" (a second stumble acted like a hiccough) "cellar."

"Wine-cellar," I thought; "and what then?"

"In the ——." A third stumble was followed by a round German

oath. How easy it is for me now to fill up the little blanks which that unhappy pavement caused!

"You share your receipts with this butler. On the day I obtain it," he added, and I now perceived his foreign accent, "I hand you one hundred thousand francs; afterward, monthly payments till you have received the stipulated sum. But how will this butler know me, in season to prevent a mistake? Hem!——he might give it to the other!"

My hearing had been trained to such a degree that I would have promised to catch any given dialogue of the spirits themselves, but the whisper that answered him eluded me. I caught nothing but a faint sibillation. "Your ring?" was the rejoinder. "He shall be instructed to recognize it? Very well. It is too large,——no, that will do, it fits the first finger. There is nothing more. I am under infinite obligations, sir; they shall be remembered. Adieu!"

The two parted; which should I pursue? In desperation I turned my lantern upon one, and illumined a face fresh with color, whose black eyes sparkled askance after the retreating figure, under straight black brows. In a moment more he was lost in a false *cul-de-sac,* and I found it impossible to trace the other.

I was scarcely better off than before; but it seemed to me that I had obtained something, and that now it was wisest to work this vein. "The butler of Madame ———." There were hundreds of thousands of Madames in town. I might call on all, and be as old as the Wandering Jew at the last call. The cellar. Wine-cellar, of course,——that came by a natural connection with butler,——but whose? There was one under my own abode; certainly I would explore it. Meanwhile, let us see the entertainments for Wednesday. The Prefect had a list of these. For some I found I had cards; I determined to allot a fraction of time to as many as possible; my friends in the Secret Service would divide the labor. Among others, Madame de St. Cyr gave a dinner, and, as she had been in the affair, I determined not to neglect her on this occasion, although having no definite idea of what had been, or plan of what should be done. I decided not to speak of this occurrence to Hay, since it might only bring him off some trail that he had struck.

Having been provided with keys, early on the following evening I entered the wine-cellar, and, concealed in an empty cask that would have held a dozen of me, waited for something to turn up. Really, when I think of myself, a diplomate, a courtier, a man-about-town, curled in a dusty, musty wine-barrel, I am moved with vexation and laughter. Nothing, however, turned up,—and at length I retired baffled. The next night came,— no news, no identification of my black-browed man, no success; but I felt certain that something must transpire in that cellar. I don't know why I had pitched upon that one in particular, but, at an earlier hour than on the previous night, I again donned the cask. A long time must have elapsed; dead silence filled the spacious vaults, except where now and then some Sillery cracked the air with a quick explosion, or some newer wine bubbled round the bung of its barrel with a faint effervescence. I had no intention of leaving this place till morning, but it suddenly appeared like the most woeful waste of time. The master of this tremendous affair should be abroad and active; who knew what his keen eyes might detect; what loss his absence might occasion in this nick of time? And here he was, shut up and locked in a wine-cellar! I began to be very nervous; I had already, with aid, searched every crevice of the cellar; and now I thought it would be some consolation to discover the thief, if I never regained the diamond. A distant clock tolled midnight. There was a faint noise,—a mouse?—no, it was too prolonged;—nor did it sound like the fiz of Champagne;—a great iron door was turning on its hinges; a man with a lantern was entering; another followed, and another. They seated themselves. In a few moments, appearing one by one and at intervals, some thirty people were in the cellar. Were they all to share in the proceeds of the diamond? With what jaundiced eye we behold things! I myself saw all that was only through the lens of this diamond, of which not one of these men had ever heard. As the lantern threw its feeble glimmer on this group, and I surveyed them through my loophole, I thought I had never seen so wild and savage a picture, such enormous shadows, such bold outline, such a startling flash on the face of their leader, such light retreating up the threatening arches. More resolute brows, more determined words, more unshrinking hearts, I had not met. In fact, I found myself in the centre of a conspiracy, a society as vindictive as the Jacobins, as unknown and terrible as the Marianne of to-day.[13] I was thunderstruck, too, at the countenances on which the light fell,—men the loyalest in estimation, ministers and senators, millionnaires who had no reason for discontent, dandies whose reason was supposed to be devoted to their tailors, poets and artists of generous aspiration and suspected tendencies, and one woman,—Delphine de St. Cyr. Their plans were brave, their determination lofty, their conclave serious and fine; yet as slowly they shut up their hopes and fears in the black masks, one man bent toward the lantern to adjust his. When he lifted his face before concealing it, I recognized him also. I had met him frequently at the Bureau of Police; he was, I believe, Secretary of the Secret Service.

I had no sympathy with these people. I had sufficient liberty myself, I was well enough satisfied with the world, I did not care to revolutionize France; but my heart rebelled at the mockery, as this traitor and spy, this creature of a system by which I gained my fame, showed his revolting face and veiled it again. And Delphine, what had she to do with them? One by one, as they entered, they withdrew, and I was left alone again. But all this was not my diamond.

Another hour elapsed. Again the door opened, and remained ajar. Some one entered, whom I could not see. There was a pause,—then a rustle,—the door creaked ever so little. "Art thou there?" lisped a shrill whisper,—a woman, as I could guess.

"My angel, it is I," was returned, a semitone lower. She approached, he advanced, and the consequence was a salute resonant as the smack with which a Dutch burggomaster may be supposed to set down his mug. I was prepared for anything. Ye gods! if it should be Delphine! But the base suspicion was birth-strangled as they spoke again. The conversation which now ensued between these lovers under difficulties was tender and affecting beyond expression. I had felt guilty enough when an unwilling auditor of the conspirators,—since, though one employs spies, one does not therefore act that part one's self, but on emergencies,—an unwillingness which would not, however, prevent my turning to advantage the information gained; but here, to listen to this rehearsal of woes and blisses, this *ah mon Fernand,* this aria in an area, growing momently more fervent, was too much. I overturned the cask, scrambled upon my feet, and fled from the cellar, leaving the astounded lovers to follow, while, agreeably to my instincts, and regardless of the diamond, I escaped the embarrassing predicament.

At length it grew to be noon of the appointed day. Nothing had transpired; all our labor was idle. I felt, nevertheless, more buoyant than usual,—whether because I was now to put my fate to the test, or that to-day was the one of which my black-browed man had spoken, and I therefore entertained a presentiment of good fortune, I cannot say. But when, in unexceptionable toilet, I stood on Mme. de St. Cyr's steps, my heart sunk. G. was doubtless already within, and I thought of the *marchand des armures'* exclamation, "Queen of Heaven, Monsieur! how shall I meet him!" I was plunged at once into the profoundest gloom. Why had I undertaken the business at all? This interference, this good-humor, this readiness to oblige,—it would ruin me yet! I forswore it, as Falstaff forswore honor. Why needed I to meddle in the *mêlée?* Why— But I was no catechumen. Questions were useless now. My emotions are not chronicled on my face, I flatter myself; and with my usual repose I saluted our hostess. Greeting G. without any allusion to the diamond, the absence of which allusion he received as a point of etiquette, I was conversing with Mrs. Leigh, when the Baron Stahl was announced. I turned to look at his Excellency. A glance electrified me. There was my dark-browed man of the midnight streets. It must, then, have been concerning the diamond that I had heard him speak. His countenance, his eager glittering eye, told that to-day was as eventful to him as to me. If he were here, I could well afford to be. As he addressed me in English, my certainty was confirmed; and the instant in which I observed the ring, gaudy and coarse, upon his finger, made confirmation doubly sure. I own I was surprised that anything could induce the Baron to wear such an ornament. Here he was actually risking his reputation as a man of taste, as an exquisite, a leader of *haut ton,* a gentleman, by the detestable vulgarity of this ring. But why do I speak so of the trinket? Do I not owe it a thrill of as fine joy as I ever knew? Faith! it was not unfamiliar to me. It had been a daily sight for years. In meeting the Baron Stahl I had found the diamond.

The Baron Stahl was, then, the thief? Not at all. My valet, as of course you have been all along aware, was the thief.

My valet, moreover, was my instructor; he taught me not again to scour Cathay for what might be lying under my hand at home. Nor have I since been so acute as to overreach myself. Yet I can explain such intolerable stupidity only by remembering that when one has been in the habit of pointing his telescope at the stars, he is not apt to turn it upon pebbles at his feet.

The Marquis of G. took down Mme. de St. Cyr; Stahl preceded me, with Delphine. As we sat at table, G. was at the right, I at the left of our hostess. Next G. sat Delphine; below her, the Baron; so that we were nearly *vis-à-vis.* I was now as fully convinced that Mme. de St. Cyr's cellar was the one, as the day before I had been that the other was; I longed to reach it. Hay had given the stone to a butler—doubtless this—the moment of its theft; but, not being aware of Mme. de St. Cyr's previous share in the adventure, had probably not afforded her another. And thus I concluded her to be ignorant of the game we were about to play; and I imagined, with the interest that one carries into a romance, the little preliminary scene between the Baron and Madame that must have already taken place, being charmed by the cheerfulness with which she endured the loss of the promised reward.

As the Baron entered the dining-room, I saw him withdraw his glove, and move the jewelled hand across his hair while passing the solemn butler, who gave it a quick recognition;—the next moment we were seated. There were only wines on the table, clustered around a central ornament,—a bunch of tall silver rushes and flagleaves, on whose airy tip danced *fleurs-de-lis* of frosted silver, a design of Delphine's,—the dishes being on sidetables, from which the guests were served as they signified their choice of the variety on their cards. Our number not being large, and the custom so informal, rendered it pleasant.

I had just finished my oysters and was pouring out a glass of Chablis, when another plate was set before the Baron.

"His Excellency has no salt," murmured the butler,—at the same time placing one beside him. A glance, at entrance, had taught me that most of the service was uniform; this dainty little *salière* I had noticed on the buffet, solitary, and unlike the others. What a fool had I been! Those gaps in the Baron's remarks caused by the pavingstones, how easily were they to be supplied!

"Madame?"

Madame de St. Cyr.

"The cellar?"

A salt-cellar.

How quick the flash that enlightened me while I surveyed the *salière!*

"It is exquisite! Am I never to sit at your table but some new device charms me?" I exclaimed. "Is it your design, Mademoiselle?" I said, turning to Delphine.

Delphine, who had been ice to all the Baron's advances, only curled her lip. "*Des babioles!*"[14] she said.

"Yes, indeed!" cried Mme. de St. Cyr, extending her hand for it. "But none the less her taste. Is it not a fairy thing? A Cellini![15] Observe this curve, these lines! but one man could have drawn them!"—and she held it for our scrutiny. It was a tiny hand and arm of ivory, parting the foam of a wave and holding a golden shell, in which the salt seemed to have crusted itself as if in some secretest ocean-hollow. I looked at the Baron a moment; his eyes were fastened upon the *salière,* and all the color had forsaken his cheeks,—his face counted his years. The diamond was in that little shell. But how to obtain it? I had no novice to deal with; nothing but *finesse* would answer.

"Permit me to examine it?" I said. She passed it to her left hand for me to take. The butler made a step forward.

"Meanwhile, Madame," said the Baron, smiling, "I have no salt."

The instinct of hospitality prevailed;—she was about to return it. Might I do an awkward thing? Unhesitatingly. Reversing my glass, I gave my arm a wider sweep than necessary, and, as it met her hand with violence, the *salière* fell. Before it touched the floor I caught it. There was still a pinch of salt left,—nothing more.

"A thousand pardons!" I said, and restored it to the Baron.

His Excellency beheld it with dismay; it was rare to see him bend over and scrutinize it with starting eyes.

"Do you find there what Count Arnaldos begs in the song," asked Delphine,—"the secret of the sea, Monsieur?"

He handed it to the butler, observing, "I find here no—"

"Salt, Monsieur?" replied the man, who did not doubt but all had gone right, and replenished it.

Had one told me in the morning, that no intricate manœuvres, but a simple blunder, would effect this, I might have met him in the Bois de Boulogne.

"We will not quarrel," said my neighbor, lightly, with reference to the popular superstition.

"Rather propitiate the offended deities by a crumb tossed over the shoulder," added I.

"Over the left?" asked the Baron, to intimate his knowledge of another idiom, together with a reproof for my *gaucherie*.

"*À gauche,—quelquefois c'est justement à droit,*" I replied.[16]

"Salt in any pottage," said Madame, a little uneasily, "is like surprise in an individual; it brings out the flavor of every ingredient, so my cook tells me."

"It is a preventive of palsy," I remarked, as the slight trembling of my adversary's finger caught my eye.

"And I have noticed that a taste for it is peculiar to those who trace their blood," continued Madame.

"Let us, therefore, elect a deputation to those mines near Cracow," said Delphine.

"To our cousins, the slaves there?" laughed her mother.

"I must vote to lay your bill on the table, Mademoiselle," I rejoined.

"But with a *boule blanche,* Monsieur?"[17]

"As the salt has been laid on the floor," said the Baron.

Meanwhile, as this light skirmishing proceeded, my sleeve and Mme. de St. Cyr's dress were slightly powdered, but I had not seen the diamond. The Baron, bolder than I, looked under the table, but made no discovery. I was on the point of dropping my napkin to accomplish a similar movement, when my accommodating neighbor dropped hers. To restore it, I stooped. There it lay, large and glowing, the Sea of Splendor, the Moon of Milk, the Torment of my Life, on the carpet, within half an inch of a lady's slipper. Mademoiselle de St. Cyr's foot had prevented the Baron from seeing it; now it moved and unconsciously covered it. All was as I wished. I hastily restored the napkin, and looked steadily at Delphine,—so steadily, that she perceived some meaning, as she had already suspected a game. By my sign she understood me, pressed her foot upon the stone and drew it nearer. In France we do not remain at table until unfit for a lady's society,—we rise with them. Delphine needed to drop neither napkin nor handkerchief; she composedly stooped and picked up the stone, so quickly that no one saw what it was.

"And the diamond?" said the Baron to the butler, rapidly, as he passed.

"It was in the *salière!*" whispered the astonished creature.

IN THE DRAWING-ROOM I sought the Marquis.

"To-day I was to surrender you your property," I said; "it is here."

"Do you know," he replied, "I thought I must have been mistaken?"

"Any of our volatile friends here might have been," I resumed; "for us it is impossible. Concerning this, when you return to France, I will relate the incidents; at present, there are those who will not hesitate to take life to obtain its possession. A conveyance leaves in twenty minutes; and if I owned the diamond, it should not leave me behind. Moreover, who knows what a day may bring forth? To-morrow there may be an *émeute*. Let me restore the thing as you withdraw."

The Marquis, who is not, after all, the Lion of England, pausing a moment to transmit my words from his ear to his brain, did not afterward delay to make inquiries or adieux, but went to seek Mme. de St. Cyr and wish her good-night, on his departure from Paris. As I awaited his return, which I knew would not be immediate, Delphine left the Baron and joined me.

"You beckoned me?" she asked.

"No, I did not."

"Nevertheless, I come by your desire, I am sure."

"Mademoiselle," I said, "I am not in the custom of doing favors; I have forsworn them. But before you return me my jewel, I risk my head and render one last one, and to you."

"Do not, Monsieur, at such price," she responded, with a slight mocking motion of her hand.

"Delphine! those resolves, last night, in the cellar, were daring, they were noble, yet they were useless."

She had not started, but a slight tremor ran over her person and vanished while I spoke.

"They will be allowed to proceed no farther,—the axe is sharpened; for the last man who adjusted his mask was a spy,—was the Secretary of the Secret Service."

Delphine could not have grown paler than was usual with her of late. She flashed her eye upon me.

"He was, it may be, Monsieur himself," she said.

"I do not claim the honor of that post."

"But you were there, nevertheless,—a spy!"

"Hush, Delphine! It would be absurd to quarrel. I was there for the recovery of this stone, having heard that it was in a cellar,—which, stupidly enough, I had insisted should be a wine-cellar."

"It was, then—"

"In a salt-cellar,—a blunder which, as you do not speak English, you cannot comprehend. I never mix with treason, and did not wish to assist at your pastimes. I speak now, that you may escape."

"If Monsieur betrays his friends, the police, why should I expect a kinder fate?"

"When I use the police, they are my servants, not my friends. I simply warn you, that, before sunrise, you will be safer travelling than sleeping,—safer next week in Vienna than in Paris."

"Thank you! And the intelligence is the price of the diamond? If I had not chanced to pick it up, my throat," and she clasped it with her fingers, "had been no slenderer than the others?"

"Delphine, will you remember, should you have occasion to do so in Vienna, that it is just possible for an Englishman to have affections, and sentiments, and, in fact, sensations? that, with him, friendship can be inviolate, and to betray it an impossibility? And even were it not, I, Mademoiselle, have not the pleasure to be classed by you as a friend."

"You err. I esteem Monsieur highly."

I was impressed by her coolness.

"Let me see if you comprehend the matter," I demanded.

"Perfectly. The arrest will be used to-night, the guillotine to-morrow."

"You will take immediate measures for flight?"

"No,—I do not see that life has value. I shall be the debtor of him who takes it."

"A large debt. Delphine, I exact a promise of you. I do not care to have endangered myself for nothing. It is not worth while to make your mother unhappy. Life is not yours to throw away. I appeal to your magnanimity."

"'Affections, sentiments, sensations!'" she quoted. "Your own danger for the affection,—it is an affair of the heart! Mme. de St. Cyr's unhappiness,—there is the sentiment. You are angry, Monsieur,—that must be the sensation."

"Delphine, I am waiting."

"Ah, well. You have mentioned Vienna,—and why? Liberals are countenanced there?"

"Not in the least. But Madame l'Ambassadrice will be countenanced."

"I do not know her."

"We are not apt to know ourselves."

"Monsieur, how idle are these cross-purposes!" she said, folding her fan.

"Delphine," I continued, taking the fan, "tell me frankly which of these two men you prefer,—the Marquis or his Excellency."

"The Marquis? He is antiphlogistic,—he is ice. Why should I freeze myself? I am frozen now,—I need fire!"

Her eyes burned as she spoke, and a faint red flushed her cheek.

"Mademoiselle, you demonstrate to me that life has yet a value to you."

"I find no fire," she said, as the flush fell away.

"The Baron?"

"I do not affect him."

"You will conquer your prejudice in Vienna."

"I do not comprehend you, Monsieur;—you speak in riddles, which I do not like."

"I will speak plainer. But first let me ask you for the diamond."

"The diamond? It is yours? How am I certified of it? I find it on the floor; you say it was in my mother's *salière;* it is her affair, not mine. No, Monsieur, I do not see that the thing is yours."

Certainly there was nothing to be done but to relate the story, which I did, carefully omitting the Baron's name. At its conclusion, she placed the prize in my hand.

"Pardon, Monsieur," she said; "without doubt you should receive it.

And this agent of the government,—one could turn him like hot iron in this vice,—who was he?"

"The Baron Stahl."

All this time G. had been waiting on thorns, and, leaving her now, I approached him, displayed for an instant the treasure on my palm, and slipped it into his. It was done. I bade farewell to this Eye of Morning and Heart of Day, this thing that had caused me such pain and perplexity and pleasure, with less envy and more joy than I thought myself capable of. The relief and buoyancy that seized me, as his hand closed upon it, I shall not attempt to portray. An abdicated king was not freer.

The Marquis departed, and I, wandering round the *salon,* was next stranded upon the Baron. He was yet hardly sure of himself. We talked indifferently for a few moments, and then I ventured on the great loan. He was, as became him, not communicative, but scarcely thought it would be arranged. I then spoke of Delphine.

"She is superb!" said the Baron, staring at her boldly.

She stood opposite, and, in her white attire on the background of the blue curtain, appeared like an impersonation of Greek genius relieved upon the blue of an Athenian heaven. Her severe and classic outline, her pallor, her downcast lids, her absorbed look, only heightened the resemblance. Her reverie seemed to end abruptly, the same red stained her cheek again, her lips curved in a proud smile, she raised her glowing eyes and observed us regarding her. At too great distance to hear our words, she quietly repaid our glances in the strength of her new decision, and then, turning, began to entertain those next her with an unwonted spirit.

"She has needed," I replied to the Baron, "but one thing,—to be aroused, to be kindled. See, it is done! I have thought that a life of cabinets and policy might achieve this, for her talent is second not even to her beauty."

"It is unhappy that both should be wasted," said the Baron. "She, of course, will never marry."

"Why not?"

"For various reasons."

"One?"

"She is poor."

"Which will not signify to your Excellency. Another?"

"She is too beautiful. One would fall in love with her. And to love one's own wife—it is ridiculous!"

"Who should know?" I asked.

"All the world would suspect and laugh."

"Let those laugh that win."

"No,—she would never do as a wife; but then as—"

"But then in France we do not insult hospitality!"

The Baron transferred his gaze to me for a moment, then tapped his snuff-box, and approached the circle round Delphine.

It was odd that we, the arch enemies of the hour, could speak without the intervention of seconds; but I hoped that the Baron's conversation might be diverting,—the Baron hoped that mine might be didactic.

They were very gay with Delphine. He leaned on the back of a chair and listened. One spoke of the new gallery of the Tuileries, and the five pavilions,—a remark which led us to architecture.

"We all build our own houses," said Delphine, at last, "and then complain that they cramp us here, and the wind blows in there, while the fault is not in the order, but in us, who increase here and shrink there without reason."

"You speak in metaphors," said the Baron.

"Precisely. A truth is often more visible veiled than nude."

"We should soon exhaust the orders," I interposed; "for who builds like his neighbor?"

"Slight variations, Monsieur! Though we take such pains to conceal the style, it is not difficult to tell the order of architecture chosen by the builders in this room. My mother, for instance—you perceive that her pavilion would be the florid Gothic."

"Mademoiselle's is the Doric," I said.

"Has been," she murmured, with a quick glance.

"And mine, Mademoiselle?" asked the Baron, indifferently.

"Ah, Monsieur," she returned, looking serenely upon him, "when one has all the winning cards in hand and yet loses the stake, we allot him *un pavillon chinois.*"—which was the polite way of dubbing him Court Fool.

The Baron's eyes fell. Vexation and alarm were visible on his contracted brow. He stood in meditation for some time. It must have been evident to him that Delphine knew of the recent occurrences,—that here in Paris she could denounce him as the agent of a felony, the participant of a theft. What might prevent it? Plainly but one thing: no woman would denounce her husband. He had scarcely contemplated this step on arrival.

The guests were again scattered in groups round the room. I examined an engraving on an adjacent table. Delphine reclined as lazily in a *fauteuil* as if her life did not hang in the balance. The Baron drew near.

"Mademoiselle," said he, "you allotted me just now a cap and bells. If two should wear it?—if I should invite another into my *pavillon chinois?*—if I should propose to complete an alliance, desired by my father, with the ancient family of St. Cyr?—if, in short, Mademoiselle, I should request you to become my wife?"

"*Eh, bien, Monsieur,*—and if you should?" I heard her coolly reply.

But it was no longer any business of mine. I rose and sought Mme. de St. Cyr, who, I thought, was slightly uneasy, perceiving some mystery to be afloat. After a few words, I retired.

Archimedes, as perhaps you have never heard, needed only a lever to move the world. Such a lever I had put into the hands of Delphine, with which she might move, not indeed the grand globe, with its multiplied attractions, relations, and affinities, but the lesser world of circumstances, of friends and enemies, the circle of hopes, fears, ambitions. There is no woman, as I believe, but could have used it.

THE NEXT DAY was scarcely so quiet in the city as usual. The great loan had not been negotiated. Both the Baron Stahl and the English minister had left Paris,—and there was a *coup d'état.*

But the Baron did not travel alone. There had been a ceremony at midnight in the Church of St. Sulpice, and her Excellency the Baroness Stahl, *née* de St. Cyr, accompanied him.

It is a good many years since. I have seen the diamond in the Duchess of X.'s coronet, once, when a young queen put on her royalty,—but I have never seen Delphine. The Marquis begged me to retain the chain, and I gave myself the pleasure of presenting it, through her mother, to the Baroness Stahl. I hear, that, whenever she desires to effect any cherished object which the Baron opposes, she has only to wear this chain, and effect it. It appears to possess a magical power, and its potent spell enslaves the

Baron as the lamp and ring of Eastern tales enslaved the Afrites. The life she leads has aroused her. She is no longer the impassive Silence; she has found her fire. I hear of her as the charm of a brilliant court, as the soul of a nation of intrigue. Of her beauty one does not speak, but her talent is called prodigious. What impels me to ask the idle question, If it were well to save her life for this? Undoubtedly she fills a station which, in that empire, must be the summit of a woman's ambition. Delphine's Liberty was not a principle, but a dissatisfaction. The Baroness Stahl is vehement, is Imperialist, is successful. While she lives, it is on the top of the wave; when she dies— ah! what business has Death in such a world?

As I said, I have never seen Delphine since her marriage. The beautiful statuesque girl occupies a niche into which the blazing and magnificent *intrigante* cannot crowd. I do not wish to be disillusioned. She has read me a riddle,—Delphine is my Sphinx.

AS FOR MR. HAY,—I once said the Antipodes were tributary to me, not thinking that I should ever become tributary to the Antipodes. But such is the case; since, partly through my instrumentality, that enterprising individual has been located in their vicinity, where diamonds are not to be had for the asking, and the greatest rogue is not a Baron.

THE AMBER GODS

STORY FIRST

Flower o' the Peach

❦❦❦❦❦❦

WE'VE SOME SPLENDID old point-lace in our family, yellow and fragrant, loose-meshed. It isn't every one has point at all; and of those who have, it isn't every one can afford to wear it. I can. Why? O, because it's in character. Besides, I admire point any way,—it's so becoming. And then, you see, this amber! Now what is in finer unison, this old point-lace, all tags and tangle and fibrous and bewildering, and this amber, to which Heaven knows how many centuries, maybe, with all their changes, brought perpetual particles of increase? I like yellow things, you see.

To begin at the beginning. My name, you're aware, is Giorgione Willoughby. Queer name for a girl! Yes; but before papa sowed his wild-oats, he was one afternoon in Fiesole, looking over Florence nestled below, when some whim took him to go into a church there, a quiet place, full of twilight and one great picture, nobody within but a girl and her little slave,—the one watching her mistress, the other saying dreadfully devout prayers on an amber rosary, and of course she didn't see him, or didn't appear to. After he got there, he wondered what on earth he came for, it was so dark and poky, and he began to feel uncomfortably,—when all of a sudden a great ray of sunset dashed through the window, and drowned the place in the splendor of the illumined painting. Papa adores rich colors; and he might have been satiated here, except that such things make you want more. It was a Venus;—no, though, it couldn't have been a Venus in a church, could it? Well, then, a Magdalen, I guess, or a Madonna, or something. I fancy the man painted for himself, and christened for others. So, when I was born, some years afterward, papa, gratefully remembering this dazzling little vignette of his youth, was absurd enough to christen *me* Giorgione. That's how I came by my identity; but the folks all call me Yone,—a baby name.

I'm a blonde, you know,—none of your silver-washed things. I wouldn't give a *fico* [1] for a girl with flaxen hair; she might as well be a wax doll, and have her eyes moved by a wire; besides, they've no souls. I imagine they were remnants at *our* creation, and somehow scrambled together, and managed to get up a little life among themselves; but it's good for nothing, and everybody sees through the pretence. They're glass chips, and brittle shavings, slender pinkish scrids,—no name for them; but just you say blonde, soft and slow and rolling,—it brings up a brilliant, golden vitality, all manner of white and torrid magnificences, and you see me! I've watched little bugs—gold rose-chafers—lie steeping in the sun, till every atom of them must have been searched with the warm radiance, and have felt that, when they reached that point, I was just like them, golden all through,—not dyed, but created. Sunbeams like to follow me, I think. Now, when I stand in one before this glass, infiltrated with the rich tinge, don't I look like the spirit of it just stepped out for inspection? I seem to myself like the complete incarnation of light, full, bounteous, overflowing, and I wonder at and adore anything so beautiful; and the reflection grows finer and deeper while I gaze, till I dare not do so any longer. So, without more words, I'm a golden blonde. You see me now: not too tall,— five feet four; not slight, or I couldn't have such perfect roundings, such flexible moulding. Here's nothing of the spiny Diana and Pallas, but Clytie or Isis speaks in such delicious curves. It don't look like flesh and blood, does it? Can you possibly imagine it will ever change? Oh!

Now see the face,—not small, either; lips with no particular outline, but melting, and seeming as if they would stain yours, should you touch them. No matter about the rest, except the eyes. Do you meet such eyes often? You wouldn't open yours so, if you did. Note their color now, before the ray goes. Yellow hazel? Not a bit of it! Some folks say topaz, but they're fools. Nor sherry. There's a dark sardine base, but over it real seas of light, clear light; there isn't any positive color; and once when I was angry, I caught a glimpse of them in a mirror, and they were quite white, perfectly colorless, only luminous. I looked like a fiend, and, you may be sure, recovered my temper directly,—easiest thing in the world, when you've motive enough. You see the pupil is small, and that gives more expansion and force to the irides; but sometimes in an evening, when I'm too gay, and a true damask settles in the cheek, the pupil grows larger and crowds out the light, and under these thick brown lashes, these yellow-hazel eyes of yours, they are dusky and purple and deep with flashes, like pansies lit by fire-flies, and then common folks call them black. Be sure, I've never got such eyes for nothing, any more than this hair. That is Lucrezia Borgian, spun gold, and ought to take the world in its toils. I always wear these thick, riotous curls round my temples and face; but the great braids be-hind—O, I'll uncoil them, before my toilet is over.

Probably you felt all this before, but didn't know the secret of it. Now, the traits being brought out, you perceive nothing wanting; the thing is perfect, and you've a reason for it. Of course, with such an organization, I'm not nervous. Nervous! I should as soon fancy a dish of cream nervous. I am too rich for anything of the kind, permeated utterly with a rare golden calm. Girls always suggest little similitudes to me: there's that brunette beauty,—don't you taste mulled wine when you see her? and thinking of yourself, did you ever feel green tea? and find me in a crust of wild honey, the expressed essence of woods and flowers, with its sweet satiety?—no, that's too cloying. I'm a deal more like Mendelssohn's music,—what I know of it, for I can't distinguish tunes,—you wouldn't suspect it,—but full harmonies delight me as they do a wild beast; and so I'm like a certain adagio in B flat, that papa likes.

There, now! you're perfectly shocked to hear me go on so about myself; but you oughtn't to be. It isn't lawful for any one else, because praise is intrusion; but if the rose please to open her heart to the moth, what then? You know, too, I didn't make myself; it's no virtue to be so fair. Louise couldn't speak so of herself: first place, because it wouldn't be true; next place, she couldn't, if it were; and lastly, she made her beauty by growing a soul in her eyes, I suppose,—what you call good. I'm not good, of course; I wouldn't give a fig to be good. So it's not vanity. It's on a far grander scale; a splendid selfishness,—authorized, too; and papa and mamma brought me up to worship beauty,—and there's the fifth commandment, you know.

Dear me! you think I'm never coming to the point. Well, here's this rosary;—hand me the perfume-case first, please. Don't you love heavy fragrances, faint with sweetness, ravishing juices of odor, heliotropes, violets, water-lilies,—powerful attars and extracts that snatch your soul off your lips? Couldn't you live on rich scents, if they tried to starve you? I could, or die on them: I don't know which would be best. There! There's the amber rosary! You needn't speak; look at it!

Bah! is that all you've got to say? Why, observe the thing; turn it over; hold it up to the window; count the beads,—long, oval, like some seaweed bulbs, each an amulet. See the tint; it's very old; like clots of sunshine,— aren't they? Now bring it near; see the carving, here corrugated, there faceted, now sculptured into hideous, tiny, heathen gods. You didn't notice that before! How difficult it must have been, when amber is so friable! Here's one with a chessboard on his back, and all his kings and queens and pawns slung round him. Here's another with a torch, a flaming torch, its fire pouring out inverted. They are grotesque enough;—but this, this is matchless: such a miniature woman, one hand grasping the round rock behind, while she looks down into some gulf, perhaps, beneath, and will let herself fall. O, you should see *her* with a magnifying-glass! You want to think of calm, satisfying death, a mere exhalation, a voluntary slipping into another element? There it is for you. They are all gods and goddesses. They are all here but one; I've lost one, the knot of all, the love of the thing. Well! wasn't it queer for a Catholic girl to have at prayer? Don't you wonder where she got it? Ah! but don't you wonder where I got it? I'll tell you.

Papa came in, one day, and with great mystery commenced unrolling, and unrolling, and throwing tissue papers on the floor, and scraps of colored wool; and Lu and I ran to him,—Lu stooping on her knees to look up, I bending over his hands to look down. It was so mysterious! I began to suspect it was diamonds for me, but knew I never could wear them, and was dreadfully afraid that I was going to be tempted, when slowly, bead by bead, came out this amber necklace. Lu fairly screamed; as for me, I just drew breath after breath, without a word. Of course they were for me;— I reached my hands for them.

"Oh, wait!" said Papa. "Yone or Lu?"

"Now how absurd, papa!" I exclaimed. "Such things for Lu!"

"Why not?" asked Lu,—rather faintly, for she knew I always carried my point.

"The idea of you in amber, Lu! It's too foreign; no sympathy between you!"

"Stop, stop!" said papa. "You sha'n't crowd little Lu out of them. What do you want them for, Lu?"

"To wear," quavered Lu,—"like the balls the Roman ladies carried for coolness."

"Well, then, you ought to have them. What do you want them for, Yone?"

"Oh, if Lu's going to have them, I *don't* want them."

But give a reason, child."

"Why, to wear, too,—to look at,—to have and to hold, for better, for worse,—to say my prayers on," for a bright idea struck me,—"to say my prayers on, like the Florence rosary." I knew that would finish the thing.

"Like the Florence rosary?" said papa, in a sleepy voice. "Why, this *is* the Florence rosary."

Of course, when we knew that, we were both more crazy to obtain it.

"Oh, sir," just fluttered Lu, "where did you get it?"

"I got it; the question is, Who's to have it?"

"I must and will, potential and imperative," I exclaimed, quite on fire. "The nonsense of the thing! Girls with lucid eyes, like shadowy shallows in quick brooks, can wear crystallizations. As for me, I can wear only concretions and growths; emeralds and all their cousins would be shockingly inharmonious on me; but you know, Lu, how I use Indian spices, and scarlet and white berries, and flowers, and little hearts and notions of beautiful copal that Rose carved for you,—and I can wear sandal-wood and ebony and pearls, and now this amber. But you, Lu, you can wear every kind of precious stone, and you may have Aunt Willoughby's rubies that she promised me; they are all in tone with you; but I must have this."

"I don't think you're right," said Louise, rather soberly. "You strip yourself of great advantages. But about the rubies, I don't want anything so flaming, so you may keep them; and I don't care at all about this. I think, sir, on the whole, they belong to Yone for her name."

"So they do," said papa. "But not to be bought off! That's my little Lu!"

And somehow Lu, who had been holding the rosary, was sitting on papa's knee, as he half knelt on the floor, and the rosary was in my hand. And then he produced a little kid box, and there lay, inside, a star with a thread of gold for the forehead, circlets for wrist and throat, two drops, and a ring. O such beauties! You've never seen them.

"The other one shall have these. Aren't you sorry, Yone?" he said.

"Oh no indeed! I'd much rather have mine, though these are splendid. What are they?"

"Aqua-marina," sighed Lu, in an agony of admiration.

"Dear, dear! how did you know?"

Lu blushed, I saw,—but I was too much absorbed with the jewels to remark it.

"Oh, they are just like that ring on your hand! You don't want two rings alike," I said. "Where did you get that ring, Lu?"

But Lu had no senses for anything beyond the casket.

If you know aqua-marina, you know something that's before every other stone in the world. Why, it is as clear as light, white, limpid, dawn light; sparkles slightly and seldom; looks like pure drops of water, sea-water, scooped up and falling down again; just a thought of its parent beryl-green hovers round the edges; and it grows more lucent and sweet to the centre, and there you lose yourself in some dream of vast seas, a glory of unimagined oceans; and you say that it was crystallized to any slow flute-like tune, each speck of it floating into file with a musical grace, and carrying its sound with it. There! it's very fanciful, but I'm always feeling the tune in aqua-marine, and trying to find it,—but I shouldn't know it was a tune, if I did, I suppose. How magnificent it would be, if every atom of creation sprang up and said its one word of abracadabra, the secret of its existence, and fell silent again. O dear! you'd die, you know; but what a pow-wow! Then, too, in aqua-marina proper, the setting is kept out of sight, and you have the unalloyed stone with its sea-rims and its clearness and steady sweetness. It wasn't the thing for Louise to wear; it belongs rather to highly nervous, excitable persons; and Lu is as calm as I, only so different! There is something more pure and simple about it than about anything else; others may flash and twinkle, but this just glows with an unvarying power, is planetary and strong. It wears the moods of the sea, too: once in a while a warm amethystine mist suffuses it like a blush; sometimes a white morning fog breathes over it: you long to get into the heart of it. That's the charm of gems, after all! You feel that they are fashioned through dissimilar processes from yourself,—that there's a mystery about them, mastering which would be like mastering a new life, like having the freedom of other stars. I give them more personality than I would a great white spirit. I like amber that way, because I know how it was made, drinking the primeval weather, resinously beading each grain of its rare wood, and dripping with a plash to filter through and around the fallen cones below. In some former state I must have been a fly embalmed in amber.

"O Lu!" I said, "this amber's just the thing for me, such a great noon creature! And as for you, you shall wear mamma's Mechlin and that aqua-marina; and you'll look like a mer-queen just issuing from the wine-dark deeps and glittering with shining water-spheres."

I never let Lu wear the point at all; she'd be ridiculous in it,—so flimsy and open and unreserved; that's for me; Mechlin, with its whiter, closer, chaster web, suits here to a T.

I must tell you, first, how this rosary came about. You know we've a million of ancestors, and one of them, my great-grandfather, was a sea-captain, and actually did bring home cargoes of slaves! But once he fetched to his wife a little islander, an Asian imp, six years old, and wilder than the wind. She spoke no word of English, and was full of short shouts and screeches, like a thing of the woods. My great-grandmother couldn't do a bit with her; she turned the house topsy-turvy, cut the noses out of the old portraits, and chewed the jewels out of the settings, killed the little home animals, spoiled the dinners, pranced in the garden with Madam Willoughby's farthingale, and royal stiff brocades rustling yards behind,— this atom of a shrimp,—or balanced herself with her heels in the air over the curb of the well, scraped up the dead leaves under one corner of the house and fired them,—a favorite occupation,—and if you left her stir-ring a mess in the kitchen, you met her, perhaps, perched in the china-closet and mumbling all manner of demoniacal prayers, twisting and

writhing and screaming over a string of amber gods that she had brought
with her and always wore. When winter came and the first snow, she was
furious, perfectly mad. One might as well have had a ball of fire in the
house, or chain-lightning; every nice old custom had been invaded, the
ancient quiet broken into a Bedlam of outlandish sounds, and as Captain
Willoughby was returning, his wife packed the sprite off with him,—to
cut, rip, and tear in New Holland, if she liked, but not in New England,—
and rejoiced herself that she would find that little brown skin cuddled up
in her best down beds and among her lavendered sheets no more. She had
learned but two words all that time,—Willoughby, and the name of
the town.

You may conjecture what heavenly peace came in when the Asian
went out, but there is no one to tell what havoc was wrought on board
ship; in fact, if there could have been such a thing as a witch, I should
believe that imp sunk them, for a stray Levantine brig picked her—still
agile as a monkey—from a wreck off the Cape de Verdes and carried her
into Leghorn, where she took—will you mind, if I say?—leg-bail, and
escaped from durance. What happened on her wanderings I'm sure is of no
consequence, till one night she turned up outside a Fiesolan villa, scorched
with malaria fevers and shaken to pieces with tertian and quartan and all
the rest of the agues. So, after having shaken almost to death, she decided
upon getting well; all the effervescence was gone; she chose to remain with
her beads in that family, a mysterious tame servant, faithful, jealous, inde-
fatigable. But she never grew; at ninety she was of the height of a yard-
stick,—and nothing could have been finer than to have a dwarf in those
old palaces, you know.

In my great-grandmother's home, however, the tradition of the
Asian sprite with her string of amber gods was handed down like a legend,
and, no one knowing what had been, they framed many a wild picture of
the Thing enchanting all her spirits from their beads about her, and calling
and singing and whistling up the winds with them till storm rolled round
the ship, and fierce fog and foam and drowning fell upon her capturers. But
they all believed, that, snatched from the wreck into islands of Eastern
archipelagoes, the vindictive child and her quieted gods might yet be
found. Of course my father knew this, and when that night in the church
he saw the girl saying such devout prayers on an amber rosary, with a

demure black slave so tiny and so old behind her, it flashed back on him, and he would have spoken, if, just then, the ray had not revealed the great painting, so that he forgot all about it, and when at last he turned, they were gone. But my father had come back to America, had sat down quietly in his elder brother's house, among the hills where I am to live, and was thought to be a sedate young man and a good match, till a freak took him that he must go back and find that girl in Italy. How to do it, with no clew but an amber rosary? But do it he did,—stationing himself against a pillar in that identical church and watching the worshippers, and not having long to wait before in she came, with little Asian behind. Papa isn't in the least romantic; he is one of those great fertilizing temperaments, golden hair and beard, and *hazel* eyes, if you will. He's a splendid old fellow! It's absurd to delight in one's father,—so bread-and-buttery,—but I can't help it. He's far stronger than I; none of the little weak Italian traits that streak me, like water in thick, sirupy wine. No,—he isn't in the least romantic, but he says he was fated to this step, and could no more have resisted than his heart could have refused to beat. When he spoke to the devotee, little Asian made sundry belligerent demonstrations; but he confronted her with the two words she had learned here, Willoughby and the town's name. The dwarf became livid, seemed always after haunted by a dreadful fear of him, pursued him with a rancorous hate, but could not hinder his marriage.—The Willoughbys are a cruel race.—Her only revenge was to take away the amber beads, which had long before been blessed by the pope for her young mistress, refusing herself to accompany my mother, and declaring that neither should her charms ever cross the water,—that all their blessing would be changed to banning, and that bane would burn the bearer, should the salt-sea spray again dash round them. But when, in process of Nature, the Asian died,—having become classic through her longevity, taking length of days for length of stature,—then the rosary belonged to mamma's sister, who by and by sent it, with a parcel of other things, to papa for me. So I should have had it at all events, you see;—papa is such a tease! The other things were mamma's wedding-veil, that point there, which once was her mother's, and some pearls.

I was born upon the sea, in a calm, far out of sight of land, under sweltering suns; so, you know, I'm a cosmopolite, and have a right to all my fantasies. Not that they are fantasies, at all; on the contrary, they are parts of my nature, and I couldn't be what I am without them, or have one and not have all. Some girls go picking and scraping odds and ends of ideas together, and by the time they are thirty get quite a bundle of whims and crotchets on their backs; but they are all at sixes and sevens, uneven and knotty like fagots, and won't lie compactly, don't belong to them, and anybody might surprise them out of them. But for me, you see, mine are harmonious; in my veins; I was born with them. Not that I was always what I am now. Oh, bless your heart! plums and nectarines and luscious things that ripen and develop all their rare juices, were green once, and so was I. Awkward, tumble-about, near-sighted, till I was twenty, a real raw-head-and-bloody-bones to all society; then mamma, who was never well in our diving-bell atmosphere, was ordered to the West Indies, and papa said it was what I needed, and I went, too,—and oh, how sea-sick! Were you ever? You forget all about who you are, and have a vague notion of being Universal Disease. I have heard of a kind of myopy that is biliousness, and when I reached the islands my sight was as clear as my skin; all that tropical luxuriance snatched me to itself at once, recognized me for kith and kin; and mamma died, and I lived. We had accidents between wind and water, enough to have made me considerate for others, Lu said; but I don't see that I'm any less careful not to have my bones spilt in the flood than ever I was. Slang? No,—poetry. But if your nature had such a wild, free tendency as mine, and then were boxed up with proprieties and civilities from year's end to year's end, maybe you, too, would escape now and then in a bit of slang.

We always had a little boy to play with, Lu and I, or rather Lu,—because, though he never took any dislike to me, he was absurdly indifferent, while he followed Lu about with a painful devotion. I didn't care, didn't know; and as I grew up and grew awkwarder, I was the plague of their little lives. If Lu had been my sister instead of my orphan cousin, as mamma was perpetually holding up to me, I should have bothered them twenty times more; but when I got larger and began to be really distasteful to his fine artistic perception, mamma had the sense to keep me out of his way; and he was busy at his lessons, and didn't come so much. But Lu just fitted him then, from the time he daubed little adoring blotches of her face on every barn-door and paling, till when his scrap-book was full of her in

46

all fancies and conceits, and he was old enough to go away and study Art. Then he came home occasionally, and always saw us; but I generally contrived, on such occasions, to do some frightful thing that shocked every nerve he had, and he avoided me instinctively, as he would an electric torpedo; but—do you believe?—I never had an idea of such a fact till, when sailing from the South, so changed, I remembered things, and felt intuitively how it must have been. Shortly after I went away, he visited Europe. I had been at home a year, and now we heard he had returned; so for two years he hadn't seen me. He had written a great deal to Lu,— brotherly letters they were,—he is so peculiar,—determining not to give her the least intimation of what he felt, if he did feel anything, till he was able to say all. And now he had earned for himself a certain fame, a promise of greater; his works sold; and if he pleased, he could marry. I merely presume this might have been his thought; he never told me. A certain fame! But that's nothing to what he will have. How can he paint gray, faint, half-alive things now? He must abound in color,—be rich, exhaustless: wild sea-sketches,—sunrise,—sunset,—mountain mists rolling in turbid crimson masses, breaking in a milky spray of vapor round lofty peaks, and letting out lonely glimpses of a melancholy moon,—South American splendors,—pomps of fruit and blossom,—all this affluence of his future life must flash from his pencils now. Not that he will paint again directly. Do you suppose it possible that I should be given him merely for a phase of wealth and light and color, and then taken,—taken, in some dreadful way, to teach him the necessary and inevitable result of such extravagant luxuriance? It makes me shiver.

It was that very noon when papa brought in the amber, that he came for the first time since his return from Europe. He hadn't met Lu before. I ran, because I was in my morning wrapper. Don't you see it there, that cream-colored, undyed silk, with the dear palms and ferns swimming all over it? And half my hair was just flung into a little black net that Lu had made me; we both had run down as we were when we heard papa. I scampered; but *he* saw only Lu, and grasped her hands. Then, of course, I stopped on the baluster to look. They didn't say anything, only seemed to be reading up for the two years in each other's eyes; but Lu dropped her kid box, and as he stooped to pick it up, he held it, and then took out the ring, looked at her and smiled, and put it on his finger. The one she had always worn was no more a mystery. He has such little hands! they don't seem made for anything but slender crayons and water-colors, as if oils would weight them down with the pigment; but there is a nervy strength about them that could almost bend an ash.

Papa's breezy voice blew through the room next minute, welcoming him; and then he told Lu to put up her jewels, and order luncheon, at which, of course, the other wanted to see the jewels nearer; and I couldn't stand that, but slipped down and walked right in, lifting my amber, and saying, "Oh, but this is what you must look at!"

He turned, somewhat slowly, with such a lovely indifference, and let his eyes idly drop on me. He didn't look at the amber at all; he didn't look at me; I seemed to fill his gaze without any action from him, for he stood quiet and passive; my voice, too, seemed to wrap him in a dream,—only an instant though; then I had reached him.

"You've not forgotten Yone," said papa, "who went persimmon and came apricot?"

"I've not forgotten Yone," answered he, as if half asleep. "But who is this?"

"Who is this?" echoed papa. "Why, this is my great West Indian magnolia, my Cleopatra in light colors, my—"

"Hush, you silly man!"

"This is she," putting his hands on my shoulders,—"Miss Giorgione Willoughby."

By this time he had found his manners.

"Miss Giorgione Willoughby," he said, with a cool bow, "I never knew you."

"Very well, sir," I retorted. "Now you and my father have settled the question, know my amber!" and lifting it again, it got caught in that curl.

I have good right to love my hair. What was there to do, when it snarled in deeper every minute, but for him to help me? and then, at the friction of our hands, the beads gave out slightly their pungent smell that breathes all through the Arabian Nights, you know; and the perfumed curls were brushing softly over his fingers, and I a little vexed and flushed as the blind blew back and let in the sunshine and a roistering wind;—why, it was all a pretty scene, to be felt then and remembered afterward. Lu, I believe, saw at that instant how it would be, and moved away to do as papa had asked; but no thought of it came to me.

"Well, if you can't clear the tangle," I said, "you can see the beads."

But while with delight he examined their curious fretting, he yet saw me.

I am used to admiration now, certainly; it is my food; without it I should die of inanition; but do you suppose I care any more for those who give it to me than a Chinese idol does for whoever swings incense before it? Are you devoted to your butcher and milkman? We desire only the unpossessed or unattainable, "something afar from the sphere of our sorrow." But, though unconsciously, I may have been piqued by this manner of his. It was new; not a word, not a glance; I believed it was carelessness, and resolved—merely for the sake of conquering, I fancied, too—to change all that. By and by the beads dropped out of the curl, as if they had been possessed of mischief and had held there of themselves. He caught them.

"Here, Circe," he said.

That was the time I was so angry; for, at the second, he meant all it comprehended. He saw, I suppose, for he added at once,—

"Or what was the name of the Witch of Atlas,

> 'The magic circle of whose voice and eyes
> All savage natures did imparadise'?" [2]

I wonder what made me think him mocking me. Frequently since then he has called me by that word.

"I don't know much about geography," I said. "Besides, these didn't come from there. Little Asian—the imp of my name, you remember—owned them."

"Ah?" with the utmost apathy; and turning to my father, "I saw the painting that enslaved you, sir," he said.

"Yes, yes," said papa, gleefully. "And then why didn't you make me a copy?"

"Why?" Here he glanced round the room, as if he weren't thinking at all of the matter in hand. "The coloring is more than one can describe, though faded. But I don't think you would like it so much now. Moreover, sir, I cannot make copies."

I stepped towards them, quite forgetful of my pride. "Can't?" I exclaimed. "Oh, how splendid! Because then no other man comes between you and Nature; your ideal hangs before you, and special glimpses open and shut on you, glimpses which copyists never obtain."

"I don't think you are right," he said, coldly, his hands loosely crossed behind him, leaning on the corner of the mantel, and looking unconcernedly out of the window.

Wasn't it provoking? I remembered myself,—and remembered, too, that I never had made a real exertion to procure anything, and it wasn't worth while to begin then; besides not being my forte,—things must come to me. Just then Lu re-entered, and one of the servants brought a tray, and we had lunch. Then our visitor rose to go.

"No, no," said papa. "Stay the day out with the girls. It's May-day, and there are to be fireworks on the other bank to-night."

"Fireworks for May-day?"

"Yes, to be sure. Wait and see."

"It would be so pleasant!" pleaded Lu.

"And a band, I forgot to mention. I have an engagement myself, so you'll excuse me; but the girls will do the honors, and I shall meet you at dinner."

So it was arranged. Papa went out. I curled up on a lounge,—for Lu wouldn't have liked to be left, if I had liked to leave her,—and soon, when he sat down by her quite across the room, I half shut my eyes and pretended to sleep. He began to turn over her workbasket, taking up her thimble, snipping at the thread with her scissors: I see now he wasn't thinking about it, and was trying to recover what he considered a proper state of feeling, but I fancied he was very gentle and tender, though I couldn't hear what they said, and I never took the trouble to listen in my life. In about five minutes I was tired of this playing 'possum, and took my observations.

What is your idea of a Louise? Mine is,—dark eyes, dark hair, decided features, pale, brown pale, with a mole on the left cheek,—and that's Louise. Nothing striking, but pure and clear, and growing always better.

For him,—he's not one of those cliff-like men against whom you are blown as a feather. I don't fancy that kind; I can stand of myself, rule myself. He isn't small, though; no, he's tall enough, but all his frame is delicate, held to earth by nothing but the cords of a strong will,—very little body, very much soul. He, too, is pale, and has dark eyes, with violet darks in them. You don't call him beautiful in the least, but you don't know him. I call him beauty itself, and I know him thoroughly. A stranger might have thought, when I spoke of those copals Rose carved, that Rose was some girl. But though he has a feminine sensibility, like Correggio or Schubert, nobody could call him womanish. "*Les races se féminisent.*" Don't you remember Matthew Roydon's Astrophill?

> "A sweet, attractive kind of grace,
> A full assurance given by looks,
> Continual comfort in a face."[3]

I always think of that flame in an alabaster vase, when I see him; "one sweet grace fed still with one sweet mind"; a countenance of another sphere: that's Vaughan Rose. It provokes me that I can't paint him myself, without other folk's words; but you see there's no natural image of him in me, and so I can't throw it strongly on any canvas. As for his manners, you've seen them;—now tell me, was there ever anything so winning when he pleases, and always a most gracious courtesy in his air, even when saying an insufferably uncivil thing? He has an art, a science, of putting the unpleasant out of his sight, ignoring or looking over it, which sometimes gives him an absent way; and that is becaue he so delights in beauty; he seems to have woven a mist over his face then, and to be shut in on his own inner loveliness; and many a woman thinks he is perfectly devoted, when, very like, he is swinging over some lonely Spanish sierra beneath the stars, or buried in noonday Brazilian forests, half stifled with the fancied breath of every gorgeous blossom of the zone. Till this time, it had been the perfection of form rather than tint that had enthralled him; he had come home with severe ideas, too severe; he needed me, you see.

But while looking at him and Lu, on that day, I didn't perceive half of this, only felt annoyed at their behavior, and let them feel that I was noticing them. There's nothing worse than that; it's a very upasbreath; it puts on the brakes; and of course a chill and a restraint overcame them till Mr. Dudley was announced.

"Dear! dear!" I exclaimed, getting upon my feet. "What ever shall we do, Lu? I'm not dressed for him." And while I stood, Mr. Dudley came in.

Mr. Dudley didn't seem to mind whether I was dressed in cobweb or sheet-iron; for he directed his looks and conversation so much to Lu, that Rose came and sat on a stool before me and began to talk.

"Miss Willoughby——"

"Yone, please."

"But you are not Yone."

"Well, just as you choose. You were going to say——?"

"Merely to ask how you liked the Islands."

"Oh, well enough."

"No more?" he said. "They wouldn't have broken your spell so, if that had been all. Do you know, I actually believe in enchantments now?"

I was indignant, but amused in spite of myself.

"Well," he continued, "why don't you say it? How impertinent am I? You won't? Why don't you laugh, then?"

"Dear me!" I replied. "You are so much on the 'subtle-souled-psychologist' line, that there's no need of my speaking at all."

"I can carry on all the dialogue? Then let *me* say how you liked the Islands."

"I shall do no such thing. I liked the West Indies because there is life there; because the air is a firmament of balm, and you grow in it like a flower in the sun; because the fierce heat and panting winds wake and kindle all latent color and fertilize every germ of delight that might sleep here forever. That's why I liked them; and you knew it just as well before as now."

"Yes; but I wanted to see if you knew it. So you think there is life there in that dead Atlantis."

"Life of the elements, rain, hail, fire, and snow."

"Snow thrice bolted by the northern blast, I fancy, by which time it becomes rather misty. Exaggerated snow."

"Everything there is an exaggeration. Coming here from England is like stepping out of a fog into an almost exhausted receiver; but you've no idea what light is, till you've been in those inland hills. You think a blue sky the perfection of bliss? When you see a white sky, a dome of colorless crystal, with purple swells of mountain heaving round you, and a wilderness in golden greens royally languid below, while stretches of a scarlet blaze, enough to ruin a weak constitution, flaunt from the rank vines that lace every thicket,—and the whole world, and you with it, seems breaking to blossom,—why, then you know what light is and can do. The very wind there by day is bright, now faint, now stinging, and makes a low wiry music through the loose sprays as if they were tense harpstrings. Nothing startles; all is like a grand composition utterly wrought out. What a blessing it is that the blacks have been imported there,—their swarthiness is in such consonance!"

"No; the native race was in better consonance. You are so enthusiastic, it is pity you ever came away."

"Not at all. I didn't know anything about it till I came back."

"But a mere animal or vegetable life is not much. What was ever done in the tropics?"

"Almost all the world's history,—wasn't it?"

"No, indeed; only the first, most trifling, and barbarian movements."

"At all events, you are full of blessedness in those climates, and that is the end and aim of all action; and if Nature will do it for you, there is no need of your interference. It is much better to be than to do;—one is strife, the other is possession."

"You mean being as the complete attainment? There is only one Being, then. All the rest of us are——"

"So you see, you are not full of blessedness there."

"O dear me! that sounds like metaphysics! Don't!"

"You ought to have been born in Abelard's time,—you've such a disputatious spirit. That's I don't know how many times you have contradicted me to-day."

"Pardon."

"I wonder if you are so easy with all women."

"I don't know many."

"I shall watch to see if you contradict Lu this way."

"I don't need. How absorbed she is! Mr. Dudley is interesting'?"

"I don't know. No. But then, Lu is a good girl, and he's her minister,—a Delphic oracle. She thinks the sun and moon set somewhere round Mr. Dudley. Oh! I mean to show him my amber!"

And I tossed it into Lu's lap, saying,—

"Show it to Mr. Dudley, Lu,—and ask him if it isn't divine!"

Of course, he was shocked, and wouldn't go into ecstasies at all; tripped on the adjective.

"There are gods enough in it to be divine," said Rose, taking it from Lu's hand and bringing it back to me. "All those very Gnostic deities who assisted at Creation. You are not afraid that the imprisoned things work their spells upon you? The oracle declares it suits your cousin best," he added, in a lower tone.

"All the oaf knows!" I responded. "I wish you'd admire it, Mr. Dudley. Mr. Rose don't like amber,—handles it like nettles."

"No," said Rose, "I don't like amber."

"He prefers aqua-marina," I continued. "Lu, produce yours!" For she had not heard him.

"Yes," said Mr. Dudley, spacing his syllables and rubbing his finger over his lip while he gazed, "every one must prefer aqua-marina."

"Nonsense! It's no better than glass. I'd as soon wear a set of window-panes. There's no expression in it. It isn't alive, like real gems."

Mr. Dudley stared. Rose laughed.

"What a vindication of amber!" he said.

He was standing now, leaning against the mantel, just as he was before lunch. Lu looked at him and smiled.

"Yone is exultant, because we both wanted the beads," she said. "I like amber as much as she."

"Nothing near so much, Lu!"

"Why didn't you have them, then?" asked Rose, quickly.

"Oh, they belonged to Yone; and uncle gave me these, which I like better. Amber is warm, and smells of the earth; but this is cool and dewy, and—"

"Smells of heaven?" asked I, significantly.

Mr. Dudley began to fidget, for he saw no chance of finishing his exposition.

"As I was saying, Miss Louisa," he began, in a different key.

I took my beads and wound them round my wrist. "You haven't as much eye for color as a poppy-bee," I exclaimed, in a corresponding key, and looking up at Rose.

"Unjust. I was thinking then how entirely they suited you."

"Thank you. Vastly complimentary from one who 'don't like amber'!"

"Nevertheless, you think so."

"Yes and no. Why don't you like it?"

"You mustn't ask me for my reasons. It is not merely disagreeable, but hateful."

"And you've been beside me like a Christian all this time, and I had it!"

"The perfume is acrid; I associate it with the lower jaw of St. Basil the Great, styled a present of immense value, you remember,—being hard, heavy, shining like gold, the teeth yet in it, and with a smell more delightful than amber,"—making a mock shudder at the word.

"Oh, it is prejudice, then."

"Not in the least. It is antipathy. Besides, the thing is unnatural; there is no existent cause for it. A bit that turns up on certain sands,—here at home, for aught I know, as often as anywhere."

"Which means Nazareth. We must teach you, sir, that there are some things at home as rare as those abroad."

"I am taught," he said, very low, and without looking up.

"Just tell me what is amber?"

"Fossil gum."

"Can you say those words and not like it? Don't it bring to you a magnificent picture of the pristine world,—great seas and other skies,—a world of accentuated crises, that sloughed off age after age, and rose fresher from each plunge? Don't you see, or long to see, that mysterious magic tree out of whose pores oozed this fine solidified sunshine? What leaf did it have? what blossom? what great wind shivered its branches? Was it a giant on a lonely coast, or thick low growth blistered in ravines and dells? That's the witchery of amber,—that it *has* no cause,—that all the world grew to produce it, maybe,—died and gave no other sign,—that its tree, which must have been beautiful, dropped all its fruits,—and how bursting with juice must they have been—"

"Unfortunately, coniferous."

"Be quiet. Stripped itself of all its lush luxuriance, and left for a vestige only this little fester of its gashes."

"No, again," he once more interrupted. "I have seen remnants of the wood and bark in a museum."

"Or has it hidden and compressed all its secret here?" I continued, obliviously. "What if in some piece of amber an accidental seed were sealed; we found, and planted, and brought back the lost æons? What a glorious world that must have been where even the gum was so precious!"

"In a picture, yes. Necessary for this. But, my dear Miss Willoughby, you convince me that the Amber Witch[4] founded your family," he said, having listened with an amused face. "Loveliest amber that ever the sorrowing sea-birds have wept," he hummed. "There! isn't that kind of stuff enough to make a man detest it?"

"Yes."

"And you are quite as bad in another way."

"Oh!"

"Just because, when we hold it in our hands, we hold also that furious epoch where rioted all monsters and poisons,—where death fecundated and life destroyed,—where superabundance demanded such existences, no souls, but fiercest animal fire;—just for that I hate it."

"Why, then, is it fitted for me?"

He laughed again, but replied: "The hues harmonize; the substances; you both are accidents; it suits your beauty."

So, then, it seemed I had beauty, after all.

"You mean that it harmonizes with me, because I am a symbol of its period. If there had been women, then, they would have been like me,—a great creature without a soul, a—"

"Pray, don't finish the sentence. I can imagine that there is something rich and voluptuous and sating about amber, its color, and its lustre, and its scent; but for others, not for me. Yes, you have beauty, after all," turning suddenly, and withering me with his eye,—"beauty, after all, as you didn't *say* just now. Why don't you put some of it into—. Mr. Willoughby is in the garden. I must go before he comes in, or he'll make me stay. There are some to whom you can't say, No."

He stopped a minute, and now, without looking,—indeed, he looked everywhere but at me, while we talked,—made a bow as if just seating me from a waltz, and, with his eyes and his smile on Louise all the way down the room, went out. Did you ever know such insolence?

PAPA MADE Mr. Dudley stay and dine, and of course we were almost bored to death, when in came Rose again, stealing behind Lu's chair, and showering her in the twilight with a rain of May-flowers.

"Now you'll have to gather them again," he said.

"Oh, how exquisite! how delicious! how I thank you!" she exclaimed, without disturbing one, however.

"You won't touch them again? Then I must," he added.

"No, no, Mr. Rose!" I cried. "I'll pick them up, and take toll."

"Don't touch them!" said Lu, "they're so sweet!"

"Yes," he murmured lower, "they share with you. I always said so, you remember."

"O yes! and every May-day but the last you have brought them to me."

"Have you the trailing-arbutus there?" asked Mr. Dudley.

"No," returned Rose.

"I thought I detected strawberries," submitted the other,—"a pleasant odor which recalls childhood to memory."

For some noses all sweet scents are lumped in one big strawberry; clovers, or hyacinths, or every laden air indifferently, the still sniff— strawberries. Commonplace!

"It's a sign of high birth to track strawberry-beds where no fruit is, Mr. Dudley," said I.

"Very true, Miss Willoughby. I was born pretty high up in the Green Mountains."

"And so keep your memory green?"

"Strawberries in June," said Rose, good-naturedly. "But fruit out of season is trouble out of reason, the Dream-Book says. It's May now, and these are its blossoms."

"Everybody makes such a fuss about ground-laurel!" said I. "I don't see why, I'm sure. They're never perfect. The leaf is hideous,—a stupid duenna! You get great green leaves, and the flowers all white; you get deep rosy flowers, and the leaves are all brown and bitten. They're neither one thing nor another. They're just like heliotropes,—no bloom at all, only scent. I've torn up myriads, to the ten stamens in their feathered case, to find where that smell comes from,—that is perfectly delicious,—and I never could. They are a cheat."

"Have you finished your tirade?" asked Rose, indifferently.

"I don't believe you mean so," murmured Lu. "They have a color of their own, almost human, infantine; and when you mass them, the tone is more soft and mellow than a flute. Everybody loves May-flowers."

"Just about. I despise flutes. I like bassoons."

"They are prophets of apple-blossoms."

"Which brings them at once into the culinary."

"They are not very showy," said Mr. Dudley; "but when we remember the Fathers—"

"There's nothing like them," said Rose, gently, as he knelt by Lu, slowly putting them into order; "nothing but pure, clear things; they're the fruit of snow-flakes, the firstlings of the year. When one thinks how sweetly they come from their warm coverts and look into this cold, breezy sky so unshrinkingly, and from what a soil they gather such a wealth of simple beauty, one feels ashamed."

"Climax worthy of the useless things!" said I.

"The moment in which first we are thoroughly ashamed, Miss Willoughby, is the sovereign one of our life. Useless things? They are worth king and bishop. Every year, weariness and depression melt away when atop of the seasons' crucible boil these little bubbles. Isn't everybody better for lavishing love? and no one merely likes these; whoever cares at all, loves entirely. We always take and give resemblances or sympathies from any close connection, and so these are in their way a type of their lovers. What virtue is in them to distil the shadow of the great pines, that wave layer after layer with a grave rhythm over them, into this delicate tint, I wonder. They have so decided an individuality,—different there from hot-house belles;—fashion strips us of our characteristics—"

"You needn't turn to me for illustration of exotics," said I.

He threw me a cluster, half-hidden in its green towers, and went on, laying one by one and bringing out little effects.

"The sweetest modesty clings to them, which Alphonse Karr denies to the violet, so that they are almost out of place in a drawing-room; one ought to give them there the shelter of their large, kind leaves."

"Hemlock's the only wear," said Louise.

"Or last year's scarlet blackberry triads. Vines together," he suggested.

"But sometimes they forget their nun-like habit," she added, "put on a frolicsome mood, and clamber out and flush all the deep ruts of the carriage-road in Follymill Woods, you remember."

"Penance next year," said I.

"No, no; you are not to bring your old world into my new," objected Rose; "they're fair little Puritans, who do no penance. Perhaps they ran out so to greet the winter-worn mariners of Plymouth, and have been pursued by the love of their descendants ever since, they getting charier. Just remember how they grow. Why, you'd never suspect a flower there, till, happening to turn up a leaf, you're in the midst of harvest. You may tramp acres in vain, and within a stone's throw they've been awaiting you. There's something very charming, too about them in this,—that when the buds are set, and at last a single blossom starts the trail, you plucking at one end of the vine, your heart's delight may touch the other a hundred miles away. Spring's telegraph. So they bind our coast with this network of flower and root."

"By no means," I asserted. "They grow in spots."

"Pshaw! I won't believe it. They're everywhere just the same, only underground preparing their little witnesses, whom they send out where most needed. You don't suppose they find much joy in the fellowship of brown pine pins and sad gray mosses, do you? Some folks say they don't grow away from the shore; but I've found them, I'm sorry to say, up in New Hampshire."

"Why sorry?" asked Lu.

"Oh, I like it best that they need our sea. They're eminently choice for this hour, too, when you scarcely gather their tint,—that tint, as if moonlight should wish to become a flower,—but their fragrance is an atmosphere all about you. How genuinely spicy it is! It's the very quintessence of those regions all whose sweetness exudes in sun-saturated balsams,—the very breath of pine woods and salt sea winds. How could it live away from the sea?"

"Why, sir," said Mr. Dudley, "you speak as if it were a creature!"

"A hard woody stem, a green robust leaf, a delicate odorous flower, Mr. Dudley, what is it all but an expression of New England character?"

"Doxology!" said I.

"Now, Miss Louise, as you have made me atone for my freedom, the task being done, let me present them in form."

"I'm sure she needn't praise them," said I.

She didn't.

"I declared people make a great fuss over them," I continued. "And you prove it. You put me in mind of a sound to be heard where one gets them,—a strange sound, like low, distant thunder, and it's nothing but the drum of a little partridge! a great song out of nothing.—Bless me! what's that?"

"Oh, the fireworks!" said Lu. And we all thronged to the windows.

"It's very good of your uncle to have them," said Rose. "What a crowd from the town! Think of the pyrotechnics among comets and aerolites some fellows may have! It's quite right, too, to make our festivals with light; it's the highest and last of all things; we never can carry our imaginations beyond light—"

"Our imaginations ought to carry us," said Lu.

"Come," I said, "you can play what pranks you please with the little May; but light is my province, my absorption; let it alone."

It grew quite dark, interrupted now and then by the glare of rockets; but at last a stream of central fire went out in a slow rain of countless violets, reflected with pale blue flashes in the river below, and then the gloom was unbroken. I saw them, in that long dim gleam, standing together at a window. Louise, her figure almost swaying as if to some inaudible music, but her face turned to him with such a steady quiet. Ah me! what a tremulous joy, what passion, and what search, lit those eyes! But you know that passion means suffering, and, tracing it in the original through its roots, you come to pathos, and still farther, to lamentation, I've heard. But he was not looking down at her, only out and away, paler than ever in the blue light, sad and resolved. I ordered candles.

"Sing to me, Louise," said Rose, at length. "It is two years since I heard you."

"Sing 'What's a' the steer, kimmer,'" I said. But instead, she gave the little ballad, "And bring my love again, for he lies among the Moors."

Rose went and leaned over the piano-forte while she sang, bending, and commanding her eyes. He seemed to wish to put himself where he was before he ever left her, to awaken everything lovely in her, to bring her before him as utterly developed as she might be,—not only to afford her, but to force upon her, every chance to master him. He seemed to wish to love, I thought.

"Thank you," he said, as she ceased. "Did you choose it purposely, Louise?"

Lu sang very nicely, and, though I dare say she would rather not then, when Mr. Dudley asked for the "Vale of Avoca," and the "Margin of Zürich's Fair Waters," she gave them just as kindly. Altogether, quite a damp programme. Then papa came in, bright and blithe, whirled me round in a *pas de deux,* and we all very gay and hilarious slipped into the second of May.

Dear me! how time goes! I must hurry.—After that, I didn't see so much of Rose; but he met Lu everywhere, came in when I was out, and, if I returned, he went, perfectly regardless of my existence, it seemed. They rode, too, all round the country; and she sat to him, though he never filled out the sketch. For weeks he was devoted; but I fancied, when I saw them, that there lingered in his manner the same thing as on the first evening while she sang to him. Lu was so gay and sweet and happy that I hardly knew her; she was always very gentle, but such a decided body,—that's the Willoughby, her mother. Yet during these weeks Rose had not spoken, not formally; delicate and friendly kindness was all Lu could have found, had she sought. One night, I remember, he came in and wanted us to go out and row with him on the river. Lu wouldn't go without me."

"Will you come?" said he, coolly, as if I were merely necessary as a thwart or thole-pin might have been, turning and letting his eyes fall on me an instant, then snatching them off with a sparkle and flush, and such a lordly carelessness of manner otherwise.

"Certainly not," I replied.

So they remained, and Lu began to open a bundle of Border Ballads, which he had brought her. The very first one was "Whistle an' I'll come to you, my lad." I laughed. She glanced up quickly, then held it in her hands a moment, repeated the name, and asked if he liked it.

"Oh, yes," he said. "There couldn't be a Scotch song without that rhythm better than melody, which, after all, is Beethoven's secret."

"Perhaps," said Louise. "But I shall not sing this."

"Oh, do!" he said, turning with surprise. "You don't know what an aerial, whistling little thing it is!"

"No."

"Why, Louise! There is nobody could sing it but you."

"Of good discourse, an excellent musician, and her hair shall be of what color it please God," quoted I, and in came Mr. Dudley, as he usually did when not wanted; though I've no reason to find fault with him, not-withstanding his blank treatment of me. He never took any notice, because he was in love with Lu. Rose never took any notice of me, either. But with a difference!

Lu was singularly condescending to Mr. Dudley that evening; and Rose, sitting aside, looked so very much disturbed—whether pleasantly or otherwise didn't occur to me—that I couldn't help enjoying his discom-fiture, and watching him through it.

Now, though I told you I wasn't nervous, I never should know I had this luxurious calm, if there were nothing to measure it by; and once in a great while a perfect whirlpool seizes me,—my blood is all in turmoil,—I bubble with silent laughter, or cry with all my heart. I had been in such a strange state a good while; and now, as I surveyed Rose, it gradually grew fiercer, till I actually sprang to my feet, and exclaimed, "There! it is insup-portable! I've been in the magnetic storm long enough! it is time something took it from me!" and ran out-doors.

Rose sauntered after, by and by, as if unwillingly drawn by a load-stone, and found the heavens wrapped in a rosy flame of Northern Lights. He looked as though he belonged to them, so pale and elf-like was his face then, like one bewitched.

"Papa's fireworks fade before mine," I said. "Now we can live in the woods, as Lu has been wishing; for a dry southerly wind follows this, with a blue smoke filming all the distant fields. Won't it be delicious?"

"Or rain," he replied; "I think it will rain to-morrow,—warm, full rains." And he seemed as if such a chance would dissolve him entirely.

As for me, those shifting, silent sheets of splendor abstracted all that was alien, and left me in my normal state.

"There they come!" I said, as Lu and Mr. Dudley, and some others who had entered in my absence,—gnats dancing in the beam,—stepped down towards us. "How charming for us all to sit out here!"

"How annoying, you mean," he replied, simply for contradiction.

"It hasn't been warm enough before," I added.

"And Louise may take cold now," he said, as if wishing to exhibit his care for her. "Whom is she speaking with? Blarsaye? And who comes after?"

"Parti. A delightful person,—been abroad, too. You and he can have a crack about Louvres and Vaticans now, and leave Lu and Mr. Dudley to me."

Rose suddenly inspected me and then Parti, as if he preferred the crack to be with cudgels; but in a second the little blaze vanished, and he only stripped a weigelia branch of every blossom.

I wonder what made Lu behave so that night; she scarcely spoke to Rose, appeared entirely unconcerned while he hovered round her like an officious sprite, was all grace to the others and sweetness to Mr. Dudley. And Rose, oblivious of snubs, paraded his devotion, seemed determined to show his love for Lu,—as if any one cared a straw,—and took the pains to be positively rude to me. He was possessed of an odd restlessness; a little defiance bristled his movements, an air of contrariness; and whenever he became quiet, he seemed again like one enchanted and folded up in a dream, to break whose spell he was about to abandon efforts. He told me Life had destroyed my enchantment;—I wonder what will destroy his.— Lu refused to sit in the gardenchair he offered,—just suffered the wreath of pink bells he gave her to hang in her hand, and by and by fall,—and when the north grew ruddier and swept the zenith with lances of light, and when it faded, and a dim cloud hazed all the stars, preserved the same equanimity, kept on the *evil* tenor of her way, and bade every one an impartial farewell at separating. She is preciously well-bred.

We hadn't remained in the garden all that time, though,—but, strolling through the gate and over the field, had reached a small grove that fringes the gully worn by Wild Fall and crossed by the railway. As we emerged from that, talking gayly, and our voices almost drowned by the dash of the little waterfall and the echo from the opposite rock, I sprang across the curving track, thinking them behind, and at the same instant a thunderous roar burst all about, a torrent of hot air whizzed and eddied over me, I fell dizzied and stunned, and the night express-train shot by like a burning arrow. Of course I was dreadfully hurt by my fall and fright,—I feel the shock now,—the blow, the stroke,—but they all stood on the little mound, from which I had sprung, like so many petrifactions: Rose, just as he had caught Louise back on firmer ground when she was about to follow me, his arm wound swiftly round her waist, yet his head thrust forward eagerly, his pale face and glowing eyes bent, not on her, but me. Still he never stirred, and poor Mr. Dudley first came to my assistance. We all drew breath at our escape, and, a little slowly, on my account, turned homeward.

"You are not bruised, Miss Willoughby?" asked Blarsaye, wakened.

"Dear Yone!" Lu said, leaving Mr. Dudley's arm, "you're so very pale! It's not pain, is it?"

"I am not conscious of any. Why should I be injured, any more than you?"

"Do you know," said Rose, *sotto voce,* turning and bending merely his head to me, "I thought I heard you scream, and that you were dead."

"And what then?"

"Nothing, but that you were lying dead and torn, and I should see you," he said,—and said as if he liked to say it, experiencing a kind of savage delight at his ability to say it.

"A pity to have disappointed you!" I answered.

"I saw it coming before you leaped," he added, as a malignant finality, and drawing nearer. "You were both on the brink. I called, but probably neither you nor Lu heard me. So I snatched her back."

Now I had been next him then.

"Jove's balance," I said, taking Parti's arm.

He turned instantly to Lu, and kept by her during the remainder of the walk, Mr. Dudley being at the other side. I was puzzled a little by Lu, as I have been a good many times since; I thought she liked Rose so much. Papa met us in the field, and there the affair must be detailed to him, and then he would have us celebrate our safety in Champagne.

"Good by, Louise," said Rose, beside her at the gate, and offering his hand, somewhat later. "I'm going away to-morrow, if it's fine."

"Going?" with involuntary surprise.

"To camp out in Maine."

"Oh,—I hope you will enjoy it."

"Would you stay long, Louise?"

"If the sketching-grounds are good."

"When I come back, you'll sing my songs? Shake hands."

She just laid a cold touch on his.

"Louise, are you offended with me?"

She looked up with so much simplicity. "Offended, Rose, with you?"

"Not offended, but frozen," I could have said. Lu is like that little sensitive-plant, shrinking into herself with stiff unconsciousness at a certain touch. But I don't think he noticed the sad tone in her voice, as she said good night; I didn't, till, the others being gone, I saw her turn after his disappearing figure, with a look that would have been despairing, but for its supplication.

The only thing Lu ever said to me about this was,—

"Don't you think Rose a little altered, Yone, since he came home?"

"Altered?"

"I have noticed it ever since you showed him your beads, that day."

"Oh! it's the amber," I said. "They are amulets, and have bound him in a thrall. You must wear them, and dissolve the charm. He's in a dream."

"What is it to be in a dream?" she asked.

"To lose thought of past or future."

She repeated my words,—"Yes, he's in a dream," she said musingly.

ROSE DIDN'T COME near us for a fortnight; but he had not camped at all, as he said. It was the first stone thrown into Lu's life, and I never saw any one keep the ripples under so; but her suspicions were aroused. Finally he came in again, all as before, and I thought things might have been different, if in that fortnight Mr. Dudley had not been so assiduous; and now, to the latter's happiness, there were several ragged children and infirm old women in whom, Lu having taken them in charge, he chose to be especially interested. Lu always was housekeeper, both because it had fallen to her while mamma and I were away, and because she had an administrative faculty equal to General Jackson's; and Rose, who had frequently gone about with her, inspecting jellies and cordials and adding up her accounts, now unexpectedly found Mr. Dudley so near his former place that he disdained to resume it himself;—not entirely, because the man of course couldn't be as familiar as an old playmate; but just enough to put Rose aside. He never would compete with any one; and Lu did not know how to repulse the other.

If the amulets had ravished Rose from himself, they did it at a distance, for I had not worn them since that day.—You needn't look. Thales imagined amber had a spirit; and Pliny says it is a counter-charm for sorceries. There are a great many mysterious things in the world. Aren't there any hidden relations between us and certain substances? Will you tell me something impossible?—But he came and went about Louise, and she sung his songs, and all was going finely again, when we gave our midsummer party.

Everybody was there, of course, and we had enrapturing music. Louise wore—no matter—something of twilight purple, and begged for the amber, since it was too much for my toilette,—a double India muslin, whose snowy sheen scintillated with festoons of gorgeous green beetles' wings flaming like fiery emeralds. A family dress, my dear, and worn by my aunt before me,—only that individual must have been frightened out of her wits by it. A cruel, savage dress, very like, but ineffably gorgeous. So I wore her aqua-marina, though the other would have been better; and when I sailed in, with all the airy folds in a hoar-frost mistiness fluttering round me and the glitter of Lu's jewels,—

"Why!" said Rose, "you look like the moon in a halo."

But Lu disliked a hostess out-dressing her guests.

It was dull enough till quite late, and then I stepped out with Mr. Parti, and walked up and down a gardenpath. Others were outside as well, and the last time I passed a little arbor I caught a yellow gleam of amber. Lu, of course. Who was with her? A gentleman, bending low to catch her words, holding her hand in an irresistible pressure. Not Rose, for he was flitting in beyond. Mr. Dudley. And I saw then that Lu's kindness was too great to allow her to repel him angrily; her gentle conscience let her wound no one. Had Rose seen the pantomime? Without doubt. He had been seeking her, and he found her, he thought, in Mr. Dudley's arms. After a while we went in, and, finding all smooth enough, I slipped through the balcony-window and hung over the balustrade, glad to be alone a moment. The wind, blowing in, carried the gay sounds away from me, even the music came richly muffled through the heavy curtains, and I wished to breathe balm and calm. The moon, round and full, was just rising, making the gloom below more sweet. A full moon is poison to some; they shut it out at every crevice, and do not suffer a ray to cross them; it has a chemical or magnetic effect; it sickens them. But I am never more free and royal than when the subtile celerity of its magic combinations, whatever they are, is at work. Never had I know the mere joy of being, so intimately as to-night. The river slept soft and mystic below the woods, the sky was full of light, the air ripe with summer. Out of the yellow honeysuckles that climbed around, clouds of delicious fragrance stole and swathed me; long wafts of faint harmony gently thrilled me. Dewy and dark and uncertain was all beyond. I, possessed with a joyousness so deep through its contented languor as to counterfeit serenity, forgot all my wealth of nature, my pomp of beauty, abandoned myself to the hour.

A strain of melancholy dance-music pierced the air and fell. I half turned my head, and my eyes met Rose. He had been there before me, perhaps. His face white and shining in the light, shining with a strange sweet smile of relief, of satisfaction, of delight, his lips quivering with unspoken words, his eyes dusky with depth after depth of passion. How long did my eyes swim on his? I cannot tell. He never stirred; still leaned there against the pillar, still looked down on me like a marble god. The sudden tears dazzled my gaze, fell down my hot cheek, and still I knelt fascinated by that smile. In that moment I felt that he was more beautiful than the night, than the music, than I. Then I knew that all this time, all summer, all past summers, all my life long, I had loved him.

Some one was waiting to make his adieux; I heard my father seeking me; I parted the curtains and went in. One after one those tedious people left, the lights grew dim, and still he stayed without. I ran to the window, and, lifting the curtain, I bent forward, crying,—

"Mr. Rose! do you spend the night on the balcony?"

Then he moved, stepped down, murmured something to my father, bowed loftily to Louise, passed me without a sign, and went out. In a moment, Lu's voice, a quick sharp exclamation, touched him; he turned, came back. She, wondering at him, had stood toying with the amber, and at last crushing the miracle of the whole, a bell-wort wrought most delicately with all the dusty pollen grained upon its anthers, crushing it between her fingers, breaking the thread, and scattering the beads upon the carpet. He stooped with her to gather them again, he took from her hand and restored to her afterward the shattered fragments of the bell-wort, he helped her disentangle the aromatic string from her falling braids,—for I kept apart,—he breathed the penetrating incense of each separate amulet, and I saw that from that hour, when every atom of his sensation was tense and vibrating, she would be associated with the loathed amber in his undefined consciousness, would be surrounded with an atmosphere of its perfume, that Lu was truly sealed from him in it, sealed into herself. Then again, saying no word, he went out.

Louise stood like one lost,—took aimlessly a few steps,—retraced them,—approached a table,—touched something,—left it.

"I am so sorry about your beads!" she said, apologetically,—when she looked up and saw me astonished,—putting the broken pieces into my hand.

"Goodness! Is that what you are fluttering about so for?"

"They can't be mended," she continued, "but I will thread them again."

"I don't care about them, I'm sick of amber," I answered consolingly. "You may have them, if you will."

"No. I must pay too great a price for them," she replied.

"Nonsense! when they break again, I'll pay you back," I said, without in the least knowing what she meant. "I didn't suppose you were too proud for a 'thank you'!"

She came and put both her arms round me neck, laid her cheek beside mine a minute, kissed me, and went up stairs. Lu always rather worshipped me.

Dressing my hair that night, Carmine, my maid, begged for the remnants of the bell-wort to "make a scent-bag with, Miss."

Next day, no Rose; it rained. But at night he came and took possession of the room, with a strange, airy gayety never seen in him before. It was so chilly, that I had heaped the wood-boughs, used in the yesterday's decorations, on the hearth, and lighted a fragrant crackling flame that danced up wildly at my touch,—for I have the faculty of fire. I sat at one side, Lu at the other, papa was holding a skein of silk for her to wind, the amber beads were twinkling in the firelight,—and when she slipped them slowly on the thread, bead after bead warmed through and through by the real blaze, they crowded the room afresh with their pungent spiciness. Papa had called Rose to take his place at the other end of the silk, and had gone out; and when Lu finished, she fastened the ends, cut the thread, Rose likening her to Atropos, and put them back into her basket. Still playing with the scissors, following down the lines of her hand, a little snap was heard.

"Oh!" said Louise, "I have broken my ring!"

"Can't it be repaired?" I asked.

"No," she returned briefly, but pleasantly, and threw the pieces into the fire.

"The hand must not be ringless," said Rose; and slipping off the ring of hers that he wore, he dropped it on the amber, then got up and threw an armful of fresh boughs upon the blaze.

So that was all done. Then Rose was gayer than before. He is one of those people to whom you must allow moods,—when their sun shines, dance,—and when their vapors rise, sit in the shadow. Every variation of the atmosphere affects him, though by no means uniformly; and so sensitive is he, that, when connected with you by any intimate *rapport,* even if but momentary, he almost divines your thoughts. He is full of perpetual surprises. I am sure he was a nightingale before he was Rose. An iridescence like sea-foam sparkled in him that evening, he laughed as lightly as the little tinkling massbells at every moment, and seemed to diffuse a rosy glow wherever he went in the room. Yet gayety was not his peculiar specialty, and at length he sat before the fire, and, taking Lu's scissors, commenced cutting bits of paper in profiles. Somehow they all looked strangely like and unlike Mr. Dudley. I pointed one out to Lu, and if he had needed confirmation, her changing color gave it. He only glanced at her askance, and then broke into the merriest description of his life in Rome, of which he declared he had not spoken to us yet, talking fast and laughing as gleefully as a child, and illustrating people and localities with scissors and paper as he went on, a couple of careless snips putting a whole scene before us.

The floor was well strewn with such chips,—fountains, statues, baths, and all the persons of his little drama,—when papa came in. He held an open letter, and, sitting down, read it over again. Rose fell into silence, clipping the scissors daintily in and out the white sheet through twinkling intricacies. As the design dropped out, I caught it,—a long wreath of honeysuckle-blossoms. Ah, I knew where the honeysuckles grew! Lu was humming a little tune. Rose joined, and hummed the last bars, then bade us good-night.

"Yone," said papa, "your Aunt Willoughy is very ill,—will not recover. She is my elder brother's widow; you are her heir. You must go and stay with her."

Now it was very likely that just at this time I was going away to nurse Aunt Willoughby! Moreover, illness is my very antipodes,—its nearness is invasion,—we are utterly antipathetic,—it disgusts and repels me. What sympathy can there be between my florid health, my rank redundant life, and any wasting disease of death? What more hostile than focal concentration and obscure decomposition? You see, we cannot breathe the same atmosphere. I banish the thought of such a thing from my feeling, from my memory. So I said,—

"It's impossible. I'm not going an inch to Aunt Willoughby's. Why, papa, it's more than a hundred miles, and in this weather!"

"Oh, the wind has changed."

"Then it will be too warm for such a journey."

"A new idea, Yone! Too warm for the mountains?"

"Yes, papa. I'm not going a step."

"Why, Yone, you astonish me! Your sick aunt!"

"That's the very thing. If she were well, I might,—perhaps. Sick! What can I do for her? I never go into a sick-room. I hate it. I don't know how to do a thing there. Don't say another word, papa. I can't go."

"It is out of the question to let it pass so, my dear. Here you are nursing all the invalids in town, yet—"

"Indeed, I'm not, papa. I don't know and don't care whether they're dead or alive."

"Well, then, it's Lu."

"Oh, yes, she's hospital agent for half the country."

"Then it is time that you also got a little experience."

"Don't, papa! I don't want it. I never saw anybody die, and I never mean to."

"Can't I do as well, uncle?" asked Lu.

"You, darling? Yes; but it isn't your duty."

"I thought, perhaps," she said, "you would rather Yone went."

"So I would."

"Dear papa, don't vex me! Ask anything else!"

"It is so unpleasant to Yone," Lu murmured, "that maybe I had better go. And if you've no objection, sir, I'll take the early train to-morrow."

Wasn't she an angel?

LU WAS AWAY a month. Rose came in, expressing his surprise. I said, "Othello's occupation's gone?"

"And left him room for pleasure now," he retorted.

"Which means seclusion from the world, in the society of lakes and chromes."

"Miss Willoughby," said he, turning and looking directly past me, "may I paint you?"

"Me? Oh, you can't."

"No; but may I try?"

"I cannot go to you."

"I will come to you."

"Do you suppose it will be like?"

"Not at all, of course. It is to be, then?"

"Oh, I've no more right than any other piece of Nature to refuse an artist a study in color."

He faced about, half pouting, as if he would go out, then returned and fixed the time.

So he painted. He generally put me into a broad beam that slanted from the top of the veiled window, and day after day he worked. Ah, what glorious days they were! how gay! how full of life! I almost feared to let him image me on canvas, do you know? I had a fancy it would lay my soul so bare to his inspection. What secrets might be searched, what depths fathomed, at such times, if men knew! I feared lest he should see me as I am, in those great masses of warm light lying before him, as I feared he saw when he said amber harmonized with me,—all being things not polarized, not organized, without centre, so to speak. But it escaped him, and he wrought on. Did he succeed? Bless you! he might as well have painted the sun; and who could do that? No; but shades and combinations that he had hardly touched or known, before, he had to lavish now; he learned more than some years might have taught him; he, who worshipped beauty, saw how thoroughly I possessed it; he has told me that through me he learned the sacredness of color. "Since he loves beauty so, why does he not love me?" I asked myself; and perhaps the feverish hope and suspense only lit up that beauty and fed it with fresh fires. Ah, the July days! Did you ever wander over barren, parched stubble-fields, and suddenly front a knot of red Turk's-cap lilies, flaring as if they had drawn all the heat and brilliance from the land into their tissues? Such were they. And if I were to grow old and gray, they would light down all my life, and I could be willing to lead a dull, grave age, looking back and remembering them, warming myself forever in their constant youth. If I had nothing to hope, they would become my whole existence. Think, then, what it will be to have all days like those!

He never satisfied himself, as he might have done, had he known me better,—and he never *shall* know me!—and used to look at me for the secret of his failure, till I laughed; then the look grew wistful, grew enamored. By and by we left the pictures. We went into the woods, warm dry woods; we stayed there from morning till night. In the burning noons, we hung suspended between two heavens, in our boat on glassy forest-pools, where now and then a shoal of white lilies rose and crowded out the under-sky. Sunsets burst like bubbles over us. When the hidden thrushes were breaking one's heart with music, and the sweet fern sent up a tropical fragrance beneath our crushing steps, we came home to rooms full of guests and my father's genial warmth. What a month it was!

One day papa went up into New Hampshire; Aunt Willoughby was dead; and one day Lu came home.

She was very pale and thin. Her eyes were hollow and purple.

"There is some mistake, Lu," I said. "It is you who are dead, instead of Aunt Willoughby."

"Do I look so wretchedly?" she asked, glancing at the mirror.

"Dreadfully! Is it all watching and grief?"

"Watching and grief," said Lu.

How melancholy her smile was! She would have crazed me in a little while, if I had minded her.

"Did you care so much for fretful, crabbed Aunt Willoughby?"

"She was very kind to me," Lu replied.

There was an odd air with her that day. She didn't go at once and get off her travelling-dress, but trifled about in a kind of expectancy, a little fever going and coming in her cheeks, and turning at any noise.

Will you believe it?—though I knew Lu had refused to marry him,—who met her at the half-way junction, saw about her luggage, and drove home with her, but Mr. Dudley, and was with us, a half-hour afterward, when Rose came in? Lu didn't turn at his step, but the little fever in her face prevented his seeing her as I had done. He shook hands with her and asked after her health, and shook hands with Mr. Dudley (who hadn't been near us during her absence), and seemed to wish she should feel that he recognized without pain a connection between herself and that personage. But when he came back to me, I was perplexed again at that be-witched look in his face,—as if Lu's presence made him feel that he was in a dream, I the enchantress of that dream. It did not last long, though. And soon she saw Mr. Dudley out, and went up-stairs.

When Lu came down to the table, she had my beads in her hand again.

"I went into your room and got them, dear Yone," she said, "because I have found something to replace the broken bell-wort," and she showed us a little amber bee, black and golden. "Not so lovely as the bellwort," she resumed, "and I must pierce it for the thread; but it will fill the number. Was I not fortunate to find it?"

But when at a flame she heated a long slender needle to pierce it, the little winged wonder shivered between her fingers, and under the hot steel filled the room with the honeyed smell of its dusted substance.

"Never mind," said I again. "It's a shame, though,—it was so much prettier than the bell-wort! We might have known it was too brittle. It's just as well, Lu."

The room smelt like a chancel at vespers. Rose sauntered to the window, and so down the garden, and then home.

73

"Yes. It cannot be helped," she said, with a smile. "But I really counted upon seeing it on the string. I'm not lucky at amber. You know little Asian said it would bring bane to the bearer."

"Dear! dear! I had quite forgotten!" I exclaimed. "O Lu, keep it, or give it away, or something! I don't want it any longer."

"You're very vehement," she said, laughing now. "I am not afraid of your gods. Shall I wear them?"

So the rest of the summer Lu twined them round her throat,— amulets of sorcery, orbs of separation; but one night she brought them back to me. That was last night. There they lie.

The next day, in the high golden noon, Rose came. I was on the lounge in the alcove parlor, my hair half streaming out of Lu's net; but he didn't mind. The light was toned and mellow, the air soft and cool. He came and sat on the opposite side, so that he faced the wall table with its dish of white, stiflingly sweet lilies, while I looked down the drawing-room. He had brought a book, and by and by opened at the part commenc-ing, "Do not die, Phene."[5] He read it through,—all that perfect, perfect scene. From the moment when he said,

> "I overlean
> This length of hair and lustrous front—they turn
> Like an entire flower upward,"—

his voice low, sustained, clear,—till he reached the line,

> "Look at the woman here with the new soul,"—

till he turned the leaf and murmured,

> "Shall to produce form out of unshaped stuff
> Be art,—and, further, to evoke a soul
> From form, be nothing? This new soul is mine!"—

till then, he never glanced up. Now, with a proud grace, he raised his head,—not to look at me, but across me, at the lilies, to satiate himself with their odorous snowiness. When he again pronounced words, his voice was husky and vibrant; but what music dwelt in it and seemed to prolong rather than break the silver silence, as he echoed,

"Some unsuspected isle in the far seas"!

How many read, to descend to a prosaic life! how few to meet one as rich and full beside them! The tone grew ever lower; he looked up slowly, fastening his glance on mine.

"And you are ever by me while I gaze,—
Are in my arms as now—as now—as now!"

he said. He swayed forward with those wild questioning eyes,—his breath blew over my cheek; I was drawn,—I bent; the full passion of his soul broke to being, wrapped me with a blinding light, a glowing kiss on linger-ing lips, a clasp strong and tender as heaven. All my hair fell down like a shining cloud and veiled us, the great rolling folds in wave after wave of crisp splendor. I drew back from that long, silent kiss, I gathered up each gold thread of the straying tresses, blushing, defiant. He also, he drew back. But I knew all then. I had no need to wait longer; I had achieved. Rose loved me. Rose had loved me from that first day.—You scarcely hear what I say, I talk so low and fast? Well, no matter, dear, you wouldn't care.—For a moment that gaze continued, then the lids fell, the face grew utterly white. He rose, flung the book, crushed and torn, upon the floor, went out, speaking no word to me, nor greeting Louise in the next room. Could he have seen her? No. I, only, had that. For, as I drew from his arm, a meteoric crimson, shooting across the pale face bent over work there, flashed upon me, and then a few great tears, like sudden thunder-drops, falling slowly and wetting the heavy fingers. The long mirror opposite her reflected the interior of the alcove parlor. No,—he could not have seen, he must have felt her.

I wonder whether I should have cared, if I had never met him any more,—happy in this new consciousness. But in the afternoon he re-turned, bright and eager.

"Are you so very busy, dear Yone," he said, without noticing Lu, "that you cannot drive with me to-day?"

Busy! In five minutes I whirled down the avenue beside him. I had not been Yone to him before. How quiet we were! he driving on, bent forward, seeing out and away; I leaning back, my eyes closed, and, when-ever a remembrance of that instant at noon thrilled me, a stinging blush staining my cheek. I, who had believed myself incapable of love, till that night on the balcony, felt its floods welling from my spirit,—who had believed myself so completely cold, was warm to my heart's core. Again that breath fanned me, those lips touched mine, lightly, quickly.

"Yone, my Yone!" he said. "Is it true? No dream within dream? Do you love me?"

Wistful, longing, tender eyes.

"Do I love you? I would die for you!"

AH, ME! If the July days were such, how perfect were the August and September nights! their young moon's lingering twilight, their full broad bays of silver, their interlunar season! The winds were warm about us, the whole earth seemed the wealthier for our love. We almost lived upon the river, he and I alone,—floating seaward, swimming slowly up with late tides, reaching home drenched with dew, parting in passionate silence. Once he said to me,—

"Is it because it is so much larger, more strange and beautiful, than any other love could be, that I feel guilty, Yone,—feel as if I sinned in loving you so, my great white flower?"

I OUGHT TO TELL you how splendid papa was, never seemed to consider that Rose had only his art, said I had enough from Aunt Willoughby for both, we should live up there among the mountains, and set off at once to make arrangements. Lu has a wonderful tact, too,—seeing at once where her path lay. She is always so well oriented! How full of peace and bliss these two months have been! Last night Lu came in here. She brought back my amber gods, saying she had not intended to keep them, and yet loitering.

"Yone," she said at last, "I want you to tell me if you love him."

Now, as if that were any affair of hers! I looked what I thought.

"Don't be angry," she pleaded. "You and I have been sisters, have we not? and always shall be. I love you very much, dear,—more than you may believe; I only want to know if you will make him happy."

"That's according," said I, with a yawn.

She still stood before me. Her eyes said, "I have a right,—I have a right to know."

"You want me to say how much I love Vaughan Rose?" I asked, finally. "Well, listen, Lu,—so much, that, when he forgets me,—and he will, Lu, one day,—I shall die."

"Prevent his forgetting you, Yone!" she returned. "Make your soul white and clear, like his."

"No! no!" I answered. "He loves me as I am. I will never change."

Then somehow tears began to come. I didn't want to cry; I had to crowd them back behind my fingers and shut lids.

"Oh, Lu!" I said, "I cannot think what it would be to live, and he not a part of me! not for either of us to be in the world without the other!"

Then Lu's tears fell with mine, as she drew her fingers over my hair. She said she was happy, too; and to-day has been down and gathered every one, so that, when you see her, her white array will be wreathed with purple heart's-ease. But I didn't tell Lu quite the truth, you must know. I don't think I should die, except to my former self, if Rose ceased to love me. I should change. Oh, I should hate him! Hate is as intense as love.

Bless me! What time can it be? There are papa and Rose walking in the garden. I turned out my maid to find chance for all this talk; I must ring for her. There, there's my hair! silken coil after coil, full of broken lights, rippling below the knees, fine and fragrant. Who could have such hair but I? I am the last of the Willoughbys, a decayed race, and from such strong decay what blossom less gorgeous should spring?

October now. All the world swings at the top of its beauty; and those hills where we shall live, what robes of color fold them! Tawny filemot gilding the valleys, each seam and rut a scroll or arabesque, and all the year pouring out her heart's blood to flush the maples, the great empurpled granites warm with the sunshine they have drunk all summer! So I am to be married to-day, at noon. I like it best so; it is my hour. There is my veil, that regal Venice point. Fling it round you. No, you would look like a ghost in one,—Lu like a corpse. Dear me! That's the second time I've rung for Carmine. I dare say the hussy is trying on my gown. You think it strange I don't delay? Why, child, why tempt Providence? Once mine, always mine. He might wake up. No, no, I couldn't have meant that! It is not possible that I have merely led him into a region of richer dyes, lapped him in this vision of color, kindled his heart to such a flame, that it may light him towards further effort. Can you believe that he will slip from me and return to one in better harmony with him? Is any one? Will he ever find himself with that love lost, this love exhausted, only his art left him? Never! *I* am his crown. See me! how singularly, gloriously beautiful! For him only! all for him! I love him! I cannot, I will not lose him! I defy all! My heart's proud pulse assures me! I defy Fate! Hush—One,—two,—twelve o'clock. Carmine!

STORY LAST

Astra Castra, Numen Lumen [6]

THE CLICK OF HER NEEDLES and the soft singing of the night-lamp are the only sounds breaking the stillness, the awful stillness, of this room. How the wind blows without! it must be whirling white gusty drifts through the split hills. If I were as free! Whistling round the gray gable, tearing the bleak boughs, crying faint hoarse moans down the chimneys! A wild, sad gale! There is a lull, a long breathless lull, before it soughs up again. Oh, it is like a pain! Pain! Why do I think the word? Must I suffer any more? Am I crazed with opiates? or am I dying? They are in that drawer,—laudanum, morphine, hyoscyamus, and all the drowsy sirups,—little drops, but soaring like a fog and wrapping the whole world in a dull ache with no salient sting to catch a groan on. They are so small, they might be lost in this long, dark room; why not the pain too, the point of pain, I? A long, dark room; I at one end, she at the other; the curtains drawn away from me that I may breathe. Ah, I have been stifled so long! They look down on me, all those old dead and gone faces, those portraits on the wall,—look all from their frames at me, the last term of the race, the vanishing summit of their design. A fierce weapon thrust into the world for evil has that race been,—from the great gray Willoughby, threatening with his iron eyes there, to me, the sharp apex of its suffering. A fierce, glittering blade! Why I alone singled for this curse? Rank blossom, rank decay, they answer, but falsely. I lie here, through no fault of mine, blasted by disease, the dread with no relief. A hundred ancestors look from my walls and see in me the centre of their lives, of all their little splendor, of their sins and follies; what slept in them wakes in me. Oh, let me sleep too!

How long could I live and lose nothing! I saw my face in the hand-glass this morning,—more lovely than health fashioned it;—transparent skin, bounding blood with its fire burning behind the eye, on cheek, on lip,—a beauty that every pang has aggravated, heightened, sharpened, to a superb intensity, flushing, rapid, unearthly,—a brilliancy to be dreamed of. Like a great autumn leaf I fall, for I am dying—dying! Yes, death finds me more beautiful than life made me; but have I lost nothing? Great Heaven, I have lost all!

A fancy comes to me, that to-day was my birthday. I have forgotten to mark time; but if it was, I am thirty-two years old. I remember birthdays of a child,—loving, cordial days. No one remembers to-day. Why should they? But I ache for a little love. Thirty-two,—that is young to die! I am too fair, too rich, for death!—not his fit spoil! Is there no one to save me? no help? can I not escape? Ah, what a vain eagerness! what an idle hope! Fall back again, heart! Escape? I do not desire to. Come, come, kind rest! I am tired.

That cap-string has loosened now, and all this golden cataract of hair has rushed out over the piled pillows. It oppresses and terrifies me. If I could speak, it seems to me that I would ask Louise to come and bind it up. Won't she turn and see? . . .

Have I been asleep? What is this in my hands? The amber gods? Oh, yes! I asked to see them again; I like their smell, I think. It is ten years I have had them. They enchant; but the charm will not last; nothing will. I rubbed a little yellow smoke out of them,—a cloud that hung between him and the world, so that he saw only me,—at least— What am I dreaming of? All manner of illusions haunt me. Who said anything about ten years? I have been married ten years. Happy, then, ten years? Oh, no! One day he woke.—How close the room is! I want some air. Why don't they do something—

Once, in the pride of a fool, I fear having made some confidence, some recital of my joy to ears that never had any. Did I say I would not lose him? Did I say I could live just on the memory of that summer? I lash myself that I must remember it! that I ever loved him! When he stirred, when the mist left him, when he found a mere passion had blinded him, when he spread his easel, when he abandoned love,—was I wretched? I, too, abandoned love!—more,—I hated! All who hate are wretched. But he was bound to me! Yes, he might move restlessly,—it only clanked his chains. Did he wound me? I was cruel. He never spoke. He became artist,—ceased to be man,—was more indifferent than the cloud. He could paint me then,—and, revealed and bare, all our histories written in me, he hung me up beside my ancestors. There I hang. Come from thy frame, thou substance, and let this troubled phantom go! Come! for he gave my life to thee. In thee he shut and sealed it all, and left me as the empty husk.—Did she—that other—join us then? No! I sent for her. I meant to teach him that he was yet a man,—to open before him a gulf of anguish; but *I* slipped down it. Then I dogged them; they never spoke alone; I intercepted the eye's language; I withered their wintry smiles to frowns; I stifled their sighs; I checked their breath, their motion. Idle words passed our lips; we three lived in a real world of silence, agonized mutes. She went. Summer by summer my father brought her to us. Always memory was kindled afresh, always sorrow kept smouldering. Once she came; I lay here; she has not left me since. He,—he also comes; he has soothed pain with that loveless eye, carried me in untender arms, watched calmly beside my delirious nights. He who loved beauty has learned disgust. Why should I care? I, from the slave of bald form, enlarged him to the master of gorgeous color; his blaze is my ashes. He studies me. I owe him nothing. . . .

Is it near morning? Have I dozed again? Night is long. The great hall-clock is striking,—throb after throb on the darkness. I remember, when I was a child, watching its lengthened pendulum swing as if time were its own and it measured the thread slowly, loath to part,—remember streaking its great ebony case with a little finger, misting it with a warm breath. Throb after throb,—is it going to peal forever? Stop, solemn clangor! hearts stop. Midnight.

The nurses have gone down; she sits there alone. Her bent side-face is full of pity. Now and then her head turns; the great brown eyes lift heavily, and lie on me,—heavily,—as if the sight of me pained her. Ah, in me perishes her youth! death enters her world! Besides, she loves me. I do not want her love,—I would fling it off; but I am faint,—I am impotent,—I am so cold! Not that she lives, and I die,—not that she has peace, and I tumult,—not for her voice's music,—not for her eye's lustre,—not for any charm of her womanly presence,—neither for her clear, fair soul,—nor that when the storm and winter pass and I am stiff and frozen, she smiles in the sun and leads new life,—not for all this I hate her; but because my going gives her what I lost,—because, I stepped aside, the light falls on her,—because from my despair springs her happiness. Poor fool! let her be happy, if she can! Her mother was a Willoughby! And what is a flower that blows on a grave? . . .

Why do I remember so distinctly one night alone of all my life,—one night, when we dance in the low room of a seaside cottage,—dance to Lu's singing? He leads me to her when the dance is through, brushing with his head the festooned nets that swing from the rafters,—and in at the open casement is blown a butterfly, a dead butterfly, from off the sea. She holds it compassionately, till I pin it on my dress,—the wings, twin magnificences, freckled and barred and powdered with gold, fluttering at my breath. Some one speaks with me; she strays to the window, he follows, and they are silent. He looks far away over the gray loneliness stretching beyond. At length he murmurs: "A brief madness makes my long misery. Louise, if the earth were dazzled aside from her constant pole-star to worship some bewildering comet, would she be more forlorn than I?"

"Dear Rose! your art remains," I hear her say.

He bends lower, that his breath may scorch her brow. "Was I wrong? Am I right?" he whispers, hurriedly. "You loved me once; you love me now, Louise, if I were free?"

"But you are not free."

She does not recoil, yet her very atmosphere repels him, while looking up with those woful eyes blanching her cheek by their gathering darkness. "And, Rose—" she sighs, then ceases abruptly, while a quiver of sudden scorn writhes spurningly down eyelid and nostril and pains the whole face.

He erects himself, then reaches his hand for the rose in her belt, glances at me,—the dead thing in my bosom rising and falling with my turbulent heart,—holds the rose to his lips, leaves her. How keen are my ears! how flushed my cheek! how eager and fierce my eyes! He approaches; I snatch the rose and tear its petals in an angry shower, and then a dim east-wind pours in and scatters my dream like flakes of foam. All dreams go; youth and hope desert me; the dark claims me. O room, surrender me! O sickness and sorrow, loose your weary hold!

It maddens me to know that the sun will shine again, the tender grass grow green, the veery sing, the crocus come. She will walk in the light and re-gather youth, and I moulder, a forgotten heap. Oh, why not all things crash to ruin with me?—

Pain, pain, pain! Where is my father? Why is he away, when they know I die? He used to hold me once; he ought to hear me when I call. He would rest me, and stroke the grief aside,—he is so strong. Where is he?

These amulets stumbling round again? Amber, amber gods, you did mischief in your day! If I clutched you hard, as Lu did once, all your spells would be broken.—It is colder than it was. I think I will go to sleep.—

What was that? How loud and resonant! It stuns me. It is too sonorous. Does sound flash? Ah! the hour. Another? How long the silver toll swims on the silent air! It is one o'clock,—a passing bell, a knell. If I were at home by the river, the tide would be turning down, down, and out to the broad, broad sea. Is it worth while to have lived?

Have I spoken? She looks at me, rises, and touches that bell-rope that always brings him. How softly he opens the door! Waiting, perhaps. Well. Ten years have not altered him much. The face is brighter, finer,—shines with the eternal youth of genius. They pause a moment; I suppose they are coming to me; but their eyes are on each other.

Why must the long, silent look with which he met her the day I got my amber strike back on me now so vindictively? I remember three looks: that, and this, and one other,—one fervid noon, a look that drank my soul, that culminated my existence. Oh, I remember! I lost it a little while ago. I have it now. You are coming? Can't you hear me? See! these costly liqueurs, these precious perfumes beside me here, if I can reach them, I will drench the coverlet in them; it shall be white and sweet as a little child's. I wish they were rich lilies of that day; it is too late for the baby May-flowers. You do not like amber? There the thread breaks again! the little cruel gods go tumbling down the floor! Come, lay my head on your breast! kiss my life off my lips! I am your Yone! I forgot a little while,—but I love you, Rose! Rose!

WHY! I thought arms held me. How clear the space is! The wind from outdoors, rising again, must have rushed in. There is the quarter striking. How free I am! No one here? No swarm of souls about me? Oh, those two faces looked from a great mist, a moment since; I scarcely see them now. Drop, mask! I will not pick you up! Out, out into the gale! back to my elements!

So I passed out of the room, down the staircase. The servants below did not see me, but the hounds crouched and whined. I paused before the great ebony clock; again the fountain broke, and it chimed the halfhour; it was half past one; another quarter, and the next time its ponderous silver hammers woke the house, it would be two. Half past one? Why, then, did not the hands move? Why cling fixed on a point five minutes before the first quarter struck? To and fro, soundless and purposeless, swung the long pendulum. And, ah! what was this thing I had become? I had done with time. Not for me the hands moved on their recurrent circle any more.

I must have died at ten minutes past one.

CIRCUMSTANCE

❦❦❦❦❦

SHE HAD REMAINED, during all that day, with a sick neighbor,—those eastern wilds of Maine in that epoch frequently making neighbors and miles synonymous,—and so busy had she been with care and sympathy that she did not at first observe the approaching night. But finally the level rays, reddening the snow, threw their gleam upon the wall, and, hastily donning cloak and hood, she bade her friends farewell and sallied forth on her return. Home lay some three miles distant, across a copse, a meadow, and a piece of woods,—the woods being a fringe on the skirts of the great forests that stretch far away into the North. That home was one of a dozen log-houses lying a few furlongs apart from each other, with their half-cleared demesnes separating them at the rear from a wilderness untrodden save by stealthy native or deadly panther tribes.

She was in a nowise exalted frame of spirit,—on the contrary, rather depressed by the pain she had witnessed and the fatigue she had endured; but in certain temperaments such a condition throws open the mental pores, so to speak, and renders one receptive of every influence. Through the little copse she walked slowly, with her cloak folded about her, lingering to imbibe the sense of shelter, the sunset filtered in purple through the mist of woven spray and twig, the companionship of growth not sufficiently dense to band against her, the sweet homefeeling of a young and tender wintry wood. It was therefore just on the edge of the evening that she emerged from the place and began to cross the meadowland. At one hand lay the forest to which her path wound; at the other the evening star hung over a tide of failing orange that slowly slipped down the earth's broad side to sadden other hemispheres with sweet regret. Walking rapidly now, and with her eyes wide-open, she distinctly saw in the air before her what was not there a moment ago, a winding-sheet,—cold, white, and ghastly, waved by the likeness of four wan hands,—that rose with a long inflation, and fell in rigid folds, while a voice, shaping itself from the hollowness above, spectral and melancholy, sighed,—"The Lord have mercy on the people! The Lord have mercy on the people!" Three times the sheet with its corpse-covering outline waved beneath the pale hands, and the voice, awful in its solemn and mysterious depth, sighed, "The Lord have mercy on the people!" Then all was gone, the place was clear again, the gray sky was obstructed by no deathly blot; she looked about her, shook her shoulders decidedly, and, pulling on her hood, went forward once more.

She might have been a little frightened by such an apparition, if she had led a life of less reality than frontier settlers are apt to lead; but dealing with hard fact does not engender a flimsy habit of mind, and this woman was too sincere and earnest in her character, and too happy in her situation, to be thrown by antagonism, merely, upon superstitious fancies and chimeras of the second-sight. She did not even believe herself subject to an hallucination, but smiled simply, a little vexed that her thought could have framed such a glamour from the day's occurrences, and not sorry to lift the bough of the warder of the woods and enter and disappear in their sombre path. If she had been imaginative, she would have hesitated at her first step into a region whose dangers were not visionary; but I suppose that the thought of a little child at home would conquer that propensity in the most habituated. So, biting a bit of spicy birch, she went along. Now and then she came to a gap where the trees had been partially felled, and here she found that the lingering twilight was explained by that peculiar and perhaps electric film which sometimes sheathes the sky in diffused light for many hours before a brilliant aurora. Suddenly, a swift shadow, like the fabulous flying-dragon, writhed through the air before her, and she felt herself instantly seized and borne aloft. It was that wild beast—the most savage and serpentine and subtle and fearless of our latitudes—known by hunters as the Indian Devil, and he held her in his clutches on the broad floor of a swinging fir-bough. His long sharp claws were caught in her clothing, he worried them sagaciously a little, then, finding that ineffectual to free them, he commenced licking her bare arm with his rasping tongue and pouring over her the wide streams of his hot, fœtid breath. So quick had this flashing action been that the woman had had no time for alarm; moreover, she was not of the screaming kind: but now, as she felt him endeavoring to disentangle his claws, and the horrid sense of her fate smote her, and she saw instinctively the fierce plunge of those weapons, the long strips of living flesh torn from her bones, the agony, the quivering disgust, itself a worse agony,—while by her side, and holding her in his great lithe embrace, the monster crouched, his white tusks whetting and gnashing, his eyes glaring through all the darkness like balls of red fire,—a shriek, that rang in every forest hollow, that startled every winter-housed thing, that stirred and woke the least needle of the tasselled pines, tore through her lips. A moment afterward, the beast left the arm, once white, now crimson, and looked up alertly.

She did not think at this instant to call upon God. She called upon her husband. It seemed to her that she had but one friend in the world; that was he; and again the cry, loud, clear, prolonged, echoed through the woods. It was not the shriek that disturbed the creature at his relish; he was not born in the woods to be scared of an owl, you know; what then? It must have been the echo, most musical, most resonant, repeated and yet repeated, dying with long sighs of sweet sound, vibrated from rock to river and back again from depth to depth of cave and cliff. Her thought flew after it; she knew, that, even if her husband heard it, he yet could not reach her in time; she saw that while the beast listened he would not gnaw,— and this she *felt* directly, when the rough, sharp, and multiplied stings of his tongue retouched her arm. Again her lips opened by instinct, but the sound that issued thence came by reason. She had heard that music charmed wild beasts,—just this point between life and death intensified every faculty,—and when she opened her lips the third time, it was not for shrieking, but for singing.

A little thread of melody stole out, a rill of tremulous motion; it was the cradle-song with which she rocked her baby;—how could she sing that? And then she remembered the baby sleeping rosily on the long settee before the fire,—the father cleaning his gun, with one foot on the green wooden rundle,—the merry light from the chimney dancing out and through the room, on the rafters of the ceiling with their tassels of onions and herbs, on the log walls painted with lichens and festooned with apples, on the king's-arm slung across the shelf with the old pirate's-cutlass, on the snow-pile of the bed, and on the great brass clock,—dancing, too, and lingering on the baby, with his fringed-gentian eyes, his chubby fists clenched on the pillow, and his fine breezy hair fanning with the motion of his father's foot. All this struck her in one, and made a sob of her breath, and she ceased.

Immediately the long red tongue thrust forth again. Before it touched, a song sprang to her lips, a wild sea-song, such as some sailor might be singing far out on trackless blue water that night, the shrouds whistling with frost and the sheets glued in ice,—a song with the wind in its burden and the spray in its chorus. The monster raised his head and flared the fiery eyeballs upon her, then fretted the imprisoned claws a moment and was quiet; only the breath like the vapor from some hell-pit still swathed her. Her voice, at first faint and fearful, gradually lost its quaver, grew under her control and subject to her modulation; it rose on long swells, it fell in subtle cadences, now and then its tones pealed out like bells from distant belfries on fresh sonorous mornings. She sung the song through, and, wondering lest his name of Indian Devil were not his true name, and if he would not detect her, she repeated it. Once or twice now, indeed, the beast stirred uneasily, turned, and made the bough sway at his movement. As she ended, he snapped his jaws together, and tore away the fettered member, curling it under him with a snarl,—when she burst into the gayest reel that ever answered a fiddle-bow. How many a time she had heard her husband play it on the homely fiddle made by himself from birch and cherrywood! how many a time she had seen it danced on the floor of their one room, to the patter of wooden clogs and the rustle of homespun petticoat! how many a time she had danced it herself!—and did she not remember once, as they joined clasps for eight-hands-round, how it had lent its gay, bright measure to her life? And here she was singing it alone, in the forest, at midnight, to a wild beast! As she sent her voice trilling up and down its quick oscillations between joy and pain, the creature who grasped her uncurled his paw and scratched the bark from the bough; she must vary the spell; and her voice spun leaping along the projecting points of tune of a hornpipe. Still singing, she felt herself twisted about with a low growl and a lifting of the red lip from the glittering teeth; she broke the hornpipe's thread, and commenced un-ravelling a lighter, livelier thing, an Irish jig. Up and down and round about her voice flew, the beast threw back his head so that the diabolical face fronted hers, and the torrent of his breath prepared her for his feast as the anaconda slimes his prey. Frantically she darted from tune to tune; his restless movements followed her. She tired herself with dancing and vivid national airs, growing feverish and singing spasmodically as she felt her horrid tomb yawning wider. Touching in this manner all the slogan and keen clan cries, the beast moved again, but only to lay the disengaged paw across her with heavy satisfaction. She did not dare to pause; through the clear cold air, the frosty starlight, she sang. If there were yet any tremor in the tone, it was not fear,—she had learned the secret of sound at last; nor could it be chill,—far too high a fever throbbed her pulses; it was nothing but the thought of the log-house and of what might be passing within it. She fancied the baby stirring in his sleep and moving his pretty lips,—her husband rising and opening the door, looking out after her, and wondering at her absence. She fancied the light pouring through the chink and then shut in again with all the safety and comfort and joy, her husband taking down the fiddle and playing lightly with his head inclined, playing while she sang, while she sang for her life to an Indian Devil. Then she knew he was fumbling for and finding some shining fragment and scoring it down the yellowing hair, and unconsciously her voice forsook the wild wartunes and drifted into the half-gay, half-melancholy Rosin the Bow.

Suddenly she woke pierced with a pang, and the daggered tooth penetrating her flesh;—dreaming of safety, she had ceased singing and lost it. The beast has regained the use of all his limbs, and now, standing and raising his back, bristling and foaming, with sounds that would have been like hisses but for their deep and fearful sonority, he withdrew step by step toward the trunk of the tree, still with his flaming balls upon her. She was all at once free, on one end of the bough, twenty feet from the ground. She did not measure the distance, but rose to drop herself down, careless of any death, so that it were not this. Instantly, as if he scanned her thoughts, the creature bounded forward with a yell and caught her again in his dreadful hold. It might be that he was not greatly famished; for, as she suddenly flung up her voice again, he settled himself composedly on the bough, still clasping her with invincible pressure to his rough, ravenous breast, and listening in a fascination to the sad, strange U-la-lu that now moaned forth in loud, hollow tones above him. He half closed his eyes, and sleepily reopened and shut them again.

What rending pains were close at hand! Death! and what a death! worse than any other that is to be named! Water, be it cold or warm, that which buoys up blue icefields, or which bathes tropical coasts with currents of balmy bliss, is yet a gentle conqueror, kisses as it kills, and draws you down gently through darkening fathoms to its heart. Death at the sword is the festival of trumpet and bugle and banner, with glory ringing out around you and distant hearts thrilling through yours. No gnawing disease can bring such hideous end as this; for that is a fiend bred of your own flesh, and this—is it a fiend, this living lump of appetites? What dread comes with the thought of perishing in flames! but fire, let it leap and hiss never so hotly, is something too remote, too alien, to inspire us with such loathly horror as a wild beast; if it have a life, that life is too utterly beyond our comprehension. Fire is not half ourselves; as it devours, arouses neither hatred nor disgust; is not to be known by the strength of our lower natures let loose; does not drip our blood into our faces from foaming chaps, nor mouth nor slaver above us with vitality. Let us be ended by fire, and we are ashes, for the winds to bear, the leaves to cover; let us be ended by wild beasts, and the base, cursed thing howls with us forever through the forest. All this she felt as she charmed him, and what force it lent to her song God knows. If her voice should fail! If the damp and cold should give her any fatal hoarseness! If all the silent powers of the forest did not conspire to help her! The dark, hollow night rose indifferently over her; the wide, cold air breathed rudely past her, lifted her wet hair and blew it down again; the great boughs swung with a ponderous strength, now and then clashed their iron lengths together and shook off a sparkle of icy spears or some long-lain weight of snow from their heavy shadows. The green depths were utterly cold and silent and stern. These beautiful haunts that all the summer were hers and rejoiced to share with her their bounty, these heavens that had yielded their largess, these stems that had thrust their blossoms into her hands, all these friends of three moons ago forgot her now and knew her no longer.

Feeling her desolation, wild, melancholy, forsaken songs rose thereon from that frightful aerie,—weeping, wailing tunes, that sob among the people from age to age, and overflow with otherwise unexpressed sadness,—all rude, mournful ballads,—old tearful strains, that Shakespeare heard the vagrants sing, and that rise and fall like the wind and tide,—sailor-songs, to be heard only in lone mid-watches beneath the moon and stars,—ghastly rhyming romances, such as that famous one of the Lady Margaret, when

> "She slipped on her gown of green
> A piece below the knee,—
> And 't was all a long cold winter's night
> A dead corse followed she."[1]

Still the beast lay with closed eyes, yet never relaxing his grasp. Once a half-whine of enjoyment escaped him,—he fawned his fearful head upon her; once he scored her cheek with his tongue: savage caresses that hurt like wounds. How weary she was! and yet how terribly awake! How fuller and fuller of dismay grew the knowledge that she was only prolonging her anguish and playing with death! How appalling the thought that with her voice ceased her existence! Yet she could not sing forever; her throat was dry and hard; her very breath was a pain; her mouth was hotter than any desert-worn pilgrim's;—if she could but drop upon her burning tongue one atom of the ice that glittered about her!—but both of her arms were pinioned in the giant's vice. She remembered the winding-sheet, and for the first time in her life shivered with spiritual fear. Was it hers? She asked herself, as she sang, what sins she had committed, what life she had led, to find her punishment so soon and in these pangs,—and then she sought eagerly for some reason why her husband was not up and abroad to find her. He failed her,—her one sole hope in life; and without being aware of it, her voice forsook the songs of suffering and sorrow for old Covenanting hymns,—hymns with which her mother had lulled her, which the class-leader pitched in the chimney-corners,—grand and sweet Methodist hymns,[2] brimming with melody and with all fantastic involutions of tune to suit that ecstatic worship,—hymns full of the beauty of holiness, steadfast, relying, sanctified by the salvation they had lent to those in worse extremity than hers,—for they had found themselves in the grasp of hell, while she was but in the jaws of death. Out of this strange music, peculiar to one character of faith, and than which there is none more beautiful in its degree nor owning a more potent sway of sound, her voice soared into the glorified chants of churches. What to her was death by cold or famine or wild beasts? "Though He slay me, yet will I trust in him," she sang. High and clear through the frore fair night, the level moonbeams splintering in the wood, the scarce glints of stars in the shadowy roof of branches, these sacred anthems rose,—rose as a hope from despair, as some snowy spray of flower-bells from blackest mould. Was she not in God's hands? Did not the world swing at his will? If this were in his great plan of providence, was it not best, and should she not accept it?

"He is the Lord our God; his judgments are in all the earth."

Oh, sublime faith of our fathers, where utter self-sacrifice alone was true love, the fragrance of whose unrequired subjection was pleasanter than that of golden censers swung in purple-vapored chancels!

Never ceasing in the rhythm of her thoughts, articulated in music as they thronged, the memory of her first communion flashed over her. Again she was in that distant place on that sweet spring morning. Again the congregation rustled out, and the few remained, and she trembled to find herself among them. How well she remembered the devout, quiet faces, too accustomed to the sacred feast to glow with their inner joy! how well the snowy linen at the altar, the silver vessels slowly and silently shifting! and as the cup approached and passed, how the sense of delicious perfume stole in and heightened the transport of her prayer, and she had seemed, looking up through the windows where the sky soared blue in constant freshness, to feel all heaven's balms dripping from the portals, and to scent the lilies of eternal peace! Perhaps another would not have felt so much ecstasy as satisfaction on that occasion; but it is a true, if a later disciple, who has said, "The Lord bestoweth his blessings there, where he findeth the vessels empty."

"And does it need the walls of a church to renew my communion?" she asked. "Does not every moment stand a temple four-square to God? And in that morning, with its buoyant sunlight, was I any dearer to the Heart of the World than now?—'My beloved is mine, and I am his,'" she sang over and over again, with all varied inflection and profuse tune. How gently all the winter-wrapt things bent toward her then! into what relation with her had they grown! how this common dependence was the spell of their intimacy! how at one with Nature had she become! how all the night and the silence and the forest seemed to hold its breath, and to send its soul up to God in her singing! It was no longer despondency, that singing. It was neither prayer nor petition. She had left imploring, "How long wilt thou forget me, O Lord? Lighten mine eyes, lest I sleep the sleep of death! For in death there is no remembrance of thee,"—with countless other such fragments of supplication. She cried rather, "Yea, though I walk through the valley of the shadow of death, I will fear no evil: for thou art with me; thy rod and thy staff, they comfort me,"—and lingered, and repeated, and sang again, "I shall be satisfied, when I awake, with thy likeness."

Then she thought of the Great Deliverance, when he drew her up out of many waters, and the flashing old psalm pealed forth triumphantly:—

> "The Lord descended from above,
>   and bow'd the heavens hie:
> And underneath his feet he cast
>   the darknesse of the skie.
> On cherubs and on cherubins
>   full royally he road:
> And on the wings of all the winds
>   came flying all abroad."

She forgot how recently, and with what a strange pity for her own shapeless form that was to be, she had quaintly sung,—

> "O lovely appearance of death!
>   What sight upon earth is so fair?
> Not all the gay pageants that breathe
>   Can with a dead body compare!"

She remembered instead,—"In thy presence is fulness of joy; at thy right hand there are pleasures forevermore. God will redeem my soul from the power of the grave: for he shall receive me. He will swallow up death in victory." Not once now did she say, "Lord, how long wilt thou look on; rescue my soul from their destructions, my darling from the lions,"—for she knew that the young lions roar after their prey and seek their meat from God. "O Lord, thou preservest man and beast!" she said.

She had no comfort or consolation in this season, such as sustained the Christian martyrs in the amphitheatre. She was not dying for her faith; there were no palms in heaven for her to wave; but how many a time had she declared,—"I had rather be a doorkeeper in the house of my God, than to dwell in the tents of wickedness!" And as the broad rays here and there broke through the dense covert of shade and lay in rivers of lustre on crystal sheathing and frozen fretting of trunk and limb and on the great spaces of refraction, they builded up visibly that house, the shining city on the hill, and singing, "Beautiful for situation, the joy of the whole earth, is Mount Zion, on the sides of the North, the city of the Great King," her vision climbed to that higher picture where the angel shows the dazzling thing, the holy Jerusalem descending out of heaven from God, with its splendid battlements and gates of pearls, and its foundations, the eleventh a jacinth, the twelfth an amethyst,—with its great white throne, and the rainbow round about it, in sight like unto an emerald: "And there shall be no night there,—for the Lord God giveth them light," she sang.

What whisper of dawn now rustled through the wilderness? How the night was passing! And still the beast crouched upon the bough, changing only the posture of his head, that again he might command her with those charmed eyes;—half their fire was gone; she could almost have released herself from his custody; yet, had she stirred, no one knows what malevolent instinct might have dominated anew. But of that she did not dream; long ago stripped of any expectation, she was experiencing in her divine rapture how mystically true it is that "he that dwelleth in the secret place of the Most High shall abide under the shadow of the Almighty."

Slow clarion cries now wound from the distance as the cocks caught the intelligence of day and re-echoed it faintly from farm to farm,—sleepy sentinels of night, sounding the foe's invasion, and translating that dim intuition to ringing notes of warning. Still she chanted on. A remote crash of brushwood told of some other beast on his depredations, or some night-belated traveller groping his way through the narrow path. Still she chanted on. The far, faint echoes of the chanticleers died into distance, the crashing of the branches grew nearer. No wild beast that, but a man's step,—a man's form in the moonlight, stalwart and strong,—on one arm slept a little child, in the other hand he held his gun. Still she chanted on.

Perhaps, when her husband last looked forth, he was half ashamed to find what a fear he felt for her. He knew she would never leave the child so long but for some direst need,—and yet he may have laughed at himself, as he lifted and wrapped it with awkward care, and, loading his gun and strapping on his horn, opened the door again and closed it behind him, going out and plunging into the darkness and dangers of the forest. He was more singularly alarmed than he would have been willing to acknowledge; as he had sat with his bow hovering over the strings, he had half believed to hear her voice mingling gayly with the instrument, till he paused and listened if she were not about to lift the latch and enter. As he drew nearer the heart of the forest, that intimation of melody seemed to grow more actual, to take body and breath, to come and go on long swells and ebbs of the night-breeze, to increase with tune and words, till a strange shrill singing grew ever clearer, and, as he stepped into an open space of moon-beams, far up in the branches, rocked by the wind, and singing, "How beautiful upon the mountains are the feet of him that bringeth good tidings, that publisheth peace," he saw his wife,—his wife,—but, great God in heaven! how? Some mad exclamation escaped him, but without diverting her. The child knew the singing voice, though never heard before in that unearthly key, and turned toward it through the veiling dreams. With a celerity almost instantaneous, it lay, in the twinkling of an eye, on the ground at the father's feet, while his gun was raised to his shoulder and levelled at the monster covering his wife with shaggy form and flaming gaze,—his wife so ghastly white, so rigid, so stained with blood, her eyes so fixedly bent above, and her lips, that had indurated into the chiselled pallor of marble, parted only with that flood of solemn song.

I do not know if it were the mother-instinct that for a moment lowered her eyes,—those eyes, so lately riveted on heaven, now suddenly seeing all life-long bliss possible. A thrill of joy pierced and shivered through her like a weapon, her voice trembled in its course, her glance lost its steady strength, fever-flushes chased each other over her face, yet she never once ceased chanting. She was quite aware, that, if her husband shot now, the ball must pierce her body before reaching any vital part of the beast,—and yet better that death, by his hand, than the other. But this her husband also knew, and he remained motionless, just covering the creature with the sight. He dared not fire, lest some wound not mortal should break the spell exercised by her voice, and the beast, enraged with pain, should rend her in atoms; moreover, the light was too uncertain for his aim. So he waited. Now and then he examined his gun to see if the damp were injuring its charge, now and then he wiped the great drops from his forehead. Again the cocks crowed with the passing hour,—the last time they were heard on that night. Cheerful home sound then, how full of safety and all comfort and rest it seemed! what sweet morning incidents of sparkling fire and sunshine, of gay household bustle, shining dresser, and cooing baby, of steaming cattle in the yard, and brimming milk-pails at the door! what pleasant voices! what laughter! what security! and here—

Now, as she sang on in the slow, endless, infinite moments, the fervent vision of God's peace was gone. Just as the grave had lost its sting, she was snatched back again into the arms of earthly hope. In vain she tried to sing, "There remaineth a rest for the people of God,"—her eyes trembled on her husband's, and she could only think of him, and of the child, and of happiness that yet might be, but with what a dreadful gulf of doubt between! She shuddered now in the suspense; all calm forsook her; she was tortured with dissolving heats or frozen with icy blasts; her face contracted, growing small and pinched; her voice was hoarse and sharp,—every tone cut like a knife,—the notes became heavy to lift,—withheld by some hostile pressure,—impossible. One gasp, a convulsive effort, and there was silence,—she had lost her voice.

The beast made a sluggish movement,—stretched and fawned like one awaking,—then, as if he would have yet more of the enchantment, stirred her slightly with his muzzle. As he did so, a sidelong hint of the man standing below with the raised gun smote him; he sprung round furiously, and, seizing his prey, was about to leap into some unknown airy den of the topmost branches now waving to the slow dawn. The late moon had rounded through the sky so that her gleam at last fell full upon the bough with fairy frosting; the wintry morning light did not yet penetrate the gloom. The woman, suspended in mid-air an instant, cast only one agonized glance beneath,—but across and through it, ere the lids could fall, shot a withering sheet of flame,—a rifle-crack, half-heard, was lost in the terrible yell of desperation that bounded after it and filled her ears with savage echoes, and in the wide arc of some eternal descent she was falling;—but the beast fell under her.

I think that the moment following must have been too sacred for us, and perhaps the three have no special interest again till they issue from the shadows of the wilderness upon the white hills that skirt their home. The father carries the child hushed again into slumber, the mother follows with no such feeble step as might be anticipated. It is not time for reaction,— the tension not yet relaxed, the nerves still vibrant, she seems to herself like some one newly made; the night was a dream; the present stamped upon her in deep satisfaction, neither weighed nor compared with the past; if she has the careful tricks of former habit, it is as an automaton; and as they slowly climb the steep under the clear gray vault and the paling morning star, and as she stops to gather a spray of the red-rose berries or a feathery tuft of dead grasses for the chimney-piece of the log-house, or a handful of brown cones for the child's play,—of these quiet, happy folk you would scarcely dream how lately they had stolen from under the banner and encampment of the great King Death. The husband proceeds a step or two in advance; the wife lingers over a singular foot-print in the snow, stoops and examines it, then looks up with a hurried word. Her husband stands alone on the hill, his arms folded across the babe, his gun fallen,—stands defined as a silhouette against the pallid sky. What is there in their home, lying below and yellowing in the light, to fix him with such a stare? She springs to his side. There is no home there. The log-house, the barns, the neighboring farms, the fences, are all blotted out and mingled in one smoking ruin. Desolation and death were indeed there, and benefi- cence and life in the forest. Tomahawk and scalping-knife, descending during that night, had left behind them only this work of their accom- plished hatred and one subtle foot-print in the snow.

For the rest,—the world was all before them, where to choose.[3]

IN THE MAGUERRIWOCK

MR. FURBUSH was waited upon one morning by a client, and requested to take charge of a case that was rather out of his usual beat, as he said. And though its being a good instance of mysterious disappearance, with almost nothing to start from, gave it an immediate interest to his inquisitive mind, yet the investigation, being located upon an almost uncivilized region of the frontier forest, made it a much less agreeable study than was the same line of cases when they could be worked up in the pleasant purlieus of the city, and involved no greater hardships than attendance at the opera-houses and in the drawing-rooms of fashionable ladies.

"But," said the client, "I think it will really be worth your while. The fee will be such—"

"Yes, yes," said Mr. Furbush, "but I am not so young as I was. I have a liking for my easy-chair. Perhaps my scent is not so keen as once—"

"On the contrary, habit has made it perfect."

"No dog for the chase like an old one? Well, let me have the data," said Mr. Furbush, rather pleased than otherwise—for the truth was he had been getting a little rusty—taking an enormous pinch of snuff, and then filliping his fingers till he seemed to be throwing dust in the eyes of the universe.

"Listen then," said his interlocutor. "Ten years ago a pack-peddler went through the town of Boltonby—the last large town in that part of the State, and the last town at all before you reach the Maguerriwock

district [1]—he stopped at the watchmaker's there, and exhibited the contents of his pack, a small pack, but full of valuables. There were watches
and bracelets and gold chains in it; brooches set with pearls; there were
carbuncles and amethysts and many marketable stones variously set—it
was decidedly a precious pack on the whole; and though the watchmaker
lightened it of sundry articles, he made it heavy again with the gold which
he paid for them; the peddler preferring gold, as he was going upon the
frontier and into Canada, where our own bank-bills were at a discount.

"'But do you go afoot?' asked the watchmaker.

"'Unless some team gives me a lift,' replied the peddler.

"'Dangerous business,' the watchmaker said, 'in such a neighborhood as the Maguerriwock. I wouldn't be seen there alone after dark
though I had left all my watches here in the shop behind me. And you to
walk into the lion's mouth with all your wealth upon you?'

"'Who would suspect me of wealth?' asked the peddler. 'Do you see
the patches on my boots? am I not out at elbow? do I wear fine linen? am
I not on foot stubbing along too poor to take a stage? does my pack look
like any thing more than a farm-laborer's knapsack?' And he laughed,
and asked which road led to the Third Plantation, and which to the
Maguerriwock, and went out in the direction of the Third Plantation.
There were one or two loungers in the store; I don't know their names—
I suppose they could easily be ascertained. It has been found that the
peddler, after he had gone a couple of miles in the direction of the
Third Plantation, that is, on a northwest radius, struck across the fields and
made for the road that runs in the direction of a northeast radius from
Boltonby centre, and that led into the Maguerriwock—on one side of him,
the black and white brook tumbling down with its foam; on the other, old
Maguerriwock Mountain rising dark with its firs. Whether he lost his way
and wandered round there till he starved or died, whether the bears and
wolves abounding there made an end of him, whether he was waylaid and
murdered, it is impossible to say; all we know is, that he never reached the
settlement beyond, or if he did, there is no trace of his having done so.
Now before the peddler went on his fatal journey, he having a few surplus
funds, invested them in a Bolivian Silver-mining Company's stock, the
sound of whose name happened to take his fancy, wisely as it eventuated.
This Company made dividend after dividend—first of fifty, then of a

hundred, then of five hundred per cent.; the stock has risen to an almost inestimable value, and the fortune of a prince lies ready for the peddler's hand, or for the hand of the next of kin. It is of the first importance to this next of kin to discover the peddler; if he is not forthcoming, it becomes of the second importance to establish the fact of his decease. And I, Mr. Furbush," said the client, drawing back the better to observe the effect of his announcement, "am the next of kin!"

"Yes," said Mr. Furbush, calmly, after he had sent up a ring of smoke to the ceiling, and watched it dissipate there. "Yes; I've known about that million's rusting for an owner this long time, and wondered you never came to me about it. I don't know but what I'll undertake it. Tell you to-morrow. Call again, same hour." After which the two heads were put together a moment as to terms and expenses, and the client went out; and Mr. Furbush snapped his fingers to a pleasant tune for a little while, having made his bargain all on one side. But this exultation was succeeded by a corresponding depression, for Mr. Furbush never found any pleasure in overreaching a simpleton; he liked to measure wits with some one whose blade was as long and as keen as his own; the case, too, was as simply put together as black and white; he saw it now straight before him; and although I believe in the end he exacted the fulfillment of his client's promises, yet the whole round sum which he thus obtained, and which enabled him to withdraw presently from business, had he chosen so to do, gave him far less pleasure than the pitiful salary of a detective policeman used to do when he drew it quarterly.

A gay party of gentlemen was just forming for a hunting excursion down in this very Maguerriwock district and no other; and to this Mr. Furbush, happening to know about it, had no difficulty in attaching himself. Most of the gentlemen treated Mr. Furbush with distinguished urbanity, whether they had ever had occasion to deal with him in the past, or feared they might have in the future; and while he never lost an eye to business, he contrived to enjoy himself until they reached Boltonby, the large town of which mention has been made, in as good wildwood fashion as did ever any one who wore the belted green.

In Boltonby Mr. Furbush's watch must needs get itself out of order just as the party was going into the deep woods. Of course he sought the watchmaker's without delay, in order to repair the mishap.

"Take a seat, if you please," said the artisan. "I'll not detain you a half hour, Sir. Nothing but some snuff in the works," and he applied all his dexterity. "Haven't seen a repeater here before, Sir," said he, presently, "since I looked into the pack of the peddler that was killed in the Maguerriwock."

"Killed!" exclaimed Mr. Furbush.

"Well, there's some suppose he got bewildered, and wandered round till he grew exhausted; and there even have been discovering parties out after his pack. But it's all one now. The thing that's certain is that the last time he was seen it was in this shop," said he, sensationally.

"Indeed? They never suspected you of a hand in his disappearance, then?" asked Mr. Furbush, mischievously stealing the sensation.

"Hardly, Sir," said the worthy watchmaker. "Not any one in Boltonby, Sir."

"But are you certain he was seen here then?"

"In my shop? I should think so. Let me see who saw him," said the watchmaker, reflectively. "The parson—there he sits now; Dr. Stedman, dead long ago, poor man; old Ledgefield, from over the mountain—"

"Maguerriwock?"

"The same. And one or two of the farmers that never sent, nor never received, a letter in the whole course of their lives, but who came regularly every Saturday, from far and near, to see if there were any for them, whether or no. I had the post-office here then. That was the way they kept up with the world. Let me see—the Cravens, father and son; and Billy Moore—he's a cripple—"

"You never laid the deed to old Ledgefield?"

"Bless you, no," said the watchmaker, as he blew between the wheels of the watch blasts fit to carry the vans of a bolting-mill. "Couldn't have killed a fly."

"Was the peddler such a small man that you compare him to so small an object?"

"Small? He? As much limestone in his bones as ever walked across the State of Maine. Six feet two in his stockings."

"One man alone couldn't have matched him, then, I take it?" said Mr. Furbush.

"Not unless he pinned him from behind. No, nor then either."

"It is, to my apprehension, the most probable conjecture that he is lying at the foot of the Maguerriwock rocks, and his knapsack beside him," said the parson, joining in, and warmed with the old gossip of the place.

"Yes, many's thought so. I remember the first exploring party after him. I went with them. We thought if the wolves had got him we should find parts of his clothes; and I was sure I should know an odd button I had seen in his woolen shirt. It was a wooden button, carved to represent a little Chinese god, with a head slung in his belt. He said he'd carved it himself, going along from place to place; and 'twas ugly enough for you to believe him, the button was. Dr. Stedman and a parcel of us went; made a regular spree of it. The Cravens got it up, and we slept at their farm in the settlement beyond, and drank such cider there as only the apples of Eden ever could have made before."

"Not very good cider, then, if you remember the character of the apples in that locality," said Mr. Furbush, with a wink at the parson. "Good farm?"

"Well, no, not particularly so—at that time, that is. Shiftless fellows, they used to be; fond of hunting and drinking; perked up since then, been more industrious, as Walmar finished sowing his wild oats; got the fences up every where, land improved, barns built; wonderful stock, too, now; best breed of horses in all the Maguerriwock; fine cattle, Alderneys and Jerseys; some merinos—"

"Rather unusual for this region, isn't it?"

"Rather. I've a few myself. I bought them of them, though. The parson bought some merinos. When we saw the fellows turning a short corner we just encouraged them that way. 'Tisn't good for a community to have idlers on its outskirts, you know, Sir. We feel a little as if it was our work. Better ride out and see it, Sir, before you leave these parts; only twenty miles across the woods—crack farm!"

"You would find it most interesting," said the parson.

"Thank you," answered Mr. Furbush; "I don't doubt it."

"There's your watch, all right. No, indeed, Sir, not a penny! Trifling service—stranger, too!" And Mr. Furbush retired, having decidedly the best of this bargain, as of nearly all others in which he had a hand.

Mr. Furbush lost no time in excusing himself from his party, in seeking the society of the sheriff, in hiring a team, in driving across the woods, and arriving at nightfall on the crack farm of the Cravens, which he had been so warmly advised to visit.

On the way he confided in the sheriff so much as he thought best, made that astonished and slightly unwilling individual his confederate, and though they had no precisely prepared plan of action, they had yet that concert of attention and suggestion which might prove invaluable. The leafy shadows fell around them as they rode and plotted; the soft wind blew in their faces, full of delicious flowery smells and the sun-kisses of resinous branches; the fallen boughs crackled pleasantly under their wheels in the soft forest road. It seemed impossible that any such sweet, wild region could be the seat of dark and evil deeds. It would have seemed so, rather, to any one else than the sheriff, whose daily business dealt with the doers of such deeds till there was nothing strange about them, or than Mr. Furbush, whose calculations, having finally determined toward one direction, not all the leafy shadows or flowery smells of creation could turn aside.

It was just as the red sunset changed to purple over all the clear country that they came out from the obscurity of the wood upon the long rich slopes of the Craven farm. In the distance other clearings were to be seen, but yet hardly deserving the name, since, so far as they could be discerned in the light of approaching evening, they seemed to be mere acres of tangle and brushwood, while the Craven fields were velvet with turf or billowy with grain, the fences were of mortared stone, the great open-doored barns were overflowing, mild-eyed cattle were standing contentedly about the fields which darkened so gently, and on the grass before the door a man was breaking a superb stallion that appeared to have all the fire of the mustang with all the grace of the Arab in his composition.

"It takes money to have such things as that horse," said Mr. Furbush. "You may 'perk up' and be as industrious as you please, but ten years are not enough to change the generations of a common cart-horse into such a creature as that. It takes money—watches, brooches set with pearls, carbuncles, amethysts, and gold coins that are preferred to our own bank-bills for currency on the Canadian frontier."

The sheriff laughed as Mr. Furbush spoke, and then hailed the horse-tamer; but not before Mr. Furbush had noted the singular contrast evident between the stone fences laid in plaster, the bountiful barns, and the low, rude house, with its hanging eaves, narrow windows, and entirely barbarous appearance, and had rummaged round among his reasons to find one that answered the question why so miserable a hovel was patched and painted and retained by men who evidently liked the display of a crack farm.

"Hallo, Walmar," cried the sheriff. "Got a night's lodging to spare?"

"Don't know," was the hospitable answer. "I'll ask the old man. Who's that with you?"

"Gentleman going across the clearing. Afraid of night air. Guess I'll get down and stretch my legs, any way. Mr. Furbush, Mr. Walmar Craven."

Mr. Furbush took off his hat, but coughed tenderly, and pulled up the handkerchief around his throat—carefully looked over his new acquaintance the while, and decided that he probably looked better to-day than he did ten years ago, was no stronger to-day than he was ten years ago, and was an ill-looking whelp, with his underhung jaw, ten years ago or to-day. Meanwhile Mr. Craven himself had come out to inspect the arrival. "Come in! come in!" he cried, with a certain rough heartiness, under whose lion's skin Mr. Furbush thought he could detect the fox's ears. "Lodging? Of course we have," he said. "Always a bed for you, Sheriff; and any friend of yours welcome here. Never turned a man from my door since I had one. Come in, come in!"

Mr. Furbush was not a coward; but his courage needed one or two little invitations to assert its existence as he bent his head beneath the low lintel of that man's dwelling; for, as he said to himself, he had never seen a more evil countenance belie more good profession in all his life before. It was not the burly, brutal face of the prize-fighter or the lounging plug-ugly, which he already knew so well; it had a hideousness whose die must have been broken in the stamping, and eyes that crossed at a sickening angle of strabismus gave all the original face an added sinister effect, that made the one who had seen it a single time turn and look again, that he might be sure it was an actual thing which he had seen, and no vision of an impossibility.

The house, which the three now entered, presented even a poorer appearance internally than it did without, for trees tossing their boughs overhead, and wild rose-bushes growing under the windows, decorated it in some degree outside, while inside it was bare. Carpets on the floors, prints upon the walls, soft-cushioned and luxurious seats, these are the caprices of womankind, and they were absent here. The Cravens had silver spoons for their supper-table, they wore gold watches and bright-jeweled breast-pins, they liked to dazzle beholders at the county fairs, and to take the prizes on their cattle there; but they chose for their chairs those that they could tilt back upon, for a table one that they could rest their heels upon, a floor that was not too good to ornament with elaborate designs in tobacco juice; so plain pine boards, furniture of deal, and walls once white-washed and now arabesqued with smoke stains, the marks of popping beer bottles, and the dust of years, made up the cheer of the receptionroom. One woman sat in the chimney-corner of this room, her hair combed straight away from her thin face and knotted up with a great silver comb, a dirt-colored gown apparently thrown upon her person, and a shawl pinned at her throat. She was a wretched-looking being, and she neither glanced up nor spoke when the three entered, but went on poking the fire with the walking-stick in her hands. "My wife," said Mr. Craven, with a hideous leer. "You mustn't mind her, gentlemen—she's weak," and he tapped his own head to signify the particular direction in which his wife's weakness lay. "Lost her mind," he said, briefly.

"Indeed!" exclaimed Mr. Furbush; "that is very sad. A recent thing?"

"Oh no, no," said the other, carelessly. "Some years since, when this child was born"—as the door opened, and a child shambled into the apartment—an undersized changling of a thing, with long, tow-colored elf-locks hanging round a face as white as leprosy. She sidled forward and stood looking into Mr. Furbush's eyes.

"I'm a fool," said she.

"Dear me, dear me!" exclaimed the sheriff, who felt more familiar with knaves than fools. "I never knew you had such a child, Craven! How old is she?"

"Old as her tongue, and a little older than her teeth; ain't you, Semantha?"

"No," answered Semantha, stoutly. "I'm ten year old next April-Fool

Day. Wal said so!" And with that she shuffled hurriedly round inside her mother's chair, as if afraid of a hand that might come after her, and commenced talking to herself in an unintelligible rattle that seemed to be her natural language.

"That's the way with them," said Mr. Craven, "from morning till night. The old woman, she seldom speaks at all; Semantha, she gabbles all the time. They're no good to themselves nor any body else. But there," said the benevolent being, with one of his most effective grimaces, as he opened a high cupboard-door, "you can't put them out of the way. We contrive to get along. Something to take, gentlemen? Nothing clearer this side the St. John. None of your fire and smoke, but real mountain-dew. If the sheriff wasn't here should say I smuggled it myself. Don't suppose he'll object to a drop, all the same?"

Meantime Mr. Walmar Craven, the horsetamer, a man now of some thirty-odd years, had entered and hung a kettle on the crane, had produced some slices of bacon, and a frying-pan, into which he broke several eggs, and had set out on the bare deal an apparently recent purchase of table-service, whose stout material, brilliantly flowered and butterflied, seemed to attract poor little Semantha's attention irresistibly, as she crept forward and stealthily seized one of the plates, which she commenced spinning like a top, and was immediately assisted from the room by one arm and the toe of the brotherly boot therefor. Mrs. Craven started up at the scuffle and the screams, looked around her vacantly, as if she could not make out the disturbance, smoothed her hair, and sat down again with her scared face. "Three men went down cellar," said she, "and only two came up," and would have again commenced poking the fire had not her tender husband snatched the stick away with a gesture that promised more than it performed.

"Mountain-dew is all very well, Mr. Craven," said Mr. Furbush, "for any one that has never heard of your cider. But as for me, there never was any Champagne bottled in France, if that's where they bottle it, equal to the sparkle of the real pippin cider of any new apple-orchard."

"Well, now," said Mr. Craven. "I'm your man for that. You'd never think, to look at a little pink and white apple-blossom, that it had such a tingle in it, would you? I've kept my barrel of cider every fall for a dozen years back. Some's so hard you have to use washing soda with it, and some's the pure juice of last September. Walmar, give me a dip. My cellar's full of it. What shall I bring you, gentlemen?"

" 'Twould take more mind than I've got to make up," said the sheriff.

"Suppose," said Mr. Furbush, jocosely and in good-fellowship, "suppose, since there's such a stock below, we go down and taste all round!"

Mr. Craven was blowing at a coal, which just then he dropped. He picked it up, and said nothing till his wick caught the flame—whether he was considering the proposition, or whether he had no breath to spare. If he was considering it, it is to be supposed that he reasoned that if these men had any design in going into his cellar they would get in one way or another, fair means or foul, and there was nothing like innocent unsuspiciousness to disarm suspicion.

"Won't give the gentlemen such trouble, father," said his thoughtful son, starting forward with a pitcher in either hand. "Sullars ain't such nice places for visitors."

"Don't speak of trouble!" cried Mr. Furbush. "And as for nice places, I never saw a nicer than a cider-vault. Remember when I was a boy," continued Mr. Furbush, who was making the Cravens feel very much at home with him, "going round with a straw and trying all the bung-holes. No such sport in life, except it is blowing bubbles with a clay pipe. Pity we can't stay boys! Come along, Mr. Sheriff! Got your pitcher, Craven? and the straws? Let me take your light. Stairs steep?"

There was no resisting such cheerful volubility. But with a curious expression of dogged sullenness, as Mr. Furbush thought, flashing out and smothering again on their pleasant countenance, the Cravens led the way together; and as they opened the door the woman in the chimney-corner half rose from her seat and looked after them with her frightened face. "Three men went down cellar," said she, "and only two came up. Three men went down cellar, and only two came up," and she commenced wringing her hands and moaning till she forgot about it.

Mr. Furbush's heart—for I suppose he had one—gave a bound; but his hand held the candle just as steadily, and his face looked as innocently eager after cider as if no such words as those the infirm woman uttered had ever clenched his certainty. He knew very well that when Walmar set down his pitchers and ran back he was shaking the poor thing by the shoulders till the teeth rattled in her head, and jouncing her down in her chair afterward; but not being yet prepared to interfere he called cheerily for his straw, as if that was what the gay and festive young man had run back for.

Although Mr. Furbush had given it as his opinion that there were no such nice places as cider-cellars, the present one might have changed such opinion and confirmed that of Mr. Walmar after all. The walls were a too substantial foundation to so rickety a superstructure as the cottage, and had probably been built in long after the cottage had been reared over a mere hole in the ground; but with such solid walls and arches the place would have been a nice one if it had only been a clean one. The sides were of thick stone, the floor was of brick laid in gravel, a close and compact floor, as good as the hearths of half the country roundabout.

Mr. Furbush swung the candle over his head, narrowly missing setting fire to the sheets of cobwebs that fringed the low beams above, and noting with his hurried glance that there was not one place newer than another or of fresher stone in all the masonry, and that the cellar exactly corresponded, in its appearance of size, to the two rooms which he had seen overhead.

"By George! a prime place!" said he. "It only wants a broom. If your cider is half as good, in its way, as your cellar, Mr. Craven, there's nothing more to ask!"

"Taste it and see," said Mr. Craven, handing him the straw and taking the candle, while Walmar went forward with his hatchet and started the bungs of the barrels that lay on their sides all round the cellar, as much, Mr. Furbush could not help thinking, like the pictures which he had seen in the illustrated newspapers of royal sarcophagi in their tombs as any thing else. There was something desperately suggestive, too, in the figure of the strong-armed Walmar hurling his hatchet over his head, half lighted and wholly devilish in the strange chiaroscuro of the place.

"That, now," said Mr. Furbush, giving place to the sheriff, "is a lady's tipple. I confess I like it a trifle older."

"Try this, then," said Mr. Craven. "And if it doesn't suit, there's yet another and another and another. I'm particular about my cider too. I like it hard as the hardest. I'm a hard-shell myself, I am. Any body that picks me up will find they've got a hard nut to crack."

"More like the thing—but still—" said Mr. Furbush, smacking his lips doubtfully.

"Aha—I see. Nothing for you but the genuine identical—meller as a Juneating, and the tang of a russet in April. Good for a headache in the morning. That's the talk, and here's the thing!"

Mr. Furbush's eyes had now become accustomed to the half-light. Over each straw that he had bent he had looked as a little child looks over the edge of its drinking cup, on almost as close an inspection as a sunbeam makes when a camera commands. This was to be the last, and he prepared himself for an exhaustive survey, while he took just one gurgling sip through his straw, to feel sure that the man was not making game of him.

The floor, with here a heap of straw and there some carelessly thrown vegetables, was every where dry and dusty—every where dry and dusty except in one place. Was it Mr. Furbush's vivid imagination that gave the bricks there, ever so slightly, a brighter, damper tint than the others? As Mr. Craven moved and stood just beyond it now, holding his candle low, his shadow fell there long and outstretched as any grave. If Mr. Furbush believed in any thing, it was in coincidences. A line of irregularly growing fungi, that had sprouted up here and there along its length between the bricks, just gave his eye one glimpse of themselves, common toad-stools, but of various tints—white, pale pink, and tawny orange—perhaps a half dozen or less. Mr. Furbush could have laughed aloud as he raised his head. "Never tasted any thing so pungent in my life!" said he.

"Pungent—that's the word," said Mr. Craven.

"It's a drink fit for the gods," said Mr. Furbush, wiping his mouth vigorously, for if there was one thing on earth he detested more than another it was cider.

"Why do you have such things as that growing in your cellar, though? Should think 'twould corrupt the cider; they only ought to grow on graves," said Mr. Furbush, stooping to pluck one of the unsightly stems from its nook between two bricks. It gave out a damp, deathly odor, he fancied, that made him sick; he threw it down again, but not before the candle had fallen from Mr. Craven's hand and left them all in darkness.

Mr. Furbush stood stone-still and grasped the trigger of a little bosom-friend he had, expecting to feel two hands on his throat in the next

moment. But Mr. Craven only swore an oath about his own deuced clum-
siness, strode past him, and in a moment called to them from the head of
the stairs and flared another light down by which they might see to find
their way up into the room above.

Mr. Furbush understood now, just as well as if he had the whole
horrid scene of one night ten years ago before him, why the feeble woman
in the corner of the chimney-place, who, mechanically, with a remnant of
her old housewifely instinct, turned, as she was wont to do when the savor
attracted her, the bacon with the fork that had been left in the pan—why
she moaned ever to herself without lifting her head the refrain that had
cost her her reason and made her unborn child an idiot: "Three men went
down cellar, and only two came up." But he lit the hospitable pipe after
supper, and placidly smoked away without a thought of the pipe of peace;
and retired to the room he was to share with the sheriff, when they had
partaken of a jorum of apple-toddy, without experiencing a single qualm of
sensibility at the idea of fitting a halter to these men's throats after having
eaten their salt. However, Mr. Furbush felt possibly acquitted of all indebt-
edness because the sheriff was to pay for the salt.

"Well," said the sheriff, as soon as they were alone, "what do you
think of 'em?"

"Two as damned rascals," said Mr. Furbush, drawing off his boots,
"as ever trod shoeleather."

"And what do you decide to do?"

"To go back to Boltonby," whispered Mr. Furbush, "for a posse to
help us bring to light again the body of the murdered pack-peddler, or
what there is left of it, from underneath those toad-stools."

"By the great horn-spoon!" swore the sheriff, in an intensity of admiration that could find no further words. And they said very little more as
they relieved each other from watch to watch between then and sunrise.

If old Craven's face had been disgustingly vicious on the night before,
daylight did not lend any feebleness to its purport, but rather searched out
and brought its evil things to naked shame. It was not fitting to call it
merely brutal; for no dumb brute had ever such intelligence, such cunning,
and such cruelty written in one scroll together on its face. I am afraid that
Mr. Furbush's smile borrowed a reflection from it as he thought how very
soon he should be able to put an end to that sickening leer of the man's.

They bade one another good-morning like the best of friends; the sheriff paid the reckoning; Craven begged them to come some day and take another taste of his cider; they promised to do so, and rolled rapidly away across the clearing, taking a circular direction by an old cart-path, and thus retracing their way and coming out in the woods on the Boltonby side, and driving with might and main toward Boltonby.

The sheriff's horse was unrivaled in all the Maguerriwock. Walmar Craven's stallion was not well enough broken to follow and discover the true direction of their path, had it occurred to his master to do so. But, without being definitely disconcerted, the Cravens must have seen the slight and casual incidents of the evening before in the light of warnings for precaution; since that there was some very busy work going on subsequently that day, inside their doors, there is no reason to doubt.

"It's rather too bad," said the sheriff, after two hours' silence, in which neither he nor Mr. Furbush had referred to the theme of their errand; "but it's an old story now—ten years ago—and the men are doing so well—seem to have reformed, as you may say—have introduced such breeds of cattle—done so much to improve the country—"

"Nonsense!" said Mr. Furbush, who was more familiar with sin and crime, penalty and punishment, than the sheriff was, and who knew very well that the sheriff had never yet been called upon to perform the last offices for any culprit. "I couldn't look at his vile throat without seeing the neck-tie that it needed!"

"I don't know," said the sheriff, nervously; "I couldn't say of myself that he abused any body but his wife; and a judge in Illinois decided lately that that was nothing—the wife must adopt more conciliating conduct."

"Mrs. Craven isn't very conciliating, is she?" said Mr. Furbush. "I should be exasperated myself if she kept on informing me for ten years, since the day I made her and her child idiots with horror, that three men went down cellar, and only two came up!" And Mr. Furbush shivered, and grew hot afterward, with a dull, indignant feeling that did not often mingle in the chess-playing work of his investigations. "He never wore a neck-tie that became him half so well as yours will!" he exclaimed. "There's nothing like a knot under the left ear for a finish."

"I don't know," said the sheriff; "the more I think of it, the more sorry I am I didn't just tip him a wink—"

"Then I should have been obliged to hold you as accessory."

"I've half the mind, I swear, to resign my commission and go to the Legislature and abolish capital punishment!"

"Ah, that's sensible. It takes the relish off of neat work, often, to think there's blood at the end of it," said Mr. Furbush. "Not here, though, I can assure you. But it's a stupid case, on the whole. If it wasn't for the fortune behind it, I think I'd have thrown up a thing that looked so plain on its face!"

It is a fact not very fair to the optimist's view that so many men are able to take pleasure, not only in the misfortunes of others, but in spite of them. The party that rode out of Boltonby that evening, to go on to the Craven's crack farm in the morning, did not make too solemn a night of it. But, gay as they had been when buoyed up by the consciousness of the service they were about to render justice, there was hardly one of them but wished he was somewhere else when they came out of the shadow of the woods in the early sunlight, and saw the figure of the elder Craven leaning against the door-post and smoking negligently, while Walmar exercised and trained his horse on the green, and all the upland and interval, with their tossing grain and meadow grass, lay in such perfect morning peace.

"Mr. Walmar," said the sheriff, "sorry to trouble you, but we shall have to request your company. No such thing as refusing the sheriff's requisition."

There was plainly doubt on Walmar's face as to whether this was an arrest, or merely a summons to serve on the posse with the others; but it grew into an odd, uneasy air of guilt, only half brazened over by defiance. If he had no other virtue, take him and his situation together, he had a consummate self-possession. Mr. Furbush looked at him, and felt that great talents were lost to the world in the early decease of Walmar Craven. But before he could speak his father had cried out, "Morning, gentlemen! Come back to taste that cider?" A sudden fiery imp darted up in his smile and his eye as he spoke.

"Well, Mr. Craven," answered the sheriff, "no objections if you haven't."

"Here, Wal," called the father; "go and fetch up a jug."

"Begging your pardon, Mr. Craven," said the sheriff, "I think we had better go ourselves."

"Oh, just as you please, gentlemen. If the cellar's big enough to hold you. You've all been there, I believe, at one time or another; but never all together. This way." And before they could admire his audacity, or wonder at their own, the party were below stairs, with father and son beside them, and had opened their bull's-eye lanterns, ready lighted long ago, and displayed their picks and shovels.

"Going to dig for treasure in my cellar?" cried Mr. Craven, facetiously, and presently holding his sides with laughter. "Well, now, I object to that, unless we go snacks!"

"You will have all you want of any treasure we find here, my good man," said Mr. Furbush, letting loose his metropolitan manner. And at the word, while his posse waited for their orders, the sheriff served the warrant upon the two men for the murder of the peddler ten years since.

"When I headed the fellows that for three days scoured the woods for him!" exclaimed Walmar, and was then made dumb by amazement.

"Go on, my friends," said his father, folding his arms then; "go on." And Mr. Furbush's lynx eye discerned the light of such cool conquest in his leer that for a moment he half feared there was something in the case after all.

Mr. Furbush's eye had other things to entertain it after a few seconds. He stepped forward to the place under which, on the night before, he had made sure that the murdered man lay. "This is the spot," said he. "Proceed with your work." But scarcely had they displaced a brick ere he saw that it was too late—the bricks had been displaced already, and freshly planted again in his absence. He caught Mr. Craven's eye. "I removed the crop of toad-stools, as you advised," said that personage, and with such a subtle but triumphal sneer that it was plain they had been outwitted, and the work was going to be in vain.

"What we are looking for," said Mr. Furbush, with ineffable but well-concealed vexation, "has been removed. Nevertheless, it is as well to follow out the plan;" and he bent forward eagerly with his lantern to watch each stroke of their shovels.

Yes, it was perfectly apparent now that the earth had all lately been turned over down to a certain point—soft rich loam, dark, and emitting a sort of faint miasma, differing from the air of the cellar. Was there an impression of any shape on the soil beneath? Mr. Furbush bent down to see. Not the least. Nothing but the dark earth. And the one great black beetle, nauseous object, scrambling away as fast as its countless legs would carry it.

For an instant Mr. Furbush, whose profession kept his mind active, was in danger of believing in the old fairy stories and fancying that the murdered man, enchanted into that foul black beetle, was being made away with before his face and eyes. But while the fancy was passing through his mind his glance had rested on a second object—was it another beetle? He stretched out his hand and caught it up, wiped it as clean as might be, and examined it—a button of carved wood, an ugly little Chinese god, carrying a head slung in his belt by a tiny rope. He turned about and held it up. "You should not have left this behind, Mr. Craven," said he.

The sheriff drew near to see what had so suddenly changed the note in Mr. Furbush's voice. "If that is all the evidence, Mr. Furbush," said he, somewhat irately, "I think I shall release Mr. Craven from arrest."

"It is out of your power," said Mr. Furbush, quietly.

"At any rate, we can go up from this vile place and think it over," said the sheriff.

"Better take something, gentlemen, before you go," said Mr. Craven, and surely Satan prompted him.

"Don't care if I do, Craven," replied the sheriff. "It's a mighty unpleasant business, any way—don't know why we should make it bitter."

Mr. Furbush said nothing, standing with a serene aspect, nowise crest-fallen, as perfectly convinced as he had been in the beginning, and sure that if his sight was only sharp enough he should presently see this man convict himself.

"No need of my cracking up the Craven cider, neighbors all," said Mr. Craven, with his very wickedest look; "though maybe when strangers come among us brewing trouble—However, there's the pressing of nigh upon a dozen years before you—there's the juice of the harvest just gone, and there's the juice of that one gone a half-score seasons since. That's Mr. Furbush's particular figure. He took such a pull at it night before last that I don't think it's got out of his head yet. Clear as the daylight of a winter's morning, that cider is—when you can see it, which you can't here—and sour as the sheriff's face. Here, Walmar, start the spile, will you?"

But Walmar, totally destitute of that diabolism of humor which was one of his father's characteristics, and not relishing the present proceeding in the least, declined to lift a hand.

"Do it myself, then," said Mr. Craven, in great glee, "if you're such a churl you can't throw a bone to a bear. I don't know how to hold a grudge, for my part; I always wipe out the score and cry quits. There's a glass on the shelf there. Thank you, Mr. Sheriff; your turn next—quality first!" and he drew the glass full and offered it to Mr. Furbush. If he had been a demon just up from the bottomless pit he could have shown no more hellish a grin than that with which, suddenly and unconsciously, he unmasked his face beneath Mr. Furbush's eye. "Pungent!" said Mr. Craven. "That's the word. A drink fit for the gods!"

"Stay a minute," said Mr. Furbush, gently pushing back the proffered nectar. "Sheriff, I should be sorry to spill good spirit, but there's some that's better out than in. Break up that barrel."

As the words left his lips Walmar sprung forward with a stifled howl.

"Not while I live," said Craven, in a metamorphosis such as if a black ember had become a fire-brand, "do you spill my cider in my cellar. Hands off!" and he was seated on the barrel.

"Do as I say," repeated Mr. Furbush, firmly. And there was only one hesitating moment before Mr. Craven was whirled away and held by as strong hands as those that were holding his raging and writhing son; the hoops had been knocked off the barrel, the staves had fallen apart from side to side with the fury of the outpouring liquor—and there lay the ghastly skull, the arms, the half-bleached skeleton of the murdered man they sought.

They stood around the dreadful and disgusting sight in a horrified silence. The two men saw that there was no escape. "Well," said the elder, in the wolfish audacity of his confession, "I suppose you know what that sound up stairs means now?" And listening they could hear the words of the woman on the dismal hearth above, as she rocked herself feebly to and fro, and made her moan: "Three men went down cellar, and only two came up!"

THE MOONSTONE MASS

THERE WAS a certain weakness possessed by my ancestors, though in nowise peculiar to them, and of which, in common with other more or less undesirable traits, I have come into the inheritance.

It was the fear of dying in poverty. That, too, in the face of a goodly share of pelf stored in stocks, and lands, and copper-bottomed clippers, or what stood for copper-bottomed clippers, or rather sailed for them, in the clumsy commerce of their times.

There was one old fellow in particular—his portrait is hanging over the hall stove to-day, leaning forward, somewhat blistered by the profuse heat and wasted fuel there, and as if as long as such an outrageous expenditure of caloric was going on he meant to have the full benefit of it—who is said to have frequently shed tears over the probable price of his dinner, and on the next day to have sent home a silver dish to eat it from at a hundred times the cost. I find the inconsistencies of this individual constantly cropping out in myself; and although I could by no possibility be called a niggard, yet I confess that even now my prodigalities make me shiver.

Some years ago I was the proprietor of the old family estate, unencumbered by any thing except timber, that is worth its weight in gold yet, as you might say; alone in the world, save for an unloved relative; and with a sufficiently comfortable income, as I have since discovered, to meet all reasonable wants. I had, moreover, promised me in marriage the hand of a woman without a peer, and which, I believe now, might have been mine on any day when I saw fit to claim it.

That I loved Eleanor tenderly and truly you can not doubt; that I desired to bring her home, to see her flitting here and there in my dark old house, illuminating it with her youth and beauty, sitting at the head of my table that sparkled with its gold and silver heir-looms, making my days and nights like one delightful dream, was just as true.

And yet I hesitated. I looked over my bankbook—I cast up my accounts. I have enough for one, I said; I am not sure that it is enough for two. Eleanor, daintily nurtured, requires as dainty care for all time to come; moreover, it is not two alone to be considered, for should children come, there is their education, their maintenance, their future provision and portion to be found. All this would impoverish us, and unless we ended by becoming mere dependents, we had, to my excited vision, only the cold charity of the world and the work-house to which to look forward. I do not believe that Eleanor thought me right in so much of the matter as I saw fit to explain, but in maiden pride her lips perforce were sealed. She laughed though, when I confessed my work-house fear, and said that for her part she was thankful there was such a refuge at all, standing as it did on its knoll in the midst of green fields, and shaded by broad-limbed oaks—she had always envied the old women sitting there by their evening fireside, and mumbling over their small affairs to one another. But all her words seemed merely idle badinage—so I delayed. I said—when this ship sails in, when that dividend is declared, when I see how this speculation turns out—the days were long that added up the count of years, the nights were dreary; but I believed that I was actuated by principle, and took pride to myself for my strength and self-denial.

Moreover, old Paul, my great-uncle on my mother's side, and the millionaire of the family, was a bitter misogynist, and regarded women and marriage and household cares as the three remediless mistakes of an over-ruling Providence. He knew of my engagement to Eleanor, but so long as it remained in that stage he had nothing to say. Let me once marry, and my share of his million would be best represented by a cipher. However, he was not a man to adore, and he could not live forever.

Still, with all my own effort, I amassed wealth but slowly, according to my standard; my various ventures had various luck; and one day my old

Uncle Paul, always intensely interested in the subject, both scientifically and from a commercial point of view, too old and feeble to go himself, but fain to send a proxy, and desirous of money in the family, made me an offer of that portion of his wealth on my return which would be mine on his demise, funded safely subject to my order, provided I made one of those who sought the discovery of the Northwest Passage.

I went to town, canvassed the matter with the experts—I had always an adventurous streak, as old Paul well knew—and having given many hours to the pursuit of the smaller sciences, had a turn for danger and discovery as well. And when the *Albatross*[1] sailed—in spite of Eleanor's shivering remonstrance and prayers and tears, in spite of the grave looks of my friends—I was one of those that clustered on her deck, prepared for either fate. They—my companions—it is true, were led by nobler lights; but as for me, it was much as I told Eleanor—my affairs were so regulated that they would go on uninterruptedly in my absence; I should be no worse off for going, and if I returned, letting alone the renown of the thing, my Uncle Paul's donation was to be appropriated; every thing then was assured, and we stood possessed of lucky lives. If I had any keen or eager desire of search, any purpose to aid the growth of the world or to penetrate the secrets of its formation; as indeed I think I must have had, I did not at that time know any thing about it. But I was to learn that death and stillness have no kingdom on this globe, and that even in the extremest bitterness of cold and ice perpetual interchange and motion is taking place. So we went, all sails set on favorable winds, bounding over blue sea, skirting frowning coasts, and ever pushing our way up into the dark mystery of the North.

I shall not delay here to tell of Danish posts and the hospitality of summer settlements in their long afternoon of arctic daylight; nor will I weary you with any description of the succulence of the radishes that grew under the panes of glass in the Governor's scrap of moss and soil, scarcely of more size than a lady's parlor fernery, and which seemed to our dry mouths full of all the earth's cool juices—but advance, as we ourselves hastened to do, while that chill and crystalline sun shone, up into the ice-cased dens and caverns of the Pole. By the time that the long, blue twilight fell, when the rough and rasping cold sheathed all the atmosphere, and the great stars pricked themselves out on the heavens like spears' points, the

Albatross was hauled up for winter-quarters, banked and boarded, heaved high on fields of ice; and all her inmates, during the wintry dark, led the life that prepared them for further exploits in higher latitudes the coming year, learning the dialects of the Esquimaux, the tricks of the seal and walrus, making long explorations with the dogs and Glipnu, their master, breaking ourselves in for business that had no play about it.

Then, at last, the August suns set us free again; inlets of tumultuous water traversed the great ice-floes; the *Albatross,* refitted, ruffled all her plumage and spread her wings once more for the North—for the secret that sat there domineering all its substance.

It was a year since we had heard from home; but who staid to think of that while our keel spurned into foam the sheets of steely seas, and day by day brought us nearer to the hidden things we sought? For myself I confess that, now so close to the end as it seemed, curiosity and research absorbed every other faculty; Eleanor might be mouldering back to the parent earth—I could not stay to meditate on such a possibility; my Uncle Paul's donation might enrich itself with gold-dust instead of the gathered dust of idle days—it was nothing to me. I had but one thought, one ambition, one desire in those days—the discovery of the clear seas and open passage. I endured all our hardships as if they had been luxuries: I made light of scurvy, banqueted off train-oil, and met that cold for which there is no language framed, and which might be a new element; or which, rather, had seemed in that long night like the vast void of ether beyond the uttermost star, where was neither air nor light nor heat, but only bitter negation and emptiness. I was hardly conscious of my body; I was only a concentrated search in myself.

The recent explorers had announced here, in the neighborhood of where our third summer at last found us, the existence of an immense space of clear water. One even declared that he had seen it.

My Uncle Paul had pronounced the declaration false, and the sight an impossibility. The North he believed to be the breeder of icebergs, an ever-welling fountain of cold; the great glaciers there forever form, forever fall; the ice-packs line the gorges from year to year unchanging; peaks of volcanic rock drop their frozen mantles like a scale only to display the fresher one beneath. The whole region, said he, is Plutonic, blasted by a primordial convulsion of the great forces of creation; and though it may be a few miles nearer to the central fires of the earth, allowing that there are such things, yet that would not in itself detract from the frigid power of its sunless solitudes, the more especially when it is remembered that the spinning of the earth, while in its first plastic material, which gave it greater circumference and thinness of shell at its equator, must have thickened the shell correspondingly at the poles; and the character of all the waste and wilderness there only signifies the impenetrable wall between its surface and centre, through which wall no heat could enter or escape. The great rivers, like the White and the Mackenzie, emptying to the north of the continents, so far from being enough in themselves to form any body of ever fresh and flowing water, can only pierce the opposing ice-fields in narrow streams and bays and inlets as they seek the Atlantic and the Pacific seas. And as for the theory of the currents of water heated in the tropics and carried by the rotary motion of the planet to the Pole, where they rise and melt the ice-floes into this great supposititious sea, it is simply an absurdity on the face of it, he argued, when you remember that warm water being in its nature specifically lighter than cold it would have risen to the surface long before it reached there. No, thought my Uncle Paul, who took nothing for granted; it is as I said, an absurdity on the face of it; my nephew shall prove it, and I stake half the earnings of my life upon it.

To tell the truth, I thought much the same as he did; and now that such a mere trifle of distance intervened between me and the proof, I was full of a feverish impatience that almost amounted to insanity.

We had proceeded but a few days, coasting the crushing capes of rock that every where seemed to run out in a diablerie of tusks and horns to drive us from the region that they warded, now cruising through a runlet of blue water just wide enough for our keel, with silver reaches of frost stretching away into a ghastly horizon—now plunging upon tossing seas, the sun wheeling round and round, and never sinking from the strange, weird sky above us, when again to our look-out a glimmer in the low horizon told its awful tale—a sort of smoky lustre like that which might ascend from an army of spirits—the fierce and fatal spirits tented on the terrible field of the ice-floe.

We were alone, our single little ship speeding ever upward in the midst of that untraveled desolation. We spoke seldom to one another, oppressed with the sense of our situation. It was a loneliness that seemed more than a death in life, a solitude that was supernatural. Here and now it was clear water; ten hours later and we were caught in the teeth of the cold, wedged in the ice that had advanced upon us and surrounded us, fettered by another winter in latitudes where human life had never before been supported.

We found, before the hands of the dial had taught us the lapse of a week, that this would be something not to be endured. The sun sank lower every day behind the crags and silvery horns; the heavens grew to wear a hue of violet, almost black, and yet unbearably dazzling; as the notes of our voices fell upon the atmosphere they assumed a metallic tone, as if the air itself had become frozen from the beginning of the world and they tinkled against it; our sufferings had mounted in their intensity till they were too great to be resisted.

It was decided at length—when the one long day had given place to its answering night, and in the jet-black heavens the stars, like knobs of silver, sparkled so large and close upon us that we might have grasped them in our hands—that I should take a sledge with Glipnu and his dogs, and see if there were any path to the westward by which, if the *Albatross* were forsaken, those of her crew that remained might follow it, and find an escape to safety. Our path was on a frozen sea; if we discovered land we did not know that the foot of man had ever trodden it; we could hope to find no *caché* of snow-buried food—neither fish nor game lived in this desert of ice that was so devoid of life in any shape as to seem dead itself. But, well provisioned, furred to the eyes, and essaying to nurse some hopefulness of heart, we set out on our way through this Valley of Death, relieving one another, and traveling day and night.

Still night and day to the west rose the black coast, one interminable height; to the east extended the sheets of unbroken ice; sometimes a huge glacier hung pendulous from the precipice; once we saw, by the starlight, a white, foaming, rushing river arrested and transformed to ice in its flight down that steep. A south wind began to blow behind us; we traveled on the ice; three days, perhaps, as days are measured among men, had passed, when we found that we made double progress, for the ice traveled too; the whole field, carried by some northward-bearing current, was afloat; it began to be crossed and cut by a thousand crevasses; the cakes, an acre each, tilted up and down, and made wide waves with their ponderous plashing in the black body of the sea; we could hear them grinding distantly in the clear dark against the coast, against each other. There was no retreat—there was no advance; we were on the ice, and the ice was breaking up. Suddenly we rounded a tongue of the primeval rock, and recoiled before a narrow gulf—one sharp shadow, as deep as despair, as full of aguish fears. It was just wide enough for the sledge to span. Glipnu made the dogs leap; we could be no worse off if they drowned. They touched the opposite block; it careened; it went under; the sledge went with it; I was left alone where I had stood. Two dogs broke loose, and scrambled up beside me; Glipnu and the others I never saw again. I sank upon the ice; the dogs crouched beside me; sometimes I think they saved my brain from total ruin, for without them I could not have withstood the enormity of that loneliness, a loneliness that it was impossible should be broken—floating on and on with that vast journeying company of spectral ice. I had food enough to support life for several days to come, in the pouch at my belt; the dogs and I shared it—for, last as long as it would, when it should be gone there was only death before us—no reprieve—sooner or later that; as well sooner as later—the living terrors of this icy hell were all about us, and death could be no worse.

Still the south wind blew, the rapid current carried us, the dark skies grew deep and darker, the lanes and avenues between the stars were crowded with forebodings—for the air seemed full of a new power, a strange and invisible influence, as if a king of unknown terrors here held his awful state. Sometimes the dogs stood up and growled and bristled their shaggy hides; I, prostrate on the ice, in all my frame was stung with a universal tingle. I was no longer myself. At this moment my blood seemed to sing and bubble in my veins; I grew giddy with a sort of delirious and inexplicable ecstasy; with another moment unutterable horror seized me; I was plunged and weighed down with a black and suffocating load, while evil things seemed to flap their wings in my face, to breathe in my mouth, to draw my soul out of my body and carry it careering through the frozen realm of that murky heaven, to restore it with a shock of agony. Once as I lay there, still floating, floating northward, out of the dim dark rim of the water-world, a lance of piercing light shot up the zenith; it divided the heavens like a knife; they opened out in one blaze, and the fire fell sheetingly down before my face—cold fire, curdlingly cold—light robbed of heat, and set free in a preternatural anarchy of the elements; its fringes swung to and fro before my face, pricked it with flaming spiculæ, dissolving in a thousand colors that spread every where over the low field, flashing, flickering, creeping, reflecting, gathering again in one long serpentine line of glory that wavered in slow convolutions across the cuts and crevasses of the ice, wreathed ever nearer, and, lifting its head at last, became nothing in the darkness but two great eyes like glowing coals, with which it stared me to a stound, till I threw myself face down to hide me in the ice; and the whining, bristling dogs cowered backward, and were dead.

I should have supposed myself to be in the region of the magnetic pole of the sphere, if I did not know that I had long since left it behind me. My pocket-compass had become entirely useless, and every scrap of metal that I had about me had become a loadstone. The very ice, as if it were congealed from water that held large quantities of iron in solution; iron escaping from whatever solid land there was beneath or around, the Plutonic rock that such a region could have alone veined and seamed with metal. The very ice appeared to have a magnetic quality; it held me so that I changed my position upon it with difficulty, and, as if it established a battery by the aid of the singular atmosphere above it, frequently sent thrills quivering through and through me till my flesh seemed about to resolve into all the jarring atoms of its original constitution; and again soothed me, with a velvet touch, into a state which, if it were not sleep, was at least haunted by visions that I dare not believe to have been realities, and from which I always awoke with a start to find myself still floating, floating. My watch had long since ceased to beat. I felt an odd persuasion that I had died when that stood still, and only this slavery of the magnet, of the cold, this power that locked every thing in invisible fetters and let nothing loose again, held my soul still in the bonds of my body. Another idea, also, took possession of me, for my mind was open to whatever visitant chose to enter, since utter despair of safety or release had left it vacant of a hope or fear. These enormous days and nights, swinging in their arc six months long, were the pendulum that dealt time in another measure than that dealt by the sunlight of lower zones; they told the time of what interminable years, the years of what vast generations far beyond the span that covered the age of the primeval men of Scripture—they measured time on this gigantic and enduring scale for what wonderful and mighty beings, old as the everlasting hills, as destitute as they of mortal sympathy, cold and inscrutable, handling the two-edged javelins of frost and magnetism, and served by all the unknown polar agencies. I fancied that I saw their far-reaching cohorts, marshaling and manœuvring at times in the field of an horizon that was boundless, the glitter of their spears and casques, the sheen of their white banners; and again, sitting in fearful circle with their phantasmagoria they shut and hemmed me in and watched me writhe like a worm before them.

I had a fancy that the perpetual play of magnetic impulses here gradually disintegrated the expanse of ice, as sunbeams might have done. If it succeeded in unseating me from my cold station I should drown, and there would be an end of me; it would be all one; for though I clung to life I did not cling to suffering. Something of the wild beast seemed to spring up in my nature; that ignorance of any moment but the present. I felt a certain kinship to the bear in her comfortable snowiness whom I had left in the parallels far below this unreal tract of horrors. I remembered traditions of such metempsychoses; the thought gave me a pang that none of these fierce and subtle elements had known how to give before. But all the time my groaning, cracking ice was moving with me, splitting now through all its leagues of length along the darkness, with an explosion like a cannon's shot, that echoed again and again in every gap and chasm of its depth, and seemed to be caught up and repeated by a thousand airy sprites, and snatched on from one to another till it fell dead through the frozen thickness of the air.

It was at about this time that I noticed another species of motion than that which had hitherto governed it seizing this journeying ice. It bent and bent, as a glacier does in its viscous flow between mountains; it crowded, and loosened, and rent apart, and at last it broke in every direction, and every fragment was crushed and jammed together again; and the whole mass was following, as I divined, the curve of some enormous whirlpool that swept it from beneath. It might have been a day and night, it might have been an hour, that we traveled on this vast curve—I had no more means of knowing than if I had veritably done with time. We were one expanse of shadow; not a star above us, only a sky of impenetrable gloom received the shimmering that now and again the circling ice cast off. It was a strange slow motion, yet with such a steadiness and strength about it that it had the effect of swiftness. It was long since any water, or the suspicion of any, had been visible; we might have been grinding through some gigantic hollow for all I could have told; snow had never fallen here; the mass moved you knew as if you felt the prodigious hand that grasped and impelled it from beneath. Whither was it tending, in the eddy of what huge stream that went, with the smoke of its fall hovering on the brink, to plunge a tremendous cataract over the limits of the earth into the unknown abyss of space? Far in advance there was a faint glimmering, a sort of powdery light glancing here and there. As we approached it—the ice and I—it grew fainter, and was, by-and-by, lost in a vast twilight that surrounded us on all sides; at the same time it became evident that we had passed under a roof, an immense and vaulted roof. As crowding, stretching, rending, we passed on, uncanny gleams were playing distantly above us and around us, now and then overlaying all things with a sheeted illumination as deathly as a grave-light, now and then shooting up in spires of blood-red radiance that disclosed the terrible aurora. I was in a cavern of ice, as wide and as high as the heavens; these flashes of glory, alternated with equal flashes of darkness, as you might say, taught me to perceive. Perhaps tremendous tide after tide had hollowed it with all its fantastic recesses; or had that Titantic race of the interminable years built it as a palace for their monarch, a temple for their deity, with its domes that sprung far up immeasurable heights and hung palely shining like mock heavens of hazy stars; its aisles that stretched away down colonnades of crystal columns into unguessed darkness; its high-heaved arches, its pierced and open sides? Now an aurora burned up like a blue-light, and went skimming under all the vaults far off into far and farther hollows, revealing, as it went, still loftier heights and colder answering radiances. Then these great arches glowed like blocks of beryl. Wondrous tracery of delicate vines and leaves, greener than the greenest moss, wandered over them, wreathed the great pillars, and spread round them in capitals of flowers; roses crimson as a carbuncle; hyacinths like bedded cubes of amethyst; violets bluer than sapphires—all as if the flowers had been turned to flame, yet all so cruelly cold, as if the power that wrought such wonders could simulate a sparkle beyond even the lustre of light, but could not give it heat, that principle of life, that fountain of first being. Yonder a stalactite of clustered ruby—that kept the aurora and glinted faintly, and more faintly, till the thing came again, when it grasped a whole body-full of splendor—hung downward and dropped a thread-like stem and a blossom of palest pink, like a transfigured Linnæa,[2] to meet the snow-drop in its sheath of green that shot up from a spire of aqua marine below. Here living rainbows flew from buttress to buttress and frolicked in the domes—the only things that dared to live and sport where beauty was frozen into horror. It seemed as if that shifting death-light of the aurora photographed all these things upon my memory, for I noted none of them at the time. I only wondered idly whither we were tending as we drove in deeper and deeper under that ice-roof, and curved more and more circlingly upon our course while the silent flashes sped on overhead. Now we were in the dark again crashing onward; now a cold blue radiance burst from every icicle, from every crevice, and I saw that the whole enormous mass of our motion bent and swept around a single point—a dark yet glittering form that sat as if upon the apex of the world. Was it one of those mightier than the Anakim,[3] more than the sons of God, to whom all the currents of this frozen world converged? Sooth I know not—for presently I imagined that my vision made only an exaggeration of some brown Esquimaux sealed up and left in his snow-house to die. A thin sheathing of ice appeared to clothe him and give the glister to his duskiness. Insensible as I had thought myself to any further fear, I cowered beneath the stare of those dead and icy eyes. Slowly we rounded, and ever rounded; the inside, on which my place was, moving less slowly than the outer circle of the sheeted mass in its viscid flow; and as we moved, by some fate my eye was caught by the substance on which this figure sat. It was no figure at all now, but a bare jag of rock rising in the centre of this solid whirlpool, and carrying on its summit something which held a light that not one of these icy freaks, pranking in the dress of gems and flowers, had found it possible to assume. It was a thing so real, so genuine, my breath became suspended; my heart ceased to beat; my brain, that had been a lump of ice, seemed to move in its skull; hope, that had deserted me, suddenly sprung up like a second life within me; the old passion was not dead, if I was. It rose stronger than life or death or than myself. If I could but snatch that mass of moonstone, that inestimable wealth! It was nothing deceptive, I declared to myself. What more natural home could it have than this region, thrown up here by the old Plutonic powers of the planet, as the same substance in smaller shape was thrown up on the peaks of the Mount St. Gothard, when the Alpine aiguilles first sprang into the day? There it rested, limpid with its milky pearl, casting out flakes of flame and azure, of red and leaf-green light, and holding yet a sparkle of silver in the reflections and refractions of its inner axis—the splendid Turk's-eye of the lapidaries, the cousin of the water-opal and the girasole, the precious essence of feldspar. Could I break it, I would find clusters of great hemitrope crystals. Could I obtain it, I should have a jewel in that mass of moonstone such as the world never saw! The throne of Jemschid could not cast a shadow beside it.[4]

Then the bitterness of my fate overwhelmed me. Here, with this treasure of a kingdom, this jewel that could not be priced, this wealth beyond an Emperor's—and here only to die! My stolid apathy vanished, old thoughts dominated once more, old habits, old desires. I thought of Eleanor then in her warm, sunny home, the blossoms that bloomed around her, the birds that sang, the cheerful evening fires, the longing thoughts for one who never came, who never was to come. But I would! I cried, where human voice had never cried before. I would return! I would take this treasure with me! I would not be defrauded! Should not I, a man, conquer this inanimate blind matter? I reached out my hands to seize it. Slowly it receded—slowly, and less slowly; or was the motion of the ice still carrying me onward? Had we encircled this apex? and were we driving out into the open and uncovered North, and so down the seas and out to the open main of black water again? If so—if I could live through it—I must have this thing!

I rose, and as well as I could, with my cramped and stiffened limbs, I moved to go back for it. It was useless; the current that carried us was growing invincible, the gaping gulfs of the outer seas were sucking us toward them. I fell; I scrambled to my feet; I would still have gone back, but, as I attempted it, the ice whereon I was inclined ever so slightly, tipped more boldly, gave way, and rose in a billow, broke, and piled over on another mass beneath. Then the cavern was behind us, and I comprehended that this ice-stream, having doubled its central point, now in its outward movement encountered the still incoming body, and was to pile above and pass over it, the whole expanse bending, cracking, breaking, crowding, and compressing, till its rearing tumult made bergs more mountainous than the offshot glaciers of the Greenland continent, that should ride safely down to crumble in the surging seas below. As block after block of the rent ice rose in the air, lighted by the blue and bristling aurora-points, toppled and mounted higher, it seemed to me that now indeed I was battling with those elemental agencies in the dreadful fight I had desired—one man against the might of matter. I sprang from that block to another; I gained my balance on a third, climbing, shouldering, leaping, struggling, holding with my hands, catching with my feet, crawling, stumbling, tottering, rising high and higher with the mountain ever making underneath; a power unknown to my foes coming to my aid, a blessed rushing warmth that glowed on all the surface of my skin, that set the blood to racing in my veins, that made my heart beat with newer hope, sink with newer despair, rise buoyant with new determination. Except when the shaft of light pierced the shivering sky I could not see or guess the height that I had gained. I was vaguely aware of chasms that were bottomless, of precipices that opened on them, of pinnacles rising round me in aerial spires, when suddenly the shelf, on which I must have stood, yielded, as if it were pushed by great hands, swept down a steep incline like an avalanche, stopped half-way, but sent me flying on, sliding, glancing, like a shooting-star, down, down the slippery side, breathless, dizzy, smitten with blistering pain by awful winds that whistled by me, far out upon the level ice below that tilted up and down again with the great resonant plash of open water, and conscious for a moment that I lay at last upon a fragment that the mass behind urged on, I knew and I remembered nothing more.

Faces were bending over me when I opened my eyes again, rough, uncouth, and bearded faces, but no monsters of the pole. Whalemen rather, smelling richly of train-oil, but I could recall nothing in all my life one fraction so beautiful as they; the angels on whom I hope to open my eyes when Death has really taken me will scarcely seem sights more blest than did those rude whalers of the North Pacific Sea. The North Pacific Sea—for it was there that I was found, explain it how you may—whether the *Albatross* had pierced farther to the west than her sailing-master knew, and had lost her reckoning with a disordered compass-needle under new stars—or whether I had really been the sport of the demoniac beings of the ice, tossed by them from zone to zone in a dozen hours. The whalers, real creatures enough, had discovered me on a block of ice, they said; nor could I, in their opinion, have been many days undergoing my dreadful experience, for there was still food in my wallet when they opened it. They would never believe a word of my story, and so far from regarding me as one who had proved the Northwest Passage in my own person, they considered me a mere idle maniac, as uncomfortable a thing to have on ship-board as a ghost or a dead body, wrecked and unable to account for myself, and gladly transferred me to a homeward-bound Russian man-of-war, whose officers afforded me more polite but quite as decided skepticism. I have never to this day found any one who believed my story when I told it—so you can take it for what it is worth. Even my Uncle Paul flouted it, and absolutely refused to surrender the sum on whose expectation I had taken ship; while my old ancestor, who hung peeling over the hall fire, dropped from his frame in disgust at the idea of one of his hard-cash descendants turning romancer. But all I know is that the *Albatross* never sailed into port again, and that if I open my knife to-day and lay it on the table it will wheel about till the tip of its blade points full at the North Star.

I have never found any one to believe me, did I say? Yes, there is one—Eleanor never doubted a word of my narration, never asked me if cold and suffering had not shaken my reason. But then, after the first recital, she has never been willing to hear another word about it, and if I ever allude to my lost treasure or the possibility of instituting search for it, she asks me if I need more lessons to be content with the treasure that I have, and gathers up her work and gently leaves the room. So that, now I speak of it so seldom, if I had not told the thing to you it might come to pass that I should forget altogether the existence of my mass of moonstone. My mass of moonshine, old Paul calls it. I let him have his say; he can not have that nor any thing else much longer; but when all is done I recall Galileo and I mutter to myself, "*Per si muove*—it *was* a mass of moonstone! [5] With these eyes I saw it, with these hands I touched it, with this heart I longed for it, with this will I mean to have it yet!"

THE BLACK BESS

A MAN who loves from his boyhood her who becomes his fate, hardly knows the nobility of his love, as does he who, from a lonely condition of which he thought well enough before, suddenly finds himself plunged into a new element and living the life of those already blest. With the first one, his love has grown as he has grown, and his weaknesses with him. It may be that love seldom conquers those weaknesses; but with the other love comes a heavenly tyrant and usurps the place of everything less noble; his heart is clean swept and garnished—a shrine for the object of his worship; he has undergone a purification, a sanctification that is scarcely less than that of a sacrament. It was so with me, I know, at least, when I first thought of wooing Margaret for my wife, and possession of her promise never made it otherwise.

To say that she was beautiful would fail to give even a pencilling of her presence; and just as impossible would it be for me to set down any categorical description of her loveliness; of the large, fair, pale face; the eyes, so gray and dark that they grew on you as you gazed, like the shades of evening from which the stars look out; of the features, which would have been sculptured had they been less instinct with pulsing and dilating life; of the tresses of finest, darkest hair, sweeping down the temples in countless curves; of the unspeakable sweetness of the smile—that smile which seemed to fill your heart and soul with sunshine and warmth. Never was there such another woman made as Margaret. Her mind, too, was no less peerless than her person. It had a trait like light itself, and gave color and vitality to every object that it rested on. Of humble birth, and with no means of education beyond those afforded by the village school and the church library, she had nevertheless cultivated herself to a point beyond that attained by many women when living a luxury of life and breathing the atmosphere of art.

It has always made me wonder, my relation with her, what she could have seen in me so to bestow herself as she did. I, myself, though still so young, was not entirely a boor; indeed, being a poor man, I was thought eccentric, perhaps because I was not a fool; but, though now sitting at my ease, a tolerably well-read man of wealth, having climbed easily by others' help, speculated largely and daringly, studied where I could and as I went, yet then I was only the master of an engine on the Great Interior Railway, running a night train across the State, and earning my living by the sweat of my brow, in soot and grime and smoke, and all in the midst of a wild relish of danger.

It is a singular fact that the human mind can become habituated to any experience. Though I shall never forget the night when I first drove my engine out of Waterwey, not too familiar with the route, dreading the darkness and the responsibility, tremulous, indeed, with a thousand tremors, yet now, were it twice as many years since I laid hand on lever or signalled for a station, I could take her out to-night, over marsh and meadow and drawbridge, up the long mountain grade, across the terrible trestle-work, round that curving precipice, one side sheer rock up into the stars, the other nothing but black darkness and an empty gulf of dizzy depth, through the thick, reverberating tunnels, down the long incline, and whistle for the brakes at Babylon, with as much nonchalance as when I took the reins from my groom this morning and gave my brown beauties their head for a breezy bit of business down the Park.

She was a rusher, that engine of mine, the Black Bess—they had not begun calling them then for the successful candidates—and would do her mile a minute if you asked it; though I've known the time, of a rainy five o'clock morning, when, with all steam on, her wheels made their revolutions and she stood still; and, to get her along the slippery side of an up-grade, both fireman and myself, jumping off, had to walk by her panting side and sprinkle the wet rails with sand to toll her on. But, although I've owned since then as choice specimens as ever stepped the turf, I never cared for any thoroughbred of them all as I did for the Black Bess, and I stabled her as carefully, and, in early days, handled her as daintily, as though she were the expected winner of a handicap.

Perhaps I loved my iron steed all the better for the dangers through which she had passed, since there are few whose affections are not drawn to their companion in peril; and the Black Bess and I had had it out one night, just as, clearing the Waterwey suburbs, we put on all speed for the long run across the marshes. The train was full, the steam was up, the very wind whistled behind us while we cleft it; light as a feather, the Black Bess went as if she trod the air.

Suddenly, with a sharp turn of the course from the shelter of a young thicket, we came out on a low cross-country road—a kind of causeway raised upon the meadows, and cutting diagonally across the railway track. So unfrequented was this road that I could not remember ever having noticed a vehicle on all its long and winding sweep; but at this moment an enormous load of hay, tilting heavily down on one side, rested directly across the track and blocked the way, not only for an instant's time, but was fixed there. I can see it here, if I close my eyes, with such a weird distinctness in every line as might be if a grave-light had stamped it on the plate of some supernatural camera—the four great steaming oxen, in the glow of the head-light, rising like a projection from the darkness, with wild eyes and interlocked horns, and trampling and tugging at the arrested wheels, the tilting mountain of meadow hay, the drunken teamster, half hidden in its pillowy masses, asleep, and with his jug beside him. In vain my touch upon the bell-rope or the rod; in vain the short, sharp shrieks of Black Bess; while I reached my hand to reverse the engine we should scatter all to flinders. One second the face, the face of that sleeping man, branded in on my brain as if by a searing-iron; the next, a wild thought of Margaret, a great blow, and dumb darkness. The man and his load were dust together, the Black Bess was off the track and above her wheels in meadow mud, and I lay stunned and senseless.

When a person recovers from a concussion of the brain, it would sometimes be better if he had died. I learned this to my cost one day; but I did not think so on first getting about after my long illness, through which I had ever been conscious of the tender face of Margaret hanging above me, and a part of the delirium of which had been a singular confusion of her face with that of the man asleep in the mountain of meadow hay. The world was in the full, deep flush of Summer; life seemed so good, love was so sure; Margaret was constantly beside me, the Black Bess was ready for me, and Christmas Day, when it should come wrapped in its soft snows, was to give me my wife forever.

I got up quickly, too quickly—too quickly by half; a long convalescence would have acted like a buffer to the shock I had received, and deadened its effect on all my system; but every month's salary was precious to me now; it was so much more added to that already laid up for the enriching of the humble little home whose prospect then was heaven; and before October had reddened her parallels, I drove the Black Bess again by night out of Waterwey.

Meantime my head was far from right. I knew that by the dull ache that sate upon it like a leaden cap; by the sharp pains that sometimes stabbed my eyeballs, as if needles were in the entering rays of light. Often, too, when people were speaking with me, their words sounded dully a long way off, and if I roused myself to some manner of enforced attention, I paid for it by a fresh assault of blinding pain. When in this condition, I went through many of my duties by mere mechanical routine, and I think my faithful fireman, George Rowe, did more at such times toward running the train on time than did its engineer—unless the Black Bess were herself gifted with that sort of wizardry and more than human power which I sometimes fancied belonged to her. All this annoyance of mine, however, was but intermittent; had it been otherwise, had it been constant, I should not live to remember it; and gradually I began to believe that it was wearing off, never dreaming that it was but assuming a new form.

My spirits had been greatly depressed during the period when I felt these results of my disaster the most acutely; they became as much too buoyant when I found that my natural strength and vigor were conquering the recurrence of the attacks. I had fully realized how wrong and how impossible my intended marriage with Margaret would be under such circumstances, and only when I found myself able to look the rising sun in the face, and to drive from twilight to twilight, from the gray of evening to the gray of dawn, without an extra throb in my temples, did I dare to dream fresh dreams of my long-desired home and its delights. The only trace of trouble that appeared to be remaining with me, at last, was a slightly-impaired eyesight, so that what once I could distinctly see in detail when at the distance of a mile, now became but a blur, and rendered me, on more or less seldom occasion, subject to some optical delusion. However, this did not interfere with my business, and, as I said, I went and came in such an atmosphere of expectation and assurance, that I might have seemed to any spiritual observer like one transfigured and walking in a nimbus.

Things were in this state with me, when, one night, as usual, I took the Express out of Waterwey. It was a somewhat heavier train than my ordinary one, and in the safe of the special car that went through with us was a large amount of coin and valuables. Remembering some daring robberies, in which trains had been thrown from the track by means of obstacles placed there by the villains who subsequently rifled them, I resolved on an even more particular look-out than common; I told the Black Bess, as I mounted, that she must spring to it, for there was work to do, and she answered to my hand like a live creature. I heard them sounding the irons down our long length—then the word was given, and our quivering carrier, starting well in hand, soon warmed to her work, and bounded along as if she meant to be the victor of some demoniacal race.

I have often thought, since those days, that there can be nothing like that man's sense of mastery whose hand it is which gives the first motion to some long train crowded with bustling life and tumult. All those beings, their joys, their fears, their expectations, their very futures and existences, are his, hang on the falling of his eyelid, on the turning of his finger. There is not such a potentate as he the earth over. But, when I drove an engine myself, I thought of no such thing; were my wheels oiled, my boiler fed, my valves right, were we well wooded, was I on time, should I earn my pittance a day—my fancies seldom took a higher flight. But this is aside.

It was at the close of a dark and stormy day, soon deepening into a black Autumn evening, of which I was about to speak. No stars in heaven, no lights on earth. The air was that fresh, wet coolness so delightful to breathe even when you got it, as I did, between puffs and whiffs of smoke; pools of water, everywhere on our way, waked up to flash like moons in our light as we left them; little new-made brooks were chasing each other beside us; woody places kept up a perpetual dripping and dropping; and the whole earth was soaked in running rivers of rain. The long perspective of the track, with its rails glittering in moisture, rose by all its length into heaven, and seemed to hang up shiningly before us like a ladder of light, the only fixed thing in all the changing, shimmering, calendered darkness.

As we appeared to wind our path up this splendid highway, suddenly what had been but a blot of blackness upon it a long way ahead, resolved itself to my vision into a less indistinct body, and I fancied some laborer, returning from his day's work, had fallen asleep beside the track, had, perhaps, in his slumber, rolled over upon it. Such stupid recklessness was not uncommon. I sounded the whistle to warn him, and then, as he did not stir, to put down the brakes. We had a full head of steam on, and were rushing forward with hardly-abated progress, and, straining my gaze, I discovered that the thing I had taken for a man now, by the size of the dark spot it filled, must be a woman, with her drapery blown loosely abroad by the breeze. I snatched my field-glass, and, steadying it for a moment, a face flashed in the disc—a single moment—and then, my horror-stricken eyes blinded, my tongue cleaving to the very roof of my mouth, with a mighty shock, I reversed the engine, and, the wheels revolving the other way, we slipped slowly up by our impetus, and paused within a yard of the actual place.

I leaped off to search the spot. George Rowe, likewise, leaped after me. There was nothing whatever on the track, save the shadow of a clump of bushes breaking the long glitter of its steel. I looked about me with a frantic swiftness—I could not feel convinced that no real object lay there. I heard the car windows rattling up, and turned about to see the passengers' heads thrusting out, and all the brakemen, as well, bending forward and peering into the darkness for the cause of our stand-still, and the shock that had thrown these from their seats, and those from their feet. Directly afterward, at sound of the conductor's voice, I seized an old log lying beside the ends of the sleepers, and lifted, pushed, and shoved one extremity of it as if I had just thrown it out of our path. George Rowe stared at me, but said nothing. The conductor seized on the intimated occurrence with avidity, wondered and gaped about him for an explanation of such a disaster being prepared for us, bade me run slowly, and returned with something to gossip over in every carriage of them all. But, as for me, far from heeding him the least, I increased the pressure to some such point as that I felt on the beating of my heart and the breathing of my lungs, and the Black Bess ran as if the fires of hell were blazing beneath her boilers. *It was the face of Margaret that I had seen!*

I lost no time, on that next day, in seeking Margaret. She was away from home, visiting at Brookford, a little town which was a watering station of all the trains along my own route. A shudder, foolish to the pitch of idiocy, seized me at the intelligence. If that were not verily Margaret's face, how nearly it might have been!—for Brookford was but a mile behind the place where last night I had brought our train to a pause. I telegraphed to her, and she came down, with a companion, to meet me in the evening as I returned. I saw her sweet face shining under the lamps as we drew up—but so fearfully like my vision of the night before that I hardly dared to think it real. In answer to my hurried inquiry, she said she had been out in the rain on the previous night, returning with her friend from a house where they had called, had stumbled and fallen across the railway, but had picked herself up, and was safe and dry beneath the roof-tree long and long before either down-train or up-train passed that way. She jested me on my clairvoyance, then laughed that she filled up my eye so completely.

I saw her standing there while we backed down to switch off again on the main track, gazing and smiling after me, standing so securely with her light, rustling figure, airy and supple as some glad young white-birch in the breeze—then we thundered by with our terrible tread, and I lost her! If there had been a score of faces on the track as we drove along I should have seen none of them that night, for brooding over and caressing in my happy thought the pure and perfect face that I really saw beneath the flaring station lamps.

I had almost forgotten this incident of my nightfaring—I mean, of course, the vision on the rails—when, some few weeks afterward, precisely the same thing occurred.

It was a soft, starry night of the Indian Summer, this time. There was a ceaseless glimmer of harmless sheet-lightnings through the sky, the horizon lifting every few moments with the innocent reflection of some deadly storm in the meridian beneath it. We were making about our ordinary running, when, like a quick illumination, directly in our path, the same obscurity, the same resolving—there lay the Face!

I knew as well now that it must be an illusion as that I was a breathing being. I did not essay any motion by which it should be suffered to impede our progress, but I stared at it with a fascinated gaze. The beautiful face!— its great gray eyes gleaming so softly up as the belching monster pounded down to dazzle them blind with its fierce and blazing head-light, to crush them from their sockets with its remorseless wheels. I could no more help my hands lifting then than my heart's beating.

In another instant the train was shivering with the shock of its reverse. I was off again, searching the place—on again, aware of my folly; and we spun straightway along the track as if let loose from a meteor. I heard George Rowe muttering at me in amazement, but I made him no reply. At Brookford the conductor harangued me stormily, and bade George Rowe have a charge over me. He thought that I was a drunken man, and well he might, for I felt my face so flushed, and my eyes so pained, that the latter may have glowed like flames in a bed of coals, while my brain burned and boiled, and bubbled, till it seemed like bursting. I was, indeed, well nigh beside myself.

I wrote to Margaret of this second occurrence, and asked her what it meant. Was I really becoming out of my head? Was I even out of my head already? She replied in much the same strain as before, jesting and cheerful; but it was like a transparent mask, and I could clearly detect an anxiety and alarm on her part beneath the whole of her playful petition not to turn her into a grave-light and Will-o'-the-Wisp, nor to connect her personality with such diabolical things as the flames of the St. Elmo's fire[1] that every sailor sees on his topmast, and which I had, doubtless, a thousand times beheld running before me on my rails.

I determined then that unless my mind were really affected I would take no more notice of any renewal of this apparition than I would of the copper cents and brass pins which adventurous schoolboys were in the habit of placing upon the track for the wheels to flatten out into nothingness. My resolutions, I need not say, were as worthless as the flattened pins, and quickly became pavingstones of that region where asphalt was primevally found in use.

For the Face haunted me—haunted me so that I wonder at myself now, and believe that only the grace and goodness of Heaven kept me from the endless perdition of hating the original. It never came twice in immediate succession, but at intervals of a few weeks, when it would seem to have accumulated power to expend, and, under circumstances of ingenious devilishness, it made its appearance. In many instances I was fortunate enough to have some ready excuse on hand for our delay, but sometimes the prodigy vanished before I slackened speed, and then no excuse was needed; but when that was not the case, as most frequently it happened, and I was abandoned to my own devices, and the bewilderment and consternation of the train, it began to be believed among the *employés* that I had become a hard fellow. Shortly following upon that I was summoned by the superintendent, and reprimanded for my intemperance—I, who had never drunk a drop in my life—doggedly promised him better fashions, for had I explained things, what director of them all, I asked myself, would have suffered a crazy man to take out the Night Express from Waterwey?

Meanwhile, owing solely to these affairs, my marriage had been indefinitely postponed; for, of course, while liable to these hallucinations and visitations, I was no fit subject for the assumption of new bonds and duties. Margaret remained as she had ever been—an angel of mercy; she soothed me, solaced me, and we took counsel together how best to overcome my difficulties; but, finally, when all our expedients seemed futile, she imperatively bade me resign my situation, for she felt that we were murderers, a thousand times multiplied, in continuing to hold so many lives in risk with the possibilities to which I might be driven by my mad fantasies.

This command and entreaty of hers was after a time when I had seen the face more vividly than before, more beautiful, more human, more piteous.

We were coming along an inclined plane, with the brakes down; at the foot of it the track ran curving over the mighty trestle-work of the Windriver Valley. It was impossible to stop the train, for it descended already without steam; and ahead of us lay the long, slow curve of the trestle-work, as—a sheer abutment of two hundred feet, filled in with sliding sand—it rose above the low, broad fields that slept, all purple and peaceful, in the silver flood of moonlight that fearful depth beneath us.

There was but a single alternative; I could throw the Black Bess and her train from the track as we touched the curve, and we should be dust before the valley could feel us or the river cover us; or, with the face before me, I must crash over and through that one dear thing of all my heart.

I knew, in an intimate and under consciousness, that I was deceived; but, do what I would, it came to me as if I were experiencing it myself, all the annihilating terror that must overwhelm the sufferer as that black monster and its red-hot eye advanced with the thundering tread, and shook her frame bodily and her soul with vast fear. I heard, in my fancy, her shrill shrieks, as she struggled vainly to rise, and escape, and flee, and knew that it was vainly. I felt—almost with positive and physical pain of my own—the breaking and grinding of the bone, and then—I should have done it—I had reached out my hand to do it—when, suddenly, the fair, pale face rose from the way like a dew-cloud, the floating garments of the late prostrate form were gathered together, all had disappeared—and we slid gently upon the trestle-work, and wound our way over its spider line, till kindly woods beyond took us into safety and shelter.

I stood, then, powerless, and could not have lifted my hand to my face to wipe off the beads of cold sweat there. It seems, perhaps, in the rehearsal, a little thing to have endured; but I can tell you that it was the tortures of the damned. The men and women who had given their lives into my hand that night, never knew how, for one moment, that hand, loosening its grasp, hesitated, and held them over the precipice and gulf of death, while they gazed out and down, and admired the beauty of the world, and felt their life and enjoyed their breath.

It was then Margaret said I must leave the railroad; I had no right longer to play at fast and loose with the destinies of others; each time I stepped upon my platform was a sin. The wear and tear of travel, and night travel at that, she said, had broken up my nervous system, which, added to my previous shock already sustained, might produce irreparable misfortunes, if I did not leave everything, and come down and rest with her at her mother's.

This last was pleasant enough—rest in that happy house, the low-roofed old farmhouse, standing on its verdant knoll, that always shone like some broad carpet of greenest velvet embroidered with all the golden sunshine of Summer, the house where everything was ordered to the music of peace and quietness—but then, by-and-bye, there was the time for that.

Was it a devil driving me on to stay? or was it my natural manliness refusing to yield to a devil and begging for one more trial?—I declined to go; still said nothing, and took my train out of Waterwey. I was so thoroughly myself on every other topic, that I could not believe in a monomania upon this one. I invented an apology to myself for every time that I yielded to my pursuer—the reflection of the moon in some ditch of still water, the lantern of a crossing in the woods, the round, white signboard of a switch, the signal-balls upon a drawbridge—I affirmed that in similarly deceptive lights and shadows they would have affected every man in the same way as that in which I was affected.

But, at last, the tormentor grew insupportable; it followed me from station to station, as some great, winged, stinging thing pursues a racer, its play on my emotions being all the more forcible that I could never entertain any sentiment of anger toward it—for there it always lay, lovely, appealing, and piteous, only the face of Margaret. It grew plain to me, and, reluctantly, I was forced to acknowledge either that my vision was distorted and ruined, or that some necessary spring in my mechanism had become loosened.

I determined then, at last, that I would consult a physician, to see if there were any balms in Gilead for my healing. I shudder now at remembrance of my selfish criminality—for I reasoned that I could do this the more readily, as I knew that, by the laws of his profession, he would be obliged to keep my application secret, and could make no report to my employers. I needed not have feared, as it ended. Old Dr. Blanchard had no time for mischief, and had, moreover, such a professional curiosity and searching into things, that, if my symptoms had been at all anomalous, he would have suffered me to launch a loaded train of my fellow creatures into eternity, in order that he might study their development. However, he assured me that it was a very simple and frequent form of disease with which I was afflicted; one taking its variation according to the idiosyncracies of the patient; and, being entirely upon the nerves, there was no medicine to reach it but my own will. This was cheerful, after my experience. If my spiritual identity, he said, was weaker than that of my body, it must succumb into hopeless insanity; but, could I rouse its flagging courage and whip it into action, all was safe and sure. The one, the one thing, for me to do was, when the next time I saw the Face before me, to run over it, boldly and without a remonstrance—remorselessly, if I could, but to run over it—and I should be well.

It was an easy thing to order—but, then, the face was Margaret's.

Dr. Blanchard professed himself interested in the case which I had exhibited to him, and would not take any fee. I went out from his presence, half comforted, somewhat strengthened, and resolved that I would do as he bade.

I began, in the first place, by fortifying myself daily with a simple tonic, in order that no mere debility might cause a failure, and, perhaps, it was on finding me so resolved that the subtle apparition feared a fresh encounter—so many weeks went by without its reappearance—the Winter, which I had once so looked forward to for its promised home and joy, having shifted into Spring—that I was fairly drawing fresh breath and fancying myself free—and, being off my guard one night, there it lay.

It was a starlit midnight, with a thick haze catching the starbeams and weaving them into a kind of fleece over the heavens, so that what light there was had a strange and supernatural effect, at best. With this, a wild, high wind was roaring on behind us, like the tramp of a ghostly legion on high, and blowing up some salt, tough gale from the seaboard. Owing to this great wind in our favor—which favoring wind has something as much to do with a railway carriage as with a ship, while pressing from the rear and destroying atmospheric resistance in face—we had made remarkable time, and were ahead of our table, so that I was on the point of slowing, when a white-winged night bird, startled by our approach, rose from its covert beside the track, and flew away toward the woods. In another moment something else rose, too, as if a slumbering wayfarer there had lifted head to gaze after the flying shadow, and then it lay back again—and, looking at it intently, *I saw the face once more.*

Now was my time. What if I should shut my eyes, and, not seeing it, drive on? But no, that would be cowardly—neither would it effect the object, neither could I do it. Moreover, were I able, in so doing I might fail to observe some real obstacle, and so plunge my whole train to destruc-tion. Therefore, I gazed. And gazing, it took the strength out of me—the sweet, wide-open eyes; the tender, trembling mouth; the half-fainting rose upon the cheek. As the storm swoops and snaps a bending tree, I sent a blast shrieking against the whistle's edge, and felt the answering drag of the brakes, and then, in spite of myself, the throttle valve had done its work, and we were gently slowing, and should have paused at a point several rods from the appealing sight—should have paused—but we did not.

It was as though some mighty and invisible hand, mightier than the breath of steam or the temper of steel, mocking my own, had seized us and was drawing us on at its wicked will. My heart refused to beat—stood still with horror; the shiver that ran even through the roots of my hair hardened there; we were close upon the place, grinding with all our hefty iron over it; we had passed it, and we paused.

The wind had dragged the whole train for that distance. If you doubt me, the books of my profession will tell you that it is no remarkable instance, for a sudden flaw of contrary wind has been known to do so much as to bring to a stop a train under full headway. I would that sudden flaws of contrary wind had been blowing one cruel day for me!

We had passed the place then. Till I could rouse me from the benumbing faintness, could draw a breath, and then could steady my voice, I did not attempt to move. But the instant I mastered myself I went through my customary drama on these occasions—was off, running behind and swinging my lantern over the vacant track, finding nothing, back again, and leaning on my handles before the conductor had reached me. I told him then that we were ahead of time by reason of the wind, and I was waiting on the side-track for the downtrain to pass. Fortunately, facts upheld me, or my flushed face and shaking hands would have betrayed the truth, or the falsehood, behind.

I questioned with myself now if the ghost was laid. Yet how could it be? We had run over the face, it was true, but by no volition of mine. Indeed, I had decided exactly the opposite; I had refused to do so; I had stopped. My will had again been cowed and conquered—not yet had it pricked the bubble of this phantasm and caused it to explode into empty and innoxious air.

It would be idle to rehearse the passing of the Summer and the coming of the Winter, with their continued visitations that then, indeed, came more seldom, but every time with increased power. I had struck work for a season, and had been up resting with Margaret, at her mother's, for two delicious months—resting, just closing my eyes in peace. I had begged her then, before I came away, to marry me; for I thought if I had the dear real face my daily companion, to come home to, to go out from, the fictitious one would perforce die a natural death. But, even had Margaret herself entirely consented, her mother had too many scruples to suffer her only child to leave her for such precarious protection as mine might be. So I went back to solitary life again.

My trouble had now become so much a chronic thing that, except when its manifestations, or their results, were extraordinary, I took no serious note of them; only the possibility of their future coming, and the actuality of their past, hung over me like a black, suffocating cloud, awake or asleep. In fact, though, I had no sleep that deserved the beneficent name. In place of the sweet oblivion and rest of forgetfulness that other men knew, I had for my part a long and living nightmare.

In all this time I had failed to find sufficient strength to obey the physician's order, to cut through the cursed thing that was killing me, with the sharp flange of my wheels, and annihilate it. But Dr. Blanchard had found me out, although in consulting him I had given no name, and one afternoon he accosted me in the street, on my way to the station, not to ascertain what progress I had made—for that was visible enough in my haggard and jaded appearance—but to ask me if I was to be on duty that night. I responded in the affirmative, and, on hearing my reply, he said, gently, that he should have the pleasure of trusting himself to my guidance for that trip, and, if I had no objection, and could find room for him, he would be my companion upon the Black Bess. Of course I perceived his intention sufficiently well; and perhaps it was an unwise thing for him to propose, for his mere presence was more likely to conjure up the appearance than to help me overcome it.

If, now, I tell the rest of the story as it appeared to me then, and as my troubled brain received it, it is because remembrance is nearly as vivid as the suffering, and I can hardly say to-day where reason ends and phantasms begin.

We had a snowy night for this excursion of Dr. Blanchard's, so much is certain; not like that great, white, whirling storm in which the face, all wrapped in folds of bridal lace, flitted before me and rested till I stopped, and not all the big ploughs in the company's use could then have advanced the snowed-up train an inch; but a night of gusty flaws, when a light down dropped on the track and was gone, and velvety flakes draped spray and twig of the woodland and shook off showeringly as we passed, and snow-squalls dashed blindingly across our path and vanished, and all the sky was a gray and dazzling bewilderment.

I knew that, whatever the weather was, Margaret would not fail me at the station, and then I told the doctor, as we neared Brookford, what sight there was in store for him at that place, and remarked that it was, may be, fortunate for me that night that Margaret had really to cross the track in order to reach the spot where she was to await us, as in looking out that no danger befell herself I should be less likely to encounter that wraith of hers, nor could I see them both together. But Dr. Blanchard shook his head, and bade me mind my own business, and have that degree of confidence in Margaret to believe her capable of taking care of herself.

And looking out into the wavering whiteness lit by the glare of the head-light, while he shouted forth his gruff advice, all at once—"*There! There!*" I cried. "*There it is!*"

"Where?" demanded the doctor, springing to gaze over my shoulder, as if his untrained vision could have discerned so much as an outline in that thick air. "Damn it! Don't be a fool! Drive on!"

"Where?" I answered. "There! right before us. A woman walking. See! she has turned her head; she sees us; she did not hear us in that gust, we have frightened her; she stumbles, she falls, she is lying on the track, she cannot get up—that face, that white face—it is Margaret's!"

"By God! there is no woman there!" he replied, before I had finished. "My eyes are as keen as yours. I tell you there is not a single object before us till we reach the Brookford lights there, a mile away!"

I hardly heard him. I had stretched out my hand to pull up, when I caught a sidelong glimpse of him, brandishing an iron bar above my head. "Touch that handle," he cried, "and I will knock you down!" And then he interposed himself between my hand and it.

"You are mad," I said, calmly, and believing what I said. "Do you suppose I fear your billy? While I am master of the Black Bess she does not run down a woman—least of all that one."

The whole of this was so hurried that not even George Rowe, who stood staring and gaping and hearkening with all his might, could make out a syllable.

"Very well," said the doctor then, reversing his method, and yelling out his words in my ear till he must have been purple. "You are convinced that you see this face, and as both your fireman and I myself can assure you what we see nothing there, you must feel equally convinced that it is your pursuing phantom, as you call it. Now, then, is the time to put an end to it. Destroy it. Exert your will. You have only to fold your hands behind you. Nothing else in the world to do. Give them here to me. The engine will do the rest. Be a man now—remember that, this once done, all your peace begins—Margaret and marriage—home and happiness. There is nothing there! Drive on!"

I heard him now, but as a hollow voice might speak far, far outside of the world in which I was.

I had fixed my will, as much as it was possible to fix so loose and weak and shaking a thing, a bundle of broken links—I was determined to obey him.

But all the time I saw only her, only her sweet face in the snowy light, as I never should see it again—the hood had fallen back from it, the wet rings of the dark hair were blowing out from it, a tint like the flush of the tea-rose was lying on its cheek—not that I noted all such items then, I remember them to-day, they were impressed like the work of a die—the ripe and lovely lips of the tender, trembling mouth were parted as if calling to me by some old fond name, the eyes suffused through all their depth with the light we cast before us, the sweet, gray eyes, like those of the deserted German girl, shone up at me like two great tears. Ah! how many times before had they gazed into mine with long and lovely looks—and now for the last time—had I returned their gaze with all the protestations of passion—and standing here to bray them into nothingness—oh, all the meetings and the partings of days that could dawn no more—the dear embraces of those arms never to be felt again, the warm, full kisses of the meeting mouth—and I myself blotting all out! To save me the vexing sting of a gadfly I was crashing down on the best-beloved thing of the world with all the mighty revolutions of my ponderous, red-hot iron, with dropping coals and the blasting breath of steam, with all the murderous purpose of this jumping, plunging fiend that I alone controlled, with a shrouding, deafening fury that to the waiting victim drowned the universe in its roar.

All these horrors came one by one before my mind, and dropped into my resolve like grains into the weighing-scale. I suffered agony. My knees were shaking under me. I doubt if I could have lifted my hand—I did not try; it hung nerveless by my side; the life was dying out of me. I only stared through my window, along the track, at the woman's face with the fright hardening into it, the blank terror there, death thundering down in the fierce wild throes of sundering socket and mangling flesh, that in one instant would have their hellish grip on every live nerve and spurting vein. Then my ears were ringing with shrieks—I fancied that even through the hot roar and reverberation of our flight I heard the rest. When would the last car be over, the last wheel turned? was that swift hiss the severing of a tress upon the rail?

It was passed. We rolled into Brookford station; George Rowe's hand had slipped before me and slowed the Black Bess to her usual point. We stopped. Then the blood bounded back to my heart, to my throat, to my face, the strength of an army to my single hand.

I seized Dr. Blanchard by the shoulder as if he had been made of cardboard. "Come back with me!" I hoarsely yelled. "If we find nothing, I am well once more—but if it is as I am sure it is, then you are dead!"

And, regardless of my train, swinging my lantern to this side and to that, I rushed back with him to the spot where the highway crossed the track, and where I swore some torn, crushed thing might lie. Never, never had I been so sure—and there—yes, yes—sob and strangle, you fool!—oh, God! oh God!—it was Margaret!

Four whitewashed walls, and a clank of chains, and a fair devil going and coming about me, and night and day and night speeding by in whirling flame.

And still the phantom face, fixed on the wall, on the trencher, on the floor, if I climb to my grated window, a seal and blotch on all the wide blue heaven! And then it grows into reality, and hides itself in flesh, it lays a cool hand on my burning brow, it puts water to my parching lip, it sings me songs which, somewhere, I fancy, that once long ago I have heard; and it smiles till it almost seems that I have seen and felt the same smile with thrills of deep, delightful joy in a life ere this. And then it sighs, a tear gathers; I grow enraged at all the lovely counterfeit; I spring upon it, and would beat it down bodily, when the fixed gray eyes arrest my arm—eyes like two tears—and after that I hear whenever I move the clanking of the chain.

One day a thundergust has swept across the sky. I have watched its purple masses fold and lap and let their fire down to earth, and, as if I were myself metallic, have felt the electric current coursing down the countless rods that protect my prison-house. A curious sensation has come over me, as if the blood had turned about and were running the right way in my veins, I am conscious of its fresh, free tingling, as if I were just made.

I look at the lovely fiend sitting there beside me, so unmoved by the wild commotion of the elements; I mind the spray of tea-roses in her hair, falling over one ear, and lending their tint to all the delicate skin below. "Let me see you, fair devil, if you are shadow or substance!" I exclaim. "You pursuing phantom, if you are not all an evil spirit, let me see if there is any blood in your veins!"

The tint upon her skin grows paler, but she smiles on me, and lifts the sleeve from the bare ivory of her rounded arm. She takes from some hidden place a tiny toy-knife, and gives it me.

Then she looks up at me again with her beautiful, fearless eyes. I do not hesitate for all they say. I scan the fair, faint veinery—I choose—and the red, red blood is trickling down, and all the tint upon her cheeks is gone, and she falls forward upon my breast. "Margaret!" I cry.

"He speaks my name," she murmurs, as one enters. "Oh! all is well!"

And all is well, indeed. From that hour I am myself. The old trouble arising from the concussion that I so long ago experienced is entirely done away with, the ghost that so long stalked through the chambers of my brain is laid to rest, and never have I seen a trace of it; but Margaret, long since recovered from her injury—Margaret herself, in the beautiful body of her flesh and blood, is seldom out of my sight.

When I came from my whitewashed prison-room, Dr. Blanchard himself took me in hand, had me at his own house till strong enough again to fight my way, and then established me in a different occupation from that in which he originally found me. I ventured out from that, in time, into deeper water. I have prospered, as you know—improved myself, as you may imagine; my house, my retinue, my equipage are worthy of my wife—for the mother of many children is more beautiful in her maturity than in her maidenhood, and if any material comfort, pride, or pleasure, can atone to her for all the trouble of her youth, the earth shall be ransacked but it shall be hers!

HER STORY

WELLNIGH the worst of it all is the mystery.

If it were true, that accounts for my being here. If it were not true, then the best thing they could do with me was to bring me here. Then, too, if it were true, they would save themselves by hurrying me away; and if it were not true— You see, just as all roads lead to Rome, all roads led me to this Retreat. If it were true, it was enough to craze me; and if it were not true, I was already crazed. And there it is! I can't make out, sometimes, whether I am really beside myself or not; for it seems that whether I was crazed or sane, if it were true, they would naturally put me out of sight and hearing—bury me alive, as they have done, in this Retreat. They? Well, no—he. She stayed at home, I hear. If she had come with us, doubtless I should have found reason enough to say to the physician at once that she was the mad woman, not I—she, who, for the sake of her own brief pleasure, could make a whole after-life of misery for three of us. She— Oh no, don't rise, don't go. I am quite myself, I am perfectly calm. Mad! There was never a drop of crazy blood in the Ridgleys or the Bruces, or any of the generations behind them, and why should it suddenly break out like a smothered fire in me? That is one of the things that puzzle me—why should it come to light all at once in me if it were not true?

Now, I am not going to be incoherent. It was too kind in you to be at such trouble to come and see me in this prison, this grave. I will not cry out once: I will just tell you the story of it all exactly as it was, and you shall judge. If I can, that is—oh, if I can! For sometimes, when I think of it, it seems as if Heaven itself would fail to take my part if I did not lift my own voice. And I cry, and I tear my hair and my flesh, till I know my anguish weighs down their joy, and the little scale that holds that joy flies up under the scorching of the sun, and God sees the festering thing for what it is! Ah, it is not injured reason that cries out in that way: it is a breaking heart!

How cool your hand is, how pleasant your face is, how good it is to see you! Don't be afraid of me: I am as much myself, I tell you, as you are. What an absurdity! Certainly any one who heard me make such a speech would think I was insane and without benefit of clergy. To ask you not to be afraid of me because I am myself. Isn't it what they call a vicious circle? And then to cap the climax by adding that I am as much myself as you are myself! But no matter—you know better. Did you say it was ten years? Yes, I knew it was as much as that—oh, it seems a hundred years! But we hardly show it: your hair is still the same as when we were at school; and mine— Look at this lock— I cannot understand why it is only sprinkled here and there: it ought to be white as the driven snow. My babies are almost grown women, Elizabeth. How could he do without me all this time? Hush now! I am not going to be disturbed at all; only that color of your hair puts me so in mind of his: perhaps there was just one trifle more of gold in his. Do you remember that lock that used to fall over his forehead and which he always tossed back so impatiently. I used to think that the golden Apollo of Rhodes had just such massive, splendid locks of hair as that; but I never told him; I never had the face to praise him; she had. She could exclaim how like ivory the forehead was—that great wide forehead—how that keen aquiline was to be found in the portrait of the Spencer of two hundred years ago. She could tell of the proud lip, of the fire burning in the hazel eye. She knew how, by a silent flattery, as she shrank away and looked up at him, to admire his haughty stature, and make him feel the strength and glory of his manhood and the delicacy of her womanhood.

She was a little thing—a little thing, but wondrous fair. Fair, did I say? No: she was dark as an Egyptian, but such perfect features, such rich and splendid color, such great soft eyes—so soft, so black—so superb a smile; and then such hair! When she let it down, the backward curling ends lay on the ground and she stood on them, or the children lifted them and carried them behind her as pages carry a queen's train. If I had my two hands twisted in that hair! Oh, how I hate that hair! It would make as good a bowstring as ever any Carthaginian woman's made.

Ah, that is atrocious! I am sure you think so. But living all these lonesome years as I have done seems to double back one's sinfulness upon one's self. Because one is sane it does not follow that one is a saint. And when I think of my innocent babies playing with the hair that once I saw him lift and pass across his lips! But I will not think of it!

Well, well! I was a pleasant thing to look at myself once on a time, you know, Elizabeth. He used to tell me so: those were his very words. I was tall and slender, and if my skin was pale it was clear with a pearly clearness, and the lashes of my gray eyes were black as shadows; but now those eyes are only the color of tears.

I never told a syllable about it—I never could. It was so deep down in my heart, that love I had for him: it slept there so dark and still and full, for he was all I had in the world. I was alone, an orphan—if not friendless, yet quite dependent. I see you remember it all. I did not even sit in the pew with my cousin's family,—there were so many to fill it,—but down in one beneath the gallery, you know. And altogether life was a thing to me that hardly seemed worth the living. I went to church one Sunday, I recollect, idly and dreamingly as usual. I did not look off my book till a voice filled my ear—a strange new voice, a deep sweet voice, that invited you and yet commanded you—a voice whose sound divided the core of my heart, and sent thrills that were half joy, half pain, coursing through me. And then I looked up and saw him at the desk. He was reading the first lesson: "Fear not, for I have redeemed thee, I have called thee by thy name: thou art mine." And I saw the bright hair, the bright upturned face, the white surplice, and I said to myself, It is a vision, it is an angel; and I cast down my eyes. But the voice went on, and when I looked again he was still there. Then I bethought me that it must be the one who was coming to take the place of our superannuated rector—the last of a fine line, they had been saying the day before, who, instead of finding his pleasure otherwise, had taken all his wealth and prestige into the Church.

Why will a trifle melt you so—a strain of music, a color in the sky, a perfume? Have you never leaned from the window at evening, and had the scent of a flower float by and fill you with as keen a sorrow as if it had been disaster touching you? Long ago, I mean—we never lean from any windows here. I don't know how, but it was in that same invisible way that this voice melted me; and when I heard it saying, "Behold, I will do a new thing; now it shall spring forth; shall ye not know it? I will even make a way in the wilderness, and rivers in the desert," I was fairly crying. Oh, nervous tears, I dare say. The doctor here would tell you so, at any rate. And that is what I complain of here: they give a physiological reason for every emotion—they could give you a chemical formula for your very soul, I have no doubt. Well, perhaps they were nervous tears, for certainly there was nothing to cry for, and the mood went as suddenly as it came—changed to a sort of exaltation, I suppose—and when they sang the psalm, and he had swept in, in his black gown, and had mounted the pulpit stairs, and was resting that fair head on the big Bible in his silent prayer, I too was singing—singing like one possessed:

> "Then, to thy courts when I repair,
>   My soul shall rise on joyful wing,
> The wonders of thy love declare,
>   And join the strain which angels sing."

And as he rose I saw him searching for the voice unconsciously, and our eyes met. Oh, it was a fresh young voice, let it be mine or whose. I can hear it now as if it were someone else singing. Ah, ah, it has been silent so many years! Does it make you smile to hear me pity myself? It is not myself I am pitying: it is that fresh young girl that loved so. But it used to rejoice me to think that I loved him before I laid eyes on him.

He came to my cousin's in the week—not to see Sylvia or to see Laura: he talked of church-music with my cousin, and then crossed the room and sat down by me. I remember how I grew cold and trembled—how glad, how shy I was; and then he had me sing; and at first Sylvia sang with us, but by and by we sang alone—I sang alone. He brought me yellow old church music, written in quaint characters: he said those characters, those old square breves, were a text guarding secrets of enchantment as much as the text of Merlin's book did; and so we used to find it. Once he brought a copy of an old Roman hymn, written only in the Roman letters: he said it was a hymn which the ancients sang to Maia, the mother-earth, and which the Church fathers adopted, singing it stealthily in the hidden places of the Catacombs; and together we translated it into tones. A rude but majestic thing it was.

And once— The sunshine was falling all about us in the bright lonely room, and the shadows of the rose leaves at the window were dancing over us. I had been singing a Gloria while he walked up and down the room, and he came up behind me: he stooped and kissed me on the mouth. And after that there was no more singing, for, lovely as the singing was, the love was lovelier yet. Why do I complain of such a hell as this is now? I had my heaven once—oh, I had my heaven once! And as for the other, perhaps I deserve it all, for I saw God only through him: it was he that waked me to worship. I had no faith but Spencer's faith; if he had been a heathen, I should have been the same, and creeds and systems might have perished for me had he only been spared from the wreck. And he had loved me from the first moment that his eyes met mine. "When I looked at you," he said, "singing that simple hymn that first day, I felt as I do when I look at the evening star leaning out of the clear sunset lustre: there is something in your face as pure, as remote, as shining. It will always be there," he said, "though you should live a hundred years." He little knew, he little knew!

But he loved me then—oh yes, I never doubted that. There were no happier lovers trod the earth. We took our pleasure as lovers do: we walked in the fields; we sat on the river's side; together we visited the poor and sick; he read me the passages he liked best in his writing from week to week; he brought me the verse from which he meant to preach, and up in the organ-loft I improvised to him the thoughts that it inspired in me. I did that timidly indeed: I could not think my thoughts were worth his hearing till I forgot myself, and only thought of him and the glory I would have revealed to him, and then the great clustering chords and the full music of the diapason swept out beneath my hands—swept along the aisles and swelled up the raftered roof as if they would find the stars, and sunset and twilight stole around us there as we sat still in the succeeding silence. I was happy: I was humble too. I wondered why I had been chosen for such a blest and sacred lot. It was so blessed to be allowed to minister one delight to him. I had a little print of the angel of the Lord appearing to Mary with the lily of annunciation in his hand, and I thought— I dare not tell you what I thought. I made an idol of my piece of clay.

When the leaves had turned we were married, and he took me home.
Ah, what a happy home it was! Luxury and beauty filled it. When I first
went into it and left the chill October night without, fires blazed upon the
hearths; flowers bloomed in every room; a marble Eros held a light up,
searching for his Psyche. "*Our* love has found its soul," said he. He led me
to the music-room—a temple in itself, for its rounded ceiling towered to
the height of the house. There were golden organ-pipes and banks of keys
fit for St. Cecilia's use; [1] there were all the delightful outlines of violin and
piccolo and harp and horn for any who would use them; there was a
pianoforte near the door for me—one such as I had never touched before;
and there were cases on all sides filled with the rarest musical works. The
floor was bare and inlaid; the windows were latticed in stained glass, so
that no common light of day ever filtered through, but light bluer than the
sky, gold as the dawn, purple as the night; and then there were vast em-
bowering chairs, in any of which he could hide himself away while I made
my incantation, as he sometimes called it, of the great spirits of song. As I
tried the piano that night he tuned the old Amati [2] which he himself now
and then played upon, and together we improvised our own epithalamium.
It was the violin that took the strong assuring part with strains of piercing
sweetness, and the music of the piano flowed along in a soft cantabile of
undersong. It seemed to me as if his part was like the flight of some white
and strong-winged bird above a sunny brook.

But he had hardly created this place for the love of me alone. He
adored music as a regenerator; he meant to use it so among his people: here
were to be pursued those labors which should work miracles when
produced in the open church. For he was building a church with the half of
his fortune—a church full of restoration of the old and creation of the
new: the walls within were to be a frosty tracery of vines running to break
into the gigantic passion-flower that formed the rose-window; the lectern
a golden globe upon a tripod, clasped by a silver dove holding on outstretched wings the book.

I have feared, since I have been here, that Spencer's piety was less
piety than partisanship: I have doubted if faith were so much alive in him as
the love of a great perfect system, and the pride in it I know he always felt.
But I never thought about it then: I believed in him as I would have

believed in an apostle. So stone by stone the church went up, and stone by stone our lives followed it—lives of such peace, such bliss! Then fresh hopes came into it—sweet trembling hopes; and by and by our first child was born. And if I had been happy before, what was I then? There are some compensations in this world: such happiness could not come twice, such happiness as there was in that moment when I lay, painless and at peace, with the little cheek nestled beside my own, while he bent above us both, proud and glad and tender. It was a dear little baby—so fair, so bright! and when she could walk she could sing. Her sister sang earlier yet; and what music their two shrill sweet voices made as they sat in their little chairs together at twilight before the fire, their curls glistening and their red shoes glistening, while they sang the evening hymn, Spencer on one side of the hearth and I upon the other! Sometimes we let the dear things sit up for a later hour in the music-room—for many a canticle we tried and practised there that hushed hearts and awed them when the choir gave them on succeeding Sundays—and always afterward I heard them singing in their sleep, just as a bird stirs in his nest and sings his stave in the night. Oh, we were happy then; and it was then she came.

She was the step-child of his uncle, and had a small fortune of her own, and Spencer had been left her guardian; and so she was to live with us—at any rate, for a while. I dreaded her coming. I did not want the intrusion; I did not like the things I heard about her; I knew she would be a discord in our harmony. But Spencer, who had only seen her once in her childhood, had been told by some one who travelled in Europe with her that she was delightful and had a rare intelligence. She was one of those women often delightful to men indeed, but whom other women—by virtue of their own kindred instincts, it may be, perhaps by virtue of temptations overcome—see through and know for what they are. But she had her own way of charming: she was the being of infinite variety— to-day glad, to-morrow sad, freakish, and always exciting you by curiosity as to her next caprice, and so moody that after a season of the lowering weather of one of her dull humors you were ready to sacrifice something for the sake of the sunshine that she knew how to make so vivid and so sweet. Then, too, she brought forward her forces by detachment. At first she was the soul of domestic life, sitting at night beneath the light and embossing on weblike muslin designs of flower and leaf which she had learned in her convent, listening to Spencer as he read, and taking from the little wallet of her work-basket apropos scraps which she had preserved from the sermon of some Italian father of the Church or of some French divine. As for me, the only thing I knew was my poor music; and I used to burn with indignation when she interposed that unknown tongue between my husband and myself. Presently her horses came, and then, graceful in her dark riding-habit, she would spend a morning fearlessly subduing one of the fiery fellows, and dash away at last with plume and veil streaming behind her. In the early evening she would dance with the children— witch-dances they were—with her round arms linked above her head, and her feet weaving the measure in and out as deftly as any flashing-footed Bayadere[3] might do—only when Spencer was there to see: at other times I saw she pushed the little hindering things aside without a glance.

By and by she began to display a strange dramatic sort of power: she would rehearse to Spencer scenes that she had met with from day to day in the place, giving now the old churchwarden's voice and now the sexton's, their gestures and very faces; she could tell the ailments of half the old women in the parish who came to me with them, and in their own tone and manner to the life; she told us once of a streetscene, with the crier crying a lost child, the mother following with lamentations, the passing strangers questioning, the boys hooting, and the child's reappearance, followed by a tumult, with kisses and blows and cries, so that I thought I saw it all; and presently she had found the secret and vulnerable spot of every friend we had, and could personate them all as vividly as if she did it by necromancy.

One night she began to sketch our portraits in charcoal: the likenesses were not perfect; she exaggerated the careless elegance of Spencer's attitude; perhaps the primness of my own. But yet he saw there the ungraceful trait for the first time, I think. And so much led to more: she brought out her portfolios, and there were her pencil-sketches from the Rhine and from the Guadalquivir, rich water-colors of Venetian scenes, interiors of old churches, and sheet after sheet covered with details of church architecture. Spencer had been admiring all the others—in spite of something that I thought I saw in them, a something that was not true, a trait of her own identity, for I had come to criticise her sharply—but when his eye rested on those sheets I saw it sparkle, and he caught them up and pored over them one by one.

"I see you have mastered the whole thing," he said: "you must instruct me here." And so she did. And there were hours, while I was busied with servants and accounts or with the children, when she was closeted with Spencer in the study, criticising, comparing, making drawings, hunting up authorities; other hours when they walked away together to the site of the new church that was building, and here an arch was destroyed, and there an aisle was extended, and here a row of cloisters sketched into the plan, and there a row of windows, till the whole design was reversed and made over. And they had the thing between them, for, admire and sympathize as I might, I did not know. At first Spencer would repeat the day's achievement to me, but the contempt for my ignorance which she did not deign to hide soon put an end to it when she was present.

It was this interest that now unveiled a new phase of her character: she was devout. She had a little altar in her room; she knew all about albs and chasubles; she would have persuaded Spencer to burn candles in the chancel; she talked of a hundred mysteries and symbols; she wanted to embroider a stole to lay across his shoulders. She was full of small church sentimentalities, and as one after another she uttered them, it seemed to me that her belief was no sound fruit of any system—if it were belief, and not a mere bunch of fancies—but only, as you might say, a rotten windfall of the Romish Church: it had none of the round splendor of that Church's creed, none of the pure simplicity of ours: it would be no stay in trouble, no shield in temptation. I said as much to Spencer.

"You are prejudiced," said he: "her belief is the result of long observation abroad, I think. She has found the need of outward observances: they are, she has told me, a shrine to the body of her faith, like that commanded in the building of the tabernacle, where the ark of the covenant was enclosed in the holy of holies."

"And you didn't think it profane in her to speak so? But I don't believe it, Spencer," I said. "She has no faith: she has some sentimentalisms."

"You are prejudiced," he repeated. "She seems to me a wonderful and gifted being."

"Too gifted," I said. "Her very gifts are unnatural in their abundance. There must be scrofula there to keep such a fire in the blood and sting the brain to such action: she will die in a madhouse, depend upon it." Think of my saying such a thing as that!

"I have never heard you speak so before," he replied coldly. "I hope you do not envy her her powers."

"I envy her nothing," I cried. "For she is as false as she is beautiful!" But I did—oh I did!

"Beautiful?" said Spencer. "Is she beautiful? I never thought of that."

"You are very blind, then," I said with a glad smile.

Spencer smiled too. "It is not the kind of beauty I admire," said he.

"Then I must teach you, sir," said she. And we both started to see her in the doorway, and I, for one, did not know, till shortly before I found myself here, how much or how little she had learned of what we said.

"Then I must teach you, sir," said she again. And she came deliberately into the firelight and paused upon the rug, drew out the silver arrows and shook down all her hair about her, till the great snake-like coils unrolled upon the floor.

"Hyacinthine," said Spencer.

"Indeed it is," said she. "The very color of the jacinth, with that red tint in its darkness that they call black in the shade and gold in the sun. Now look at me."

"Shut your eyes, Spencer," I cried, and laughed.

But he did not shut his eyes. The firelight flashed over her: the color in her cheeks and on her lips sprang ripe and red in it as she held the hair away from them with her rosy finger-tips; her throat curved small and cream-white from the bosom that the lace of her dinner-dress scarcely hid; and the dark eyes glowed with a great light as they lay full on his.

"You mustn't call it vanity," said she. "It is only that it is impossible, looking at the picture in the glass, not to see it as I see any other picture. But for all that, I know it is not every fool's beauty: it is no daub for the vulgar gaze, but a masterpiece that it needs the educated eye to find. I could tell you how this nostril is like that in a famous marble, how the curve of this cheek is that of a certain Venus, the line of this forehead like the line in the dreamy Antinous'[4] forehead. Are you taught? Is it—?"

157

Then she twisted her hair again and fastened the arrows, and laughed and turned away to look over the evening paper. But as for Spencer, as he lay back in his lordly way, surveying the vision from crown to toe, I saw him flush—I saw him flush and start and quiver, and then he closed his eyes and pressed his fingers on them, and lay back again and said not a word.

She began to read aloud something concerning services at the recent dedication of a church. I was called out as she read. When I came back, a half hour afterward, they were talking. I stopped at my worktable in the next room for a skein of floss that she had asked me for, and I heard her saying, "You cannot expect me to treat you with reverence. You are a married priest, and you know what opinion I necessarily must have of married priests." Then I came in and she was silent.

But I knew, I always knew, that if Spencer had not felt himself weak, had not found himself stirred, if he had not recognized that, when he flushed and quivered before her charm, it was the flesh and not the spirit that tempted him, he would not have listened to her subtle invitation to austerity. As it was, he did. He did—partly in shame, partly in punishment; but to my mind the listening was confusion. She had set the wedge that was to sever our union—the little seed in a mere idle cleft that grows and grows and splits the rock asunder.

Well, I had my duties, you know. I never felt my husband's wealth a reason why I should neglect them any more than another wife should neglect her duties. I was wanted in the parish, sent for here and waited for there: the dying liked to see me comfort their living, the living liked to see me touch their dead; some wanted help, and others wanted consolation; and where I felt myself too young and unlearned to give advice, I could at least give sympathy. Perhaps I was the more called upon for such detail of duty because Spencer was busy with the greater things, the church-building and the sermons—sermons that once on a time lifted you and held you on their strong wings. But of late Spencer had been preaching old sermons. He had been moody and morose too: sometimes he seemed oppressed with melancholy. He had spoken to me strangely, had looked at me as if he pitied me, had kept away from me. But she had not regarded his moods: she had followed him in his solitary strolls, had sought him in his study; and she had ever a mystery or symbol to be interpreted, the picture of a private chapel that she had heard of when abroad, or the ground-plan of an ancient one, or some new temptation to his ambition, as I divine. And soon he was himself again.

I was wrong to leave him so to her, but what was there else for me to do? And as for those duties of mine, as I followed them I grew restive; I abridged them, I hastened home. I was impatient even with the detentions the children caused. I could not leave them to their nurses, for all that; but they kept me away from him, and he was alone with her.

One day at last he told me that his mind was troubled by the suspicion that his marriage was a mistake; that on his part at least it had been wrong; that he had been thinking a priest should have the Church only for his bride, and should wait at the altar mortified in every affection; that it was not for hands that were full of caresses and lips that were covered with kisses to touch the sacrament, to offer praise. But for answer I brought my children and put them in his arms. I was white and cold and shaking, but I asked him if they were not justification enough. And I told him that he did his duty better abroad for the heartening of a wife at home, and that he knew better how to interpret God's love to men through his own love for his children. And I laid my head on his breast beside them, and he clasped us all and we cried together, he and I.

But that was not enough, I found. And when our good bishop came, who had always been like a father to Spencer, I led the conversation to that point one evening, and he discovered Spencer's trouble, and took him away and reasoned with him. The bishop was a power with Spencer, and I think that was the end of it.

The end of that, but only the beginning of the rest. For she had accustomed him to the idea of separation from me—the idea of doing without me. He had put me away from himself once in his mind: we had been one soul, and now we were two.

One day, as I stood in my sleeping-room with the door ajar, she came in. She had never been there before, and I cannot tell you how insolently she looked about her. There was a bunch of flowers on a stand that Spencer himself placed there for me every morning. He had always done so, and there had been no reason for breaking off the habit; and I had always worn one of them at my throat. She advanced a hand to pull out a blossom. "Do not touch them," I cried: "my husband puts them there."

"Suppose he does," said she lightly. "For how long?" Then she over-looked me with a long sweeping glance of search and contempt, shrugged her shoulders, and with a French sentence that I did not understand turned back and coolly broke off the blossom she had marked and hung it in her hair. I could not take her by the shoulders and put her from the room. I could not touch the flowers that she had desecrated. I left the room myself, and left her in it, and went down to dinner for the first time without the flower at my throat. I saw Spencer's eye note the omission: perhaps he took it as a release from me, for he never put the flowers in my room again after that day.

Nor did he ask me any more into his study, as he had been used, or read his sermons to me. There was no need of his talking over the church-building with me—he had her to talk it over with. And as for our music, that had been a rare thing since she arrived, for her conversation had been such as to leave but little time for it, and somehow when she came into the music-room and began to dictate to me the time in which I should take an Inflammatus and the spirit in which I should sing a ballad, I could not bear it. Then, too, to tell you the truth, my voice was hoarse and choked with tears full half the time.

It was some weeks after the flowers ceased that our youngest child fell ill. She was very ill—I don't think Spencer knew how ill. I dared not trust her with any one, and Spencer said no one could take such care of her as her mother could; so, although we had nurses in plenty, I hardly left the room by night or day. I heard their voices down below, I saw them go out for their walks. It was a hard fight, but I saved her.

But I was worn to a shadow when all was done—worn with anxiety for her, with alternate fevers of hope and fear, with the weight of my responsibility as to her life; and with anxiety for Spencer too, with a despairing sense that the end of peace had come, and with the total sleep-lessness of many nights. Now, when the child was mending and gaining every day, I could not sleep if I would.

The doctor gave me anodynes, but to no purpose: they only nerved me wide awake. My eyes aches, and my brain ached, and my body ached, but it was of no use: I could not sleep. I counted the spots on the wall, the motes upon my eyes, the notes of all the sheets of music I could recall. I remembered the Eastern punishment of keeping the condemned awake till they die, and wondered what my crime was; I thought if I could but sleep I might forget my trouble, or take it up freshly and master it. But no, it was always there—a heavy cloud, a horror of foreboding. As I heard that woman's step go by the door I longed to rid the house of it, and I dinted my palms with my nails till she had passed.

I did not know what to do. It seemed to me that I was wicked in letting the thing go on, in suffering Spencer to be any longer exposed to her power; but then I feared to take a step lest I should thereby rivet the chains she was casting on him. And then I longed so for one hour of the old dear happiness—the days when I and the children had been all and enough. I did not know what to do; I had no one to counsel with; I was wild within myself, and all distraught. Once I thought if I could not rid the house of her I could rid it of myself; and as I went through a dark passage and chanced to look up where a bright-headed nail glittered, I questioned if it would bear my weight. For days the idea haunted me. I fancied that when I was gone perhaps he would love me again, and at any rate I might be asleep and at rest. But the thought of the children prevented me, and one other thought—I was not certain that even my sorrows would excuse me before God.

I went down to dinner again at last. How she glowed and abounded in her beauty as she sat there! And I—I must have been very thin and ghastly: perhaps I looked a little wild in all my bewilderment and hurt. His heart smote him, it may be, for he came round to where I sat by the fire afterward and smoothed my hair and kissed my forehead. He could not tell all I was suffering then—all I was struggling with; for I thought I had better put him out of the world than let him, who was once so pure and good, stay in it to sin. I could have done it, you know. For though I still lay with the little girl, I could have stolen back into our own room with the chloroform, and he would never have known. I turned the handle of the door one night, but the bolt was slipped. I never thought of killing her, you see: let her live and sin, if she would. She was the thing of slime and sin, a splendid tropical growth of the passionate heat and the slime: it was only her nature. But then we think it no harm to kill reptiles, however splendid.

But it was by that time that the voices had begun to talk with me— all night long, all day. It was they, I found, that had kept me so sleepless. Go where I might, they were ever before me. If I went to the woods, I heard them in the whisper of every pine tree. If I went down to the seashore, I heard them in the plash of every wave. I heard them in the wind, in the singing of my ears, in the children's breath as I hung above them,—for I had decided that if I went out of the world I would take the children with me. If I sat down to play, the things would twist the chords into discords; if I sat down to read, they would come between me and the page.

Then I could see the creatures: they had wings like bats. I did not dare speak of them, although I fancied she suspected me, for once she said, as I was kissing my little girl, "When you are gone to a madhouse, don't think they'll have many such kisses." Did she say it? or did I think she said it? I did not answer her, I did not look up: I suppose I should have flown at her throat if I had.

I took the children out with me on my rambles: we went for miles; sometimes I carried one, sometimes the other. I took such long, long walks to escape those noisome things: they would never leave me till I was quite tired out. Now and then I was gone the whole day; and all the time that I was gone he was with her, I knew, and she was tricking out her beauty and practising her arts.

I went to a little festival with them, for Spencer insisted. And she made shadow-pictures on the wall, wonderful things with her perfect profile and her perfect arms and her subtle curves—she out of sight, the shadow only seen. Now it was Isis, I remember, and now it was the head and shoulders and trailing hair of a floating sea-nymph. And then there were charades in which she played; and I can't tell you the glorious thing she looked when she came on as Helen of Troy with all her "beauty shadowed in white veils," you know—that brown and red beauty with its smiles and radiance under the wavering of the flower-wrought veil. I sat by Spencer, and I felt him shiver. He was fighting and struggling too within himself, very likely; only he knew that he was going to yield after all—only he longed to yield while he feared. But as for me, I saw one of those bat-like things perched on her ear as she stood before us, and when she opened her mouth to speak I saw them flying in and out. And I said to Spencer, "She is tormenting me. I cannot stay and see her swallowing the souls of men in this way." And I would have gone, but he held me down fast in my seat. But if I was crazy then—as they say I was, I suppose—it was only with a metaphor, for she was sucking Spencer's soul out of his body.

But I was not crazy. I should admit I might have been if I alone had seen those evil spirits. But Spencer saw them too. He never told me so, but—there are subtle ways—I knew he did; for when I opened the church door late, as I often did at that time after my long walks, they would rush in past me with a whizz, and as I sat in the pew I would see him steadily avoid looking at me; and if he looked by any chance, he would turn so pale that I have thought he would drop where he stood; and he would redden afterward as though one had struck him. He knew then what I endured with them; but I was not the one to speak of it. Don't tell me that his color changed and he shuddered so because I sat there mumbling and nodding to myself. It was because he saw those things mopping and mowing beside me and whispering in my ear. Oh what loathsomeness the obscene creatures whispered! Foul quips and evil words I have never heard before, ribald songs and oaths; and I would clap my hands over my mouth to keep from crying out at them. Creatures of the imagination, you may say. It is possible. But they were so vivid that they seem real to me even now. I burn and tingle as I recall them. And how could I have imagined such sounds, such shapes, of things I had never heard or seen or dreamed?

And Spencer was very unhappy, I am sure. I was the mother of his children, and if he loved me no more, he had an old kindness for me still, and my distress distressed him. But for all that the glamour was on him, and he could not give up that woman and her beauty and her charm. Once or twice he may have thought about sending her away, but perhaps he could not bring himself to do it—perhaps he reflected it was too late, and now it was no matter. But every day she stayed he was the more like wax in her hands. Oh, he was weaker than water that is poured out. He was abandoning himself, and forgetting earth and heaven and hell itself, before a passion—a passion that soon would cloy, and then would sting.

It was the spring season: I had been out several hours. The sunset fell while I was in the wood, and the stars came out; and at one time I thought I would lie down there on last year's leaves and never get up again. But I remembered the children, and went home to them. They were in bed and asleep when I took off my shoes and opened the door of their room— breathing so sweetly and evenly, the little yellow heads close together on one pillow, their hands tossed about the coverlid, their parted lips, their rosy cheeks. I knelt to feel the warm breath on my own cold cheek, and then the voices began whispering again: "If only they never waked! they never waked!"

And all I could do was to spring to my feet and run from the room. I ran shoeless down the great staircase and through the long hall. I thought I would go to Spencer and tell him all—all my sorrows, all the suggestions of the voices, and maybe in the endeavor to save me he would save himself. And I ran down the long dimly-lighted drawing-room, led by the sound I heard, to the music-room, whose doors were open just beyond. It was lighted only by the pale glimmer from the other room and by the moon-light through the painted panes. And I paused to listen to what I had never listened to there—the sound of the harp and a voice with it. Of course they had not heard me coming, and I hesitated and looked, and then I glided within the door and stood just by the open piano there.

She sat at the harp singing—the huge gilded harp. I did not know she sang—she had kept that for her last reserve—but she struck the harp so that it sang itself, like some great prisoned soul, and her voice followed it—oh so rich a voice! My own was white and thin, I felt, beside it. But mine had soared, and hers still clung to earth—a contralto sweet with honeyed sweetness—the sweetness of unstrained honey that has the earth-taste and the heavy blossom-dust yet in it—sweet, though it grew hoarse and trembling with passion. He sat in one of the great arm-chairs just before her: he was white with feeling, with rapture, with forgetfulness; his eyes shone like stars. He moved restlessly, a strange smile kindled all his face: he bent toward her, and the music broke off in the middle as they threw their arms around each other, and hung there lip to lip and heart to heart. And suddenly I crashed down both my hands on the keyboard before me, and stood and glared upon them.

And I never knew anything more till I woke up here.

And that is the whole of it. That is the puzzle of it—was it a horrid nightmare, an insane vision, or was it true? Was it true that I saw Spencer, my white, clean lover, my husband, a man of God, the father of our spotless babies,—was it true that I saw him so, or was it only some wild, vile conjuration of disease? Oh, I would be willing to have been crazed a lifetime, a whole lifetime, only to wake one moment before I died and find that that had never been!

Well, well, well! When time passed and I became more quiet, I told the doctor here about the voices—I never told him of Spencer or of her— and he bade me dismiss care. He said I was ill—excitement and sleep- lessness had surcharged my nerves with that strange magnetic fluid that has worked so much mischief in the world. There was no organic disease, you see; only when my nerves were rested and right, my brain would be right. And the doctor gave me medicines and books and work, and when I saw the bat-like things again I was to go instantly to him. And after a little while I was not sure that I did see them. And in a little while longer they had ceased to come altogether. And I have had no more of them. I was on my parole then in the parlor, at the table, in the grounds. I felt that I was cured of whatever had ailed me: I could escape at any moment that I wished.

And it came Christmas time. A terrible longing for home overcame me—for my children. I thought of them at this time when I had been used to take such pains for their pleasure. I thought of the little empty stock- ings, the sad faces; I fancied I could hear them crying for me. I forgot all about my word of honor. It seemed to me that I should die, that I might as well die, if I could not see my little darlings, and hold them on my knees, and sing to them while the chimes were ringing in the Christmas Eve. And winter was here and there was so much to do for them. And I walked down the garden, and looked out at the gate, and opened it and went through. And I slept that night in a barn—so free, so free and glad! And the next day an old farmer and his sons, who thought they did me a service, brought me back, and of course I shrieked and raved. And so would you.

But since then I have been in this ward and a prisoner. I have my work, my amusement. I send such little things as I can make to my girls. I read. Sometimes of late I sing in the Sunday service. The place is a sightly place; the grounds, when we are taken out, are fine; the halls are spacious and pleasant.

Pleasant—but ah, when you have trodden them ten years!

And so, you see, if I were a clod, if I had no memory, no desires, if I had never been happy before, I might be happy now. I am confident the doctor thinks me well. But he has no orders to let me go. Sometimes it is so wearisome. And it might be worse if lately I had not been allowed a new service. And that is to try to make a woman smile who came here a year ago. She is a little woman, swarthy as a Malay, but her hair, that grows as rapidly as a fungus grows in the night, is whiter than leprosy: her eyebrows are so long and white that they veil and blanch her dark dim eyes; and she has no front teeth. A stone from a falling spire struck her from her horse, they say. The blow battered her and beat out reason and beauty. Her mind is dead: she remembers nothing, knows nothing; but she follows me about like a dog: she seems to want to do something for me, to propitiate me. All she ever says is to beg me to do her no harm. She will not go to sleep without my hand in hers. Sometimes, after long effort, I think there is a gleam of intelligence, but the doctor says there was once too much intelligence, and her case is hopeless.

Hopeless, poor thing!—that is an awful word: I could not wish it said for my worst enemy.

In spite of these ten years I cannot feel that it has yet been said for me.

If I am strange just now, it is only the excitement of seeing you, only the habit of the strange sights and sounds here. I should be calm and well enough at home. I sit and picture to myself that some time Spencer will come for me—will take me to my girls, my fireside, my music. I shall hear his voice, I shall rest in his arms, I shall be blest again. For, oh, Elizabeth, I do forgive him all!

Or if he will not dare to trust himself at first, I picture to myself how he will send another—some old friend who knew me before my trouble—who will see me and judge, and carry back report that I am all I used to be—some friend who will open the gates of heaven to me, or close the gates of hell upon me—who will hold my life and my fate.

If—oh if it should be you, Elizabeth!

MISS SUSAN'S LOVE AFFAIR

✯✯✯✯✯

SHE always impressed you as a person with a history. Though she was now a maiden woman of no doubtful age, having reached that age, indeed, that turns first, on opening the paper, to the record of deaths and marriages, and experiences a sort of disappointment if the name of some acquaintance is to be found in neither; rather gaunt and spiny; dependent on her cup of tea; wearing spectacles on the sly at her fine work; clothed in fashions of three or four years ago, if, indeed, they could ever have been entitled fashions at all; with hardly any hair on her head, and a great deal of goldsmith's work in her mouth; with nothing at all to say, and nothing at all about her that to the young imagination presents an attraction; yet withal there was a quiet reserve in manner, a certain contented silence, an air of satisfaction over delightful secrets, that led you to look at her with inquiry, and presently to be assured that in the course of her experience she had played her part in some drama, had been one of the figures of some romance, had, in short, *des affaires* to remember. She seemed to be remembering them, too, all the time. She sat pricking and stitching and threading her needle, with an odd smile about her lips, and now and then pausing with a far-away look in her eyes; sometimes the needle suspended, sometimes beating with its point a delicate tattoo on the pricked left finger, as if beating time to the dream of some old tune to which her young feet once had danced, with a strong young arm about her.

167

But Miss Susan's reverie seldom ended with a sigh. If she had suffered any in her past, the suffering was all over now, and in some incomprehensible way it seemed to be compensation enough for her to remember it now. When the girls were gossiping, as girls do, sitting at their various work, jesting each other lightly, as girls will, and taking the name of this youth or of that in vain, Miss Susan joined in the gayety, yet much of the resident of a superior planet, or rather, as Fred used to say, as Helen of Troy might have smiled, years after windy Ilion went down, when the slave women went on about their particular heroes, as she sat at her weaving, conscious of certain passages.

Poor Miss Susan! there were no more tender passages for her. Let her make the most of what sweetness there had been in the past. It could hardly have been so very much, from appearances. And yet Fred said Miss Susan had been rather pretty than otherwise in her day and generation; that is, she was round and fair, with a pair of soft dark eyes, and if not positively lovely, yet not at all unlovely, and comfortable in the sense that had never happened to doubt whether or not she was the peer of such other girls as were not breathing beauties.

Perhaps she was; and perhaps it was only her exceeding shyness that rendered it difficult for any one to do more than address her a few commonplace sentences. When a person reddens and stammers if you attempt conversation, and is unable to command a thought with which to reply, and seems about to have tears spring into her eyes at another word, you naturally make your communication very brief, if only for fear of the Society for the Prevention of Cruelty to Animals; and thus, if Miss Susan had charms, there was not much opportunity for any one to discover them. Certainly Clavers M'Veigh never discovered them. Yet such is fate: it was the charms of Clavers M'Veigh that had moved Miss Susan's heart and become the subject of her dreams—not vivid, passionate dreams, be it understood, but mild, illusory visions that glanced upon her and came again, and gave her an airy region into which to mount occasionally above her work-a-day world as she went up and down with her daily task—a region with which Miss Susan was quite content for a season, without troubling herself about its baseless fabric.

Miss Susan was not the only girl of that day whose heart felt a quicker pulse when Clavers M'Veigh went by. In fact, she would have been rather an exception if her heart had not felt his beautiful and magnetic presence. He was a person of superb appearance, a Saul for stature—and perhaps as much like one's ideal of the person of that picturesque monarch as it is given a modern mortal to be—heroically strong and brave by nature, the traditions of him went, and dark and clear and brilliant-eyed in face, with a great lock of his black hair always tumbling down his white forehead: yes, Clavers M'Veigh had fired more than one young imagination, and Miss Susan left the others to think of him as Saul, or as Lucifer, Star of the Morning, or as any else in that line, and thought of him herself only as the one man of the world. It brightened life for her to know there was such a person, and the sight of him lent delight to any day. She could settle herself at no work till she had seen him go down the street in the morning to his office, and she sang like a bird long after the sight, and lived during the rest of the day in the anticipation of seeing him go back at night-fall. An hour before the time she was all aflutter, peering forth and drawing back demurely, veiled by the drapery of her aunt's curtains, watching as eagerly as any girl watches for her delaying long-acknowledged lover. If he did not come, she waited till some chiding voice obliged her to drag herself, still looking back, away. If he came, her heart began to beat, her cheek to burn. She watched him pass, erect and haughty, looking straight before him. With a long, satisfied survey she gazed after him, with clasped hands and suspended breath, and she pursued her evening duties then with as light a heart as though she felt a lover's arm about her.

As for herself, Clavers M'Veigh was not exactly aware of her existence. He had met her, to be sure, here and there with others, and had often passed her on the street; but she was one of those colorless shadows just outside of his special consciousness, like the ghosts that flit round the dim border of hell, and he never gave her a second thought. Second?—he had never given her a first thought. Yet for all that, he had given her a flower; yes, he had given her a flower. One festive night, when in a great gayety he was dividing a bouquet among the laughing bevy about him, and somewhere on the edge of the group Miss Susan, hovering, felt a hand touch hers and slip into it a spray of heather, Clavers M'Veigh had no more idea whose hand he touched than if there had been no hand there; but poor Miss Susan has that spray of heather now. She has it in the box with her ribbon, which once he kept and wore; really kept and wore, and only surrendered on compulsion. She dropped it as she walked—a pretty blue ribbon with a silver rose wrought on it; she heard his step hastening behind her; she would have given the world to stop, but the very thought made her heart beat till she was faint, and she fled with swift feet, and he coolly folded the ribbon and put it in his breast pocket till it should be inquired for, a little amused with what he considered a bit of coquetry, and never dreaming that the light swift foot belonged to that pale and colorless Miss Susan, till his cousins, happening to see it when he accidentally pulled it out, inquired with mischievous glee if he were treasuring Miss Susan's ribbon. "It belong to the Fair Incognita," he said; and he fluttered it aloft on his fingers and pressed it dramatically to his lips. "The fleetest foot, the lightest step—"

"Nonsense!" cried his cousin Rose. "It is little Susan's. You must give it to me."

"Part with it?" cried Clavers, still dramatically.

"Yes, indeed; the poor little thing can not afford to lose it—she has so few ribbons."

"Then she must ask me herself," he said. And, as it chanced, the door opened just then, and Miss Susan came in with a message from her aunt: always delighted with an errand to the house where lived Rose, for whom she cherished one of her enthusiasms.

"Clavers has your silver ribbon, Susan," cried Rose and her sisters in chorus. "And he will not let us have it for you. You must ask him yourself, he says."

How glad she would have been to have him keep it! Did he wish to keep it, and had he made the excuse so as not to be forced to surrender it? She dared not hope. But she recognized all that propriety required of her. The blush mounted her face and fluttered on her temples; she took a step in his direction, but could no more look up than if a weight sat on either eyelid. "If you please," she said, half inaudibly, and held out her little hand in its shabby glove. And Clavers laid the ribbon across it with a grand bow; and then he and his cousin Rose exchanged a laughing look; but poor Miss Susan never saw the look.

When Miss Susan was at home and in her own room again, she sat down and thought over the little scene, and it increased and magnified itself in the mirage of fancy and desire till it assumed gigantic proportions.

Clavers M'Veigh had kept her ribbon; had chosen to keep it; had refused it to Rose; had worn it, a day at least, next his heart. What possibilities all that implied, what authority it gave her dreams, what a hope it warranted to spring in her hopeless passion! Till then Miss Susan had enjoyed no vivid personal dreams: her timid dreams had all been concerning Clavers M'Veigh himself and that enchanted kingdom in which he moved, and in them she herself figured no more than any poor little supernumerary, a sort of worthless and unhonored guardian angel with nothing but wings and wishes. But now something personal crept into them in spite of herself; she was no longer a supernumerary, but of some service, of some value: Clavers M'Veigh was aware of her, was smiling on her, perhaps was thinking of her, perhaps—   Ah, no, that could not be, that was too much; yet perhaps—only perhaps—ah, what if he were dreaming of her as she had dreamed of him! The mere idea gave Miss Susan a fantastic importance she had never felt before, gave her a place in the world, a clew to the future, something to hold by, to live for. Any one who saw her then and staid to think of it, with her head high and her foot elastic, with the sparkle in her eye and the eager light on her face, would have known some great joyful hope, that was in itself almost fruition, had certainly dawned upon her and was shining over her. But nobody ever staid to look at Miss Susan—hindered by her confirmed habit of nonentity.

Yet the bold beauty, accustomed to lovers, and enamored at last of one indifferent youth, would have laughed at Miss Susan's modest dreams; they had not reached the lofty flight to which the beauty's dreams might confidently spring. She had not once thought of herself as Clavers M'Veigh's wife, she had not thought of him even as her lover; she merely walked beside him in these reveries, heard him speak, saw him turn to her with confiding smiles; in one daring moment she danced with him, and the thought of it, of the scene, the flowers and lights and music, the encircling arm, made her as giddy as though it were real; in another she sat at his feet while he read the verses he liked best, glancing at her face for opinion or approval, and her pulses quickened at the fancy; and for the moment, at any rate, she was happy—happy as though it had been true. Possibly no one had ever asked her opinion or solicited her approval in all her life; she had never expected it; and now to think of Clavers M'Veigh doing so made her blood stir. Poor fool!

But Miss Susan was held for more and greater bliss than this, if dreams could give it to her. There was to be a sailing party down the river to the beach; and of course, as nobody thought of her cousins going without their shadows, she was included in the general invitation; and Clavers M'Veigh, as one of the committee, chanced to deliver the invitation, and Miss Susan chanced to go to the door. Presuming he should see a servant, and seeing a young lady, the gentleman was not exactly startled, and certainly by no means embarrassed—the sky might have reeled from its foundation without embarrassing Clavers M'Veigh—but just sufficiently surprised to send an unexpected cordiality into his address, and cause him to take the young lady's little lifeless hand; the other hand was at her throat—she had forgotten her bosom pin; and how she regretted the bauble! Her eyes danced, she looked really for the moment almost attractive. She promised for them all with fervor; and it seemed to her, as he turned on his way, that Clavers M'Veigh had personally invited herself to the sail, and when he handed her on board next day—though he stood at the boat side for no other purpose, and had handed a score of others across the plank—she felt that she was entirely Clavers M'Veigh's guest, and experienced a generous sense of renunciation in allowing him to bestow his attentions and his society on any of the others. All the evening before—after she had trimmed and retrimmed her little hat, with discarded scraps, for the excursion—she had sat alone in the dark with her sweet dreams. Wandering down the long beach with Clavers M'Veigh, listening to his voice, stooping now to pick up a shell, venturing now to point out to him the rainbow in the spray, now standing still together and watching the light die away from some distant sail, and now—   Ah, Miss Susan's dreams were growing bolder!

It was this pleased sense of proprietorship that gave such a glad, bright smile to Miss Susan's face, such a ringing tone to her voice. Clavers M'Veigh, glancing at her as he crossed the boat, said to himself at last that that was really quite a sweet girl, and went and sat down by her side for a moment. What do you think Miss Susan did? She burst into tears. The poor starved soul could not endure such a surfeit of happiness.

"What the deuce—" cried Clavers.

"Oh, you mustn't—mustn't mind me," ejaculated Miss Susan, looking up, with the tears sparkling sunnily all over a laughing face. "I—I always cry when I'm happy."

"Well, if women are not strange creatures!" he cried, springing to his feet. And just then the great boat giving a slight lurch as they tacked to make shore, Miss Susan, with an idea that they were in danger, sprang to her feet too, and completed the danger; for she lost her balance, swung a moment, caught at something, she knew not what, and went over into deep water, having pulled Clavers M'Veigh after her. She saw in one moment what she had done, and loosed her hold and went down, determined to let him go free, and in the instant when darkness closed over her, felt only a wild rejoicing that she had saved his life; for alone he could hold himself afloat till help came. Of course he could, and her too. He caught her, as she came up, in one hand, and grasping the boat side with the other, kept up a laughing interchange of words till she was drawn in and he could follow. They were close on shore; but there was no house near, no quarters where a change of clothing could be made, and the day was as full of danger for them in their wet garments as if they had gone to the bottom for good. As soon, then, as they could cast anchor and rattle down the sails and get ashore, the friendly party laid violent hands on the two wet creatures, and making them assume a half-lying, half-sitting position on the side of a sand hill, buried them in the hot sand to dry, according to immemorial usage, and made a great business of the merriment.

"Nothing was ever more humiliating," said Clavers M'Veigh. "And now that they have placed us at the mercy of the elements, like any drift of the sand, for a wave to wash off, they are dispersing for their chowder, and will perhaps forget all about us. Do you suppose any leviathan will come up from the deeps and make a mouthful of us, or the young ravens descend and eat out our eyes? They will never have a better chance. There sits Rose—just out of hearing. We can think of her as a kindly guardian, or else as a vulture poised on that old broken keelson, and waiting for the last signs of life to disappear before attacking us. Let us sell our life dearly!" And he laughed his gay, infectious laugh, that made Miss Susan laugh too, although she felt so very solemn.

"You are a strange little body," said Clavers M'Veigh, presently. "You haven't even thanked me. Didn't you know I saved your life?"

"Didn't you know I saved yours?" asked Miss Susan, with more *espièglerie*[1] than mortal had ever seen her show before; for happiness is a developing sunshine.

"That's good! May I ask how?"

"I let go."

"You let go?"

"I let go. Indeed I did. I didn't pull you down," said Miss Susan, quaveringly.

"And you thought I would let you go?"

"Oh no, no. I didn't think at all. I only knew you mustn't drown."

"You are a stranger little body than ever," said Clavers M'Veigh, trying, ineffectually, to turn and look at her. "But I believe you are going to sleep." And he went to sleep himself.

But Miss Susan had no idea of sleep. These were not moments to waste in unconsciousness. Lying there in the sand, with Clavers M'Veigh beside her and not two yards away—lying there in the sand and watching Clavers M'Veigh's slumbers—if a gypsy had foretold it to her, she would have thought it an impudent and impossible fiction; and here! Poor silly little Miss Susan! it seemed to her as though no one had ever come quite so near to Clavers M'Veigh. Who else had let go of life to spare him? for whom else had he risked life to save hers? What an awful moment was that in which they had been together, looking eternity in the face, and yet, indeed, each thinking of the other! How could any one ever come nearer to him than that? So strangely joyous, so unaccountably exalted, it seemed to this poor silly little Miss Susan that the sacrament of marriage could be no sweeter, no more solemn, than these moments!

Her happiness quite tired her out. And when Clavers M'Veigh awoke at length, and worried out of the sand, and rose clothed and in his right mind—that is to say, well dried as to his attire, shaking off the hot yellow grains like water-drops—he looked at her, with the long baby-like lashes resting on her pale cheek, and murmured, "Poor sweet little simpleton!" and went wandering down the beach with Rose, who had just finished her novel and scented the chowder from afar.

Miss Susan was ill for some weeks after this escapade, having taken a violent cold, of course. She did not regret it, though. During every hour that confined her to her room she had the recollection of that precious day to pore over and revel in, and of the evening sail in the moonlight on the dark water, when, as a cold wind blew up, chilling her to the marrow, Clavers M'Veigh, talking with Rose, wrapped to her dimpled chin in her great soft plaids, turned to see the shivering Miss Susan sitting behind him, and, there being nothing else to do, divided with her his shaggy boat cloak; and as she accepted a modest corner, he bent and drew the rough drapery close about her himself. Could bliss go farther? Not in Miss Susan's imagination had it ever done so. She sat in contented warmth, smiling up at the god who, obliged by the courtesy to turn his back on Rose, began to join in the boat songs that the rest were piping to the winds—join with a rich deep voice, to which she thrilled as she listened. Now and then Miss Susan tuned up her little treble and sang with him, just for the joy of singing with him; but for the chief part of the time she merely gazed and hearkened, drinking at every pore the divine draught of the hour's pleasure. This was what she never had expected, what she had no more right to expect than a principality; if he should tell her all the experiences of his life, she did not feel that she could be any more intimate with him. If, indeed, she had wildly dreamed of his love, she had, on the other hand, never so much as hoped for his acquaintance; and now, sitting wrapped in the same cloak with him, and with this bond between them caused by life risked and saved! Ah! how it made her own heart beat to remember how his beat with heavy throbs in the moments when he clung to the boat side with her upon his arm! She did not dare quite to imagine that it beat for her; it did not occur to her to imagine that it beat from the exertion; she could only let the faint hope flutter and stretch its wings in her heart as she remembered it.

This unfortunate little Miss Susan! Her aunt wrapped her in bed that night with a jug of hot water at her feet, and she sat up in bed the next morning only to have flannel and goose-grease about her throat, and her diet for a time consisted of little but onion sirup, squills, and other mild expectorants. But it all availed nothing toward quenching the light of romance that shone over her; she endured her sufferings, scarcely knowing that she suffered, for her other self walked in a serene zone above the clouds and among the castles in the air.

Clavers M'Veigh had left town, she heard. Perhaps that was the reason he had not called to inquire for the health of the little girl whom he had rescued. He had gone away to make arrangements for that long lecturing tour which, since then, has made his name ring with his eloquence from one side of the land to the other. With the October weather he had launched the enterprise; and as Miss Susan sat up in her easy-chair by the fire at last, and her cousins brought her the papers, she followed his career with something of the rapture she would have felt had she been with him. What if she had been with him! Ah! ah! Earth then would have been too much like heaven for any use of Miss Susan's. The very thought of it made the blood rush to her temples, and her aunt took away the papers, saying this reading was too much exertion yet, for any thing accelerating the beating of the heart engorged the lungs to a point of danger. If her aunt only knew the reveille Miss Susan's heart was always keeping up!

Later in the year, in the winter, indeed, and when she was quite well again, she went on a brief visit to a distant city. There was the opera, there were the theatres, there were the concerts of some seraph-toned *prima donna,* there were a score of amusements; from them all she chose the lecture of Mr. Clavers M'Veigh, and spent an ecstatic night. That great hall thronged to hear him; the echoing and re-echoing applause as he came upon the platform with his polished and perfect presence—as fine a piece of art himself as his oration was—while her head swam with the delight of seeing him; the rapt silence, broken only by that voice with its silvern resonance; the kindling of answering thought, and the electric flash of swift intelligence between orator and people; the thunders that shook the very roof when he had done—to Miss Susan it was a scene from some life so much outside and beyond her sphere that it seemed like a chapter of enchantment, something too unreal, too heavenly happy, to be true. She sat thrilling through and through with love and pride and admiration; she wondered if this great being saw her little white face in all that blossoming audience; she hugged herself with delight to think she had ever been so near him, to think they might have died together in those moments in the sea, to think of the morning in the sand, of the evening in the boat cloak. And when she reticently replied, to her friends' inquiries, that she knew him very well, their loud and enthusiastic expressions made her step along as if she walked on air. How he justified her love! No hero's bride ever breathed with a loftier sense of her crowned honor as the chosen one than poor little Miss Susan in her exultation and her satisfaction over the fact that she loved this cynosure of all men's regards—that she dared to love him. As Fox said of the game of whist, that the first best enjoyment in the world was winning at whist, and the second best was losing at whist, so Miss Susan felt that if the first best thing in life would be to have Clavers M'Veigh's love, so the next best thing was the liberty to give him hers.

She had grown very bold; she had looked her emotions in the face and called them by name; and she went back presently to her little room, her flower and her ribbon, to her round of home duties, with deeper and richer dreams to dream over.

Nobody knew any thing about the world in which the child lived. If her feelings had ever been guessed, they would have been laughed to scorn, and she was more than half aware of it. Something of their sweetness, too, possibly was due to this delicious secrecy. The very fact of this secrecy seemed to her like a tie between them; it was something that nobody shared but Clavers and herself. Many people pitied her as a girl without much vivid happiness in her way; none could have imaged her as one who pitied them, indeed, once in a while, as all people might be the objects of her pity who had not the great bliss of loving Clavers M'Veigh. She brooded over her ridiculous yet touching fancies so much, over her idea of him and her love for him, that he became a portion of her life itself, and she could not conjecture any different sensations on the part of a betrothed girl in regard to her lover. And when a vague rumor reached her that Clavers M'Veigh was engaged to be married to somebody else, she dismissed it cavalierly, and found it as impossible to believe as though he had been plighted to herself, as impossible as though he belonged to her, as impossible as if it were a question of Clavers M'Veigh's breaking faith!

She used to sit by the fire in the twilight, intensely happy with the pictures that she found there—pictures that sometimes made her heart leap to her throat; pictures of the days when she would be proudly hanging on her husband's arm, and only regretful that she did him no more honor; pictures of his face when he should bend to her with answering love in his eyes, and deplore the wasted days before he loved her, or else confess that he had loved her all along; some sudden unpremeditated picture of another fire-lit hearth to which he should enter while she sat, rosy, with clustering little yellow heads of rosy children round her—poor little children that were only the shadow of shadows, born in a dream that was banished with a burning blush in the instant of its being!

Thus far in Miss Susan's love affair every thing had progressed quietly; she had loved without let or hinderance, her emotions had all been the true and deep emotions proper to the period, and her hopes, till very recently, had been so humble that she had had no disappointment; she could have felt no otherwise, nothing but a deeper, more satisfied, more fixed and permanent joy, perhaps, had the right to feel them been real instead of fanciful. But the universal course of true love being far from smooth, it was to be expected that some obstacle would make the current run into rapids and shallows and general tumult and trouble.

And so it did: a very decided obstacle. And that was the confirmation of the rumor of Clavers M'Veigh's engagement to marry another. Clavers had accepted Fred's congratulations in the street, when Fred was last in the city; but there being only five minutes for the train, Fred had heard no particulars, not even the bride's name. Of course she was some peerless thing, as all the girls exclaimed, for Clavers's taste in beauty was perfect.

It was true, then. It was horribly, fatally true. Like a puff, all Miss Susan's dreams escaped into thin air—into that of which they were made. Widowed, childless, dreamless, hopeless, in one instant, Miss Susan stood like a tropical tree in full summer stripped of its leaves and blossoms by a cruel winter gale. She was utterly bereft in that instant; the world where she had dwelt existed no longer; she was shaken from her centre; she had no refuge without, none within; she had lost her polar star, and was shivering, bewildered, in the lonely cold. She went from room to room, aimless, white, and wan. Nobody noticed it. She was always one of those people who appear to suffer from insufficient nutrition both of body and soul, and it would have entered no one's wildest fantasies to suppose that Miss Susan was disappointed in love for Clavers M'Veigh. At first her little breaking heart was full of wild reproaches of Clavers—he had seemed to her so entirely her own, and he had betrayed her. But presently the faintest flicker of sense lighted her mind, or what passed with Miss Susan for a mental process; and she then confined her reproaches to fate—and bitter, bitter ones they were; fate, that had made her poor and mean and small and plain, unintelligent, unattractive, dependent, worthless; fate, that had at last robbed her even of the right to love! She sat down in the dark and cold, and cried and cried as if she would cry her soul away.

It was at this point that Miss Susan, deprived of the enjoyment of all her other dreams, took shelter in a new and somewhat inviting one—a dream of suicide. Why should she live? who cared for her? who would sorrow for her? of what use was she? what right had the powers that had so spoiled her life to compel her to endure it? These questions and a multitude of others swept like chaff on a whirlwind through her being. She abstracted a small vial from her aunt's medicine closet, and hung over it, lost in wonder to think so few drops of the liquid could induce a sleep from which only the Judgment trump could wake her. Whether it was thought of that trump or the bitter taste of the opiate that moved her, one can not say, but she did not swallow the poison; and she began to think of some form of death that might more openly confront Clavers M'Veigh: drowning, for instance, in the brook behind the M'Veighs' garden—as soon as the weather was warmer. That was a strong sketch that she made of herself in her mind's eye, brought up from the brook on men's shoulders, with the water streaming from her long hair, and of Clavers M'Veigh pausing on his way to view his work; but then she remembered Lancelot glancing carelessly, with his idle and indifferent compassion, on the dead Lady of Shalott. "He said, 'She has a lovely face;'" and she decided not to drown herself. No; she would look this Lancelot in the face with her great sad eyes, and let the iron enter his soul! It is impossible to say that there was not, when the first and worst was over, something rather consolatory in all this to Miss Susan; it was still very romantic, and that was a satisfaction. She could not quite rid herself of the fancy that Clavers had treated her badly, and that his conscience must smite him when he saw her; and for him to be reminded of her, if only in that way, had some flavor of the old deliciousness. And so, on this total change of base, she had begun a fresh succession of dreams. He would be coming to church on Sunday, with his future bride upon his arm—this unknown dazzling beauty, very likely an idiot, but without doubt a beauty; he should meet her, Miss Susan, at the pew door, for the M'Veighs' pew would be full, and theirs was just behind; and then he could see the pale calm face that had found peace, and think of martyrs with their palms. There! there! poor Miss Susan! It grew too ineffably silly.

But it was not silly to Miss Susan. It was all too lively reality. And when it happened just as she had fancied, and she heard her cousin murmur in church that the M'Veighs' pew was full and there was Clavers coming, she felt as if fate were really meddling in the matter, and she trembled so that she dared not look up for a moment. And when she did, who was this smiling, blushing little thing he was handing into her aunt's pew—who but his cousin Rose?

If Miss Susan fainted away during the *Te Deum* that morning, the air of the church was so oppressive that it was a wonder every body else did not faint away too; and all that Clavers M'Veigh felt as he helped Fred take her out was that if an ugly woman only knew how much uglier she looked when she fainted once, she would never faint twice. How was he—how was any body—to know that they had been present at as great an act of renunciation as it is possible for any one to make? In that half hour, feeling anew all her old love and worship of Rose, she had surrendered to her with her whole heart and soul all right and title even in a dream to the affections of Clavers M'Veigh.

And that was Miss Susan's love affair. As she sat, in her eventless middle life, she had its great thrilling secret to live over, and it never became threadbare. She felt again the rapture of her hidden passion; she was once more in the sea, in the sand, in the boat cloak; she was once more all but engaged, all but receiving the great sacrament of marriage; once more neglected, once more forsaken, once more confronting the deserting lover, once more making the great renunciation of love to friendship, once more borne from the church in those strong arms. It was always as true and as ecstatic as it had seemed to her then in her seventeenth year. And reveling in its memories and in its conscious importance, she could not help impressing you as a person with a history; and she could afford to sit and smile with that quaint air of superior experience, as the girls jested each other about their lovers, aware that she had loved a greater and brighter than any of theirs, that her romance was something sweeter than any they could ever know, and that, as I said, if she had now no love affairs to enjoy, she certainly had them to remember.

OLD MADAME

✻✻✻✻✻

MISS BARBARA! Barbara, honey! Where's this you're hiding at?" cried old Phillis, tying her bandana headgear in a more flamboyant knot over her gray hair and brown face. "Where's this you're hiding at? The Old Madame's after you."

And in answer to the summons, a girl clad in homespun, but with every line of her figure the lines, one might fancy, of a wood-and-water nymph's, came slowly up from the shore and the fishing-smacks, with a young fisherman beside her.

Down on the margin, the men were hauling a seine and singing as they hauled; a drogher was dropping its dark sails; barefooted urchins were wading in the breaking roller where the boat that the men were launching dipped up and down; women walked with baskets poised lightly on their heads, calling gayly to one another; sands were sparkling, sails were glancing, winds were blowing, waves were curling, voices were singing and laughing,—it was all the scene of a happy, sunshiny, summer morning in the little fishing-hamlet of an island off the coast.

The girl and her companion wound up the stony path, passing Phillis, and paused before a low stone house that seemed only a big bowlder itself, in whose narrow, open hallway, stretching from door to door, leaned a stately old woman on her staff,—a background of the sea rising behind her.

"Did you wish for Barbara, Old Madame?" asked the fisherman, as superb a piece of rude youth and strength as any young Viking.

She fixed him with her glance an instant.

"And you are his grandson?" said the old woman. "You are called by his name—the fourth of the name—Ben Benvoisie. I am not dreaming? You are sure of it?"

"As sure as that you are called Old Madame," he replied, with a grave pride of self-respect, and an air of something solemn in his joy, as if he had but just turned from looking on death to embrace life.

"As sure as that I am called Old Madame," she repeated. "Barbara, come here. As sure as that I am called Old Madame."

BUT SHE had not always been Old Madame. A woman not far from ninety now, tall and unbent, with her great black eyes, glowing like stars in sunken wells, from her face scarred with the script of sorrow—a proud beggar, preserving in her little coffer only the money that one day should bury her with her haughty kindred—once she was the beautiful Elizabeth Champernoune, the child of noble ancestry, the heiress of unbounded wealth, the last of a great house of honor.[1]

From birth till age, nothing that surrounded her but had its relation to the family grandeur. Her estate—her grandfather's, nay, her great-grandfather's—lay on a goodly island at the mouth of a broad river; an island whose paltry fishing-village of to-day was, before her time, a community where also a handful of other dignitaries dwelt in only less splendor. There were one or two of the ancient fishermen and pilots yet living when she died, who, babbling of their memories, could recall out of their childhood the stately form of her father, the Judge Champernoune, as he walked abroad in his black robes, who came from over seas to marry her mother, the heiress of the hero for whom the King of France had sent—when, in the French and Indian wars, the echoes of his daring deeds rang across the water—to make him Baron Chaslesmarie, with famous grants and largesse.

And in state befitting one whom the King of France thus with his own hand exalted, had the prodigal Baron Chaslesmarie spent his days—never, however, discontinuing the vast fisheries of his father, in which he had himself made fortunes before the King had found him out. And although the title died with him, and the pension died before him, for the King of France had, with treacherous complaisance, ceded the island to the enemy one day when war was over, yet store of land and money were left for the sole child, who became the wife of Judge Champernoune and the mother of Elizabeth.

What a sweet old spot it was in which Elizabeth's girlhood of ideal happiness went by! The house,—a many-gabled dwelling, here of wood and there of brick, with a noble hall where the original cornices and casements had been replaced by others of carved mahogany, the panels of the doors rich with their thick gilding, and the cellars three-deep for the cordials and dainties with which the old Baron Chaslesmarie had stored them,—was, a part of it, once brought from foreign shores as the great Government-house. Set in its brilliant gardens, it was a pleasant sight to see—here a broad upper gallery giving airy shelter, there a flight of stairs running from some flower-bed to some casement, with roses and hon-eysuckles clambering about the balustrade, avenues of ash and sycamore leading away from it, an outer velvet turf surrounding it and ending in a boundary of mossy granite bowlders. The old baron slept in his proud tomb across the bay—by the fort he had defended, the chapel he had built, in the graveyard of his people, proud as he. And Ben Benvoisie, the lad whom gossips said he had snatched from the shores of some Channel Island in one of the wild voyages of his youth, slept at his feet,—but another Ben Benvoisie lived after him. In a dimple between these bowlders of the gardens' boundary, Judge Champernoune and his wife and his other child were laid away. There was always something sadly romantic to Eliza-beth in the thought of her father walking over the island from time to time, and selecting this spot for his eternal rest, where the rocky walls enclosed him, the snows of winter and the bramble-roses of summer covered him, and the waves, not far remote, sang his long lullaby.

By the time that Elizabeth inherited the place, the importance of the island town had gone up the river to a spot on the mainland, and one by one the great families had followed, the old judge buying the land of them as they went, and their houses, dismembered, with fire and with decay, of a wing here and a gable there, and keeping but little trace of them. The judge had no thought of leaving; and the people would have felt as if the hand of Providence had been withdrawn had he done so. Nor had Elizabeth any thought of it, when she came to reign in her father's stead and infuse new life into the business of her ancestors, that had continued, as it were, by its own momentum, since, although Judge Champernoune had not thought it beneath his judicial dignity to carry it on as he found it, yet, owing to his other duties, he had not given it that personal attention it had in the vigor and impetus of the Chaslesmaries. She had not a memory that did not belong to the place. Certain sunbeams that she recalled slanting down the warehouses rich with the odors of spices and sugar, through which she had wandered as a child, were living things to her; a foggy morning, when an unseen fruiter in the seamist made all the air of the island port delicious as some tropical grove, with its cargo of lemons, seemed like a journey to the ends of the earth. And the place itself was her demesne, she its acknowledged *châtelaine*; there was not a woman in the town who had not served in her mother's kitchen or hall; it was in her fishing-smacks the men went out to sea, in her brigs they ran down to the West Indian waters and over to the Mediterranean ports—perhaps, alas, the African; it was her warehouses they filled with goods from far countries, which her agents scattered over the land—for a commerce that had begun with the supplying of the fishing-fleets, had swelled into a great foreign trade. And their homes were all that she could make them in their degree; their children she herself attended in sudden illness, having been reared, as her mother was before her, in the homely surgery and herb-craft proper to those that had others in their charge; and many a stormy night, in later years, did the good Dame Elizabeth leave her own children in their downy nests, and hasten to ease some child going out of the world on the horrible hoarse breath of croup, or to bring other children into the world in scorn of doctors three miles off.

She was twenty-five when the step-son of her father's sister, her cousin by marriage but not by blood, appeared to fulfil the agreement of their parents, to take effect when he should finish his travels—which, indeed, he had been in no haste to end. She had not been without suitors, of high and low degree. Had not the heir of the Canadian governor spoken of a treaty for the hand of this fair princess? Was it not Ben Benvoisie, the bold young master of a fishing-smack, with whom she had played when a child, who once would have carried her off to sea like any Norse pirate, and who had dared to leave his kiss red on her lips? Had Elizabeth been guilty of thinking that, had she been a river-pilot's daughter, such kisses would not come amiss?

Yet long ago had she understood that she was pledged to her Cousin Louis, and she waited for his coming. His eyes were as blue as hers were brown, his hair as black as hers was red, his features as Greek as hers were Norman, his stature as commanding as her own.

"Oh, he was a beauty, my Cousin Louis was!" she used to say.

She never called him her lover, nor her husband—he was always her Cousin Louis.

"So you have come, sir," she said, when he stepped ashore, and crossed the street and met her at the gate, and would have kissed her brow. "More slowly, sir," she said, drawing back. "You have come to win, not to wear. Elizabeth Chaslesmarie Champernoune is not a ribbon or a rose, to be tossed aside and picked up at will."

"By the Lord!" cried Cousin Louis. "If I had dreamed she were the rose she is, the salt seas would not have been running all these years between me and her sweetness—and her thorns."

"This is no court, and these no courtladies, Cousin Louis," she replied. "We are plain people, used only to plain speeches."

"Plain, indeed," said Cousin Louis. "Only Helen of Troy was plainer!"

"Nor do flattering words," she said, "well befit those whose slow coming flatters ill."

But the smile with which she uttered her somewhat bitter speech was of enchanting good-humor, and Cousin Louis thought his lines had fallen in pleasant places.

He was not so sure of it when a month had passed, and the same smile sweetened an icy manner still, and he had not yet been able, in the rush of guests that surrounded her, to have a word alone with Elizabeth. He saw that jackanapes of a young West Indian planter bring the color to her cheek with his whispered word. He saw her stroll down between the sycamores, unattended by any save Captain Wentworth. But let him strive to gain her ear and one of the young officers from Fort Chaslesmarie was sure to intercept him,—strive to attend her walk, and Dorothy and Jean and Margaret and Belle seemed to spring from the ground to her side. From smiling he changed to sullen, and from sullen to savage—to abuse his folly, to abuse her coquetry, to wonder if he cared enough for the winning of her to endure these indignities, and all at once to discover that this month had taught him there was but one woman in the world for him, and all the rest were shadows. One woman in the world,—and without her, life was so incomplete, himself so halved, that death would be the better portion.

How then? What to do? Patience gave up the siege. He was thinking of desperate measures on the day when, moping around the shores alone in a boat, he espied them riding from the Beacon Hill down upon the broad ferry-boat that crossed the shallow inlet. How his heart knocked his sides as he saw that pale, dark West Indian, with his purple velvet corduroys, and his nankeen jacket and jockey-cap, riding down beside her,—as he saw Wentworth spring from the stirrup to offer a palm for her foot when they reached the door! But Cousin Louis had not waited for that; he had put some strength to his strokes and was at the door before him, was at her side before him, compelling his withdrawal, offering no palm to tread on, but reaching up and grasping her waist with his two hands.

"By heaven!" he murmured then, as Wentworth was beyond hearing, his eyes blazing on hers. "What man do you think will endure this? What man will suffer this suspense in which you keep me?"

"It is you, Cousin Louis, who are keeping me in suspense," she answered, as she hung above him there.

And was there anything in her arch tone that gave him hope? He released her then, but when an hour later he met her again, "Very well," he said, in the suppressed key of his passion. "I will keep you in the suspense you spoke of no more. You will marry me this day, or not at all. By my soul, I will wait no longer for my answer!"

"You have never asked me, sir, before," she said. "How could you have an answer? I hardly know if you have asked me now."

But, that sunset, with Belle and Margaret and Jean and Dorothy, she strolled down to the little church, that by some hidden password was half-filled with the fishing-people and her servants. And when she came back, she was leaning on Cousin Louis's arm very differently from her usual habit, and the girls were going on before.

"If I had known this Cossack fashion was the way to win," Cousin Louis was saying—when a scream from Margaret and Belle and Dorothy and Jean rang back to them, and, hurrying forward, they found the girls with their outcry between two drawn swords, for Wentworth and the West Indian had come down into the moonlit glade to finish a sudden quarrel that had arisen over their wine, as to the preference of the fair *châtelaine*.

"Put up your swords, gentlemen," said Cousin Louis, with his proud, happy smile, "unless you wish to measure them with mine. It would be folly to fight about nothing. And there is no such person as Elizabeth Champernoune."

The men turned white in the moonlight to see the lovely creature standing there, and before they had time for anger or amazement, Elizabeth said after him:

"There is no such person as Elizabeth Champernoune. She married, an hour ago, her Cousin Louis."

Ah me, that all these passions now should be but idle air! Perhaps the hearts of the gallants swelled and sank and swelled again, as they looked at her, beautiful, rosy and glowing, in the broad white beam that bathed her. They put up their swords, and went to the house and drank her health and were rowed away.

Elizabeth and Cousin Louis settled down to their long life of promised happiness, in the hospitality of an open hearth around which friends and children clustered, blest, it seemed, by fortune and by fate. Gay parties came and went from the town above, from larger and more distant towns, from the village and port across the bay. Life was all one long, sweet holiday. What pride and joy was theirs when the son Chaslesmarie was born; what tender bliss Elizabeth's when the velvet face of the little Louise first lay beneath her own and she sank away with her into a land of downy dreams, conscious only of the wings of love hovering over her! How, at once, as child after child came, they seemed to turn into water-nixies, taking to the sea as naturally as the gulls flying around the cliffs! How each loiterer in the village would make the children his own, teaching them every prank of the waves, taking them in boats far beyond the outer light, bringing them through the breakers after dark, wrapped in great pilot-coats and drenched with foam! She never knew what was fear for her five boys, the foster-brothers of all the other children in the village. Only the little maiden Louise, pale as the rose that grew beneath the oriel, she kept under her eye as she might, bringing her up in fine household arts and delicate accomplishments,—ignorant of the shadow of Ben Benvoisie stalking so close behind as to darken all her work.

Her husband had taken the great business that Elizabeth's people had so long carried on through their glories and titles, their soldiery and war, their other pursuits if they had them; his warehouses lined the shores; the offing was full of his ships; he owned almost the last rod of land on the island, and much along the main. He did not pretend to maintain the state of the old baron; but to be a guest at Chaslesmarie was to live a charmed life awhile. He was a man of singular uprightness; as he grew older apt to bursts of anger, yet to Elizabeth and to his household he was gentleness itself; some men trembled at the sound of his voice, but children never did. If he was not so beloved as his wife by the fishing-people, it was because he was not recognized master as of right, and because he exacted his due, although tossing it in the lap of the next needy one. But he was a person with whom no other took a liberty. "A king among men, was my Cousin Louis," Old Madame used to say, and sigh and sigh and sigh again as she said it.

But the hospitality of the island was not all that of pleasure and sumptuous ease. It was a place easily reached by sail from one or more of the great towns, by boat from the town above; and in the stirring and muttering of political discontent, the gentlemen who appeared and disappeared at all hours of the day, and as often by night, folded in cloaks wet with the salt sea spray, wore spurs at their heels and swords at their sides to some purpose. And when at last war came—Horror of horrors, what was this! Cousin Louis and his island had renounced allegiance to the crown, and had taken the side of the colonial rebels and the Continental Congress.

"We!" cried Elizabeth, who knew little of such things, and had a vague idea that they owed fealty still to that throne at whose foot her grandfather had knelt. "We, whom the King of France ennobled and enriched!"

"And for that price were we sold ere we were born, and do we stay slaves handed about from one ruler to another?" her husband answered her. "We have ennobled and enriched ourselves. We have twice and thrice repaid the kings of France in tribute money. Soon shall the kings of France go the way of all the world—may the kings of Britain follow them! Henceforth, the people put on the crown. I believe in the rights of man. I live under no tyranny—but yours," he said gayly.

"A Chaslesmarie! A Champernoune!" Elizabeth was saying to herself, heedless of his smile.

"We are an insignificant islet," her husband urged. "The kings of France have betrayed us. The kings of Britain have oppressed us. We renounce the one. We defy the other!" And he ran the flag under which the rebels fought, up the staff at Chaslesmarie, and it was to be seen at the peak of all his brigantines and sloops that, leaving their legitimate affairs, armed themselves and scoured the seas, and brought their prizes into port. But freely as this wealth came in, as freely it went out; for Cousin Louis did nothing by the halves. And heart and soul being in the matter, it is safe to say that not one guinea of the gold his sailors brought him in, during that long struggle, remained to him at its close.

It was during this struggle that, when one day the sloop "Adder's-tongue" sailed, the elder son of Ben Benvoisie—who had long since married a fisherman's daughter—was found on board, a stowaway. Great was Ben Benvoisie's wrath when he missed his son; but there was nothing to be done. He rejected Cousin Louis' regrets with scorn. But when the sloop brought in her prizes, and the first man ashore told him his son had died of some ailment before he sighted an enemy, then his rage rose in a flame, he towered like an angry god, and standing on the head of the wharf, in the presence of all the people, he cursed Cousin Louis, root and branch, at home and abroad,—a black cloud full of bursting lightnings rising behind him as he spoke, as if he had a confederate in evil powers,—cursed him in wild and stinging words that made the blood run cold, that cut Cousin Louis to the heart, that, when they were repeated to her, made even Elizabeth turn faint and sick. "There is a strange second-sight with those Benvoisies," she said. "God grant his curses come to naught." But she seldom saw him at a distance without an instant's prayer, and she knew that the fishing-people always after that sight of him, standing there at the head of the wharf, with his blazing eyes and streaming hair, and the rain and the lightning and thunder volleying around him, held some superstitions of their own regarding the evil eye of the Benvoisies, and kept silent watch to see what would come of it all.

But the war at last was ended, the world was trying to regain its equilibrium, and continental money was at hand on every side, and little other. Cousin Louis, who had faith in the new republic, believed with an equally hot head in its own good faith, and sent word far and near that he would redeem the current paper, dollar for dollar in gold. And he did so. There were barrels of it in his warehouse garrets, and his grandchildren had it to play with. "It is Ben Benvoisie's word," said Elizabeth, when they saw the mistake. But Cousin Louis laughed and kissed her, and said it had sunk treasure, to be sure, but asked if Ben Benvoisie's word was to out-weigh his fisheries and fleets and warehouses and hay-lands—his splendid boys, his girl Louise! And he caught the shrinking, slender creature to his heart as he spoke—this lovely young Louise, as fair and fragile as a lily on its stem, whom he loved as he loved his life, his flower-girl, as he called her, just blossoming into girlhood, with the pale rose-tint on her cheek, and her eyes like the bee-larkspur. How was he, absorbed in his counting-room, forgetful at his dinner-table, taking his pleasures with guests, with gayeties, to know that his slip of a girl, not yet sixteen, met a handsome hazel-eyed lad at the foot of the long garden every night,—Ben Benvoisie the third,—and had promised to go with him, his wife, in boy's clothes, when-ever the fruiter was ready for sea again! But old Ben Benvoisie knew it. And he could not forbear his savage jeer. And the end was that Cousin Louis, at the foot of the long garden one night, put a bullet through young Ben Benvoisie's arm, and carried off his fainting girl to her room that she showed no wish to leave again. "She will die," said Cousin Louis, one day toward the year's close, "if we do not give way."

"She would better," said Elizabeth, who knew what the misery of her child's marriage with old Ben Benvoisie's son must needs be when the first glamour of young passion should be over.

And she did. And Cousin Louis' heart went down into the grave with her.

"It is not only old Ben Benvoisie's word," said Elizabeth. "It is his hand."

Her secret tears were bitter for the child, but not so bitter as they would have been had she first passed into old Ben Benvoisie's power, and been made the instrument for humbling the pride and breaking the heart daily of her brothers Chaslesmarie and Champernoune, and of the hated owner of the "Adder's-tongue," had she lived to smart and suffer under the difference between the rude race reared in a fishing-hut, and that reared in the mansion of her ancestors. Perhaps Old Madame never saw the thing fairly; it always seemed to her that Louise died of some disease incident to childhood. "I have my boys left," said Elizabeth. "And no one can disturb my little grave."

It was two graves the second year after. For Chaslesmarie, her first-born and her darling, whose baby kisses had been sweeter than her lover's, the life in whose little limbs and whose delicious flesh had been dearer than her own, his bright head now brighter for the fresh laurels of Harvard,— Chaslesmarie, riding down from the Beacon Hill, where he had gone to see the fishing-fleet make sail, was thrown from his horse, and did not live long enough to tell who was the man starting from the covert of bayberry-bushes. But Elizabeth carried a stout heart and a high head. She could not, if she would, have bent as Cousin Louis did, nor did the proud serenity leave her eye, although his darkened with a sadness never lightened. None knew her pangs, nor saw the tears that stained her pillow in the night; she would, if she could, have hid her suffering from herself. She began to feel a terrible assurance that she was fighting fate;—but she would make a hard fight of it. Conscious of her integrity of purpose, of the justice of her claims, of her right to the children she had borne, there was something in her of the spirit of the ancients who dared, if not defy the gods, yet accept the combat offered by them. Champernoune was the heir instead, that was all. Then there were the twin boys, Max and Rex, two lawless young souls; and the youngest of all, St. Jean, whose head always wore a halo in Eliza-beth's eyes. With these, why should she grieve? Now she was also the mother of angels!

Again, after a while, the frequent festivities filled the house, and the great gold and silver plate glittered in the dark dining-room and filled it, at every touch, with melodious and tremulous vibrations. Now the Legis-lature of the State, one and all, attended a grand banqueting there, now the Governor and his Council; now navy-yard and fort and town, and far-off towns, came to the balls that did not end even with the bright outdoor breakfast, but ran into the next night's dancing, and a whole week's gayety. Now it was boating and bathing in the creeks; now it was sailing out beyond the last lights with music and flowers and cheer; and all the time it was splendor and sumptuousness and life at the breaking crest. And Elizabeth led the dance, the stateliest of the stately, the most beautiful still of the beautiful. And if sometimes she saw old Ben Benvoisie's eyes, as he leaned over the gate and looked at her a moment within the gardens and among her roses, it was not to shudder at them. What possessed Elizabeth in those days? She only felt that the currents of her blood must sweep along in this mad way, or the heart would stop.

Then came Champernoune's wedding,—he and that friend whom the chief magistrate of the land delighted to honor, marrying sisters in one night. How lovely, how gracious, how young the bride! Was it at Gonaives that year that she died dancing? Was it at Gonaives that the yellow-fever buried Champernoune in the common trench?

Elizabeth was coming up the landing from the boat, her little negro dwarf carrying her baskets, when the news reached her quick senses, as the one that spoke it meant it should. She staggered and fell. The doctors came to bind up the broken bones, and only when they said, "At last it is quite right; but, dear lady, your dancing days are over," did any see her tears. She had buried her only girl, her first-born boy, her married heir, without great signs of sorrow. She had plunged into a burning house in the village once, gathering her gauzy skirts about her, to bring out the little Louise whom an unfaithful nurse had taken there and forsaken in her fright. She had waded, torch in hand, into the wildly rolling surf of a starless night to clutch the bow of Chaslesmarie's boat that was sweeping helplessly to the breaker with the unskilled child at the helm. She had shut herself up with Champernoune, when Ben Benvoisie brought back the small-pox to the village, and had suffered no one to minister to him but herself. And when the dog all thought mad tore Cousin Louis' arm, she herself had sucked the poison from the wound.

Yet with that sentence, that absurd little sentence, that her dancing days were over, it seemed all at once to Elizabeth that everything else was over, too. With Champernoune now everything else had gone—state and splendor, peace and pleasure, hospitality and home and hearth, and all the rest. All things had been possible to her, the mastery of her inner joy itself in one form or another, while she held her forces under her. But now she herself was stricken, and who was to fight for them? Who, when the stars in their courses fought against Sisera!

But as wild as the grief of Cousin Louis was, hers was at still, though there were ashes on her heart. She went about with a cane when she got up, unable to step a minuet or bend a knee in prayer. "But see," cried old Ben Benvoisie to himself, "her head is just as high!"

Not so with Cousin Louis. He sat in his counting-room, his face bent on his hands half the time. Cargoes came in unheeded, reports were made him unregarded, ships lay at the wharf unloaded, the state of the market did not concern him—nothing seemed of any matter but those three graves. Then he roused himself to a spasmodic activity, gave orders here and orders there, but his mind was otherwhere. With the striking of the year's balance he had made bad bargains, taken bad debts, sent out bad men with his fleets, brought in his fares and his fruits and foreign goods at a bad season, lost the labor of years. A fire had reduced a great property elsewhere to ashes; a storm had scattered and destroyed his southern ships. "Something must be done," said Cousin Louis. And he looked back from his counting-room, on the fair mansion from whose windows he had so long heard song and laughter floating, with its gardens round about it, where the sweet-briar and the tall white rose climbed and looked down at the red rose blushing at their feet, where the honeysuckles shed their fragrance, where the great butterflies waved their wings over all the sweet old-fashioned flowers that had been brought from the gardens of France and summer after summer had bloomed and spiced the air, where the golden robins flashed from bough to bough of the lane of plum-trees, and the sunshine lay vivid on the encircling velvet verdure. "Her home, and the home of her people for a century behind her—the people whose blood in her veins went to make her what she is—noblest woman, sweetest wife, that ever made a man's delight. The purest, proudest, loftiest soul that looks heaven in the face. O God, bless her, my dear wife—dearer than when I wooed you or when I wedded you, by all the long increase of years! Something must be done," said Cousin Louis, "or that will go with the rest."

Perhaps Cousin Louis began to forefeel the future then. Certainly, as a little time passed on, an unused timidity overwhelmed him. Against Elizabeth's advice he began to call in various moneys from here and there where they were gathering more to themselves. "There is to be another war with the British," he said. "We must look to our fortunes." But he would not have any interference with their way of life, the way Elizabeth had always lived. There must still be the dinner to the judges, the supper to the clergy, the frequent teas to the ladies of the fort, the midsummer throng of young people, the house full for the Christmas holidays; Max and Rex were to be thought of, St. Jean was not to grow up remembering a house of mourning. Why had no one told them that, in all the festive season before Champernoune's death, the younger boys not being held then to strict account, old Ben Benvoisie, sitting with them on the sea-beaten rocks, had fired their fancy with stories of the wild sealife that had blanched his hair and furrowed his face before the time? One day St. Jean came in to break the news: Max and Rex had run away to sea. "I should have liked to go," said St. Jean, "but I could not leave my mother so."

"By the gods!" said his father. "You shall go master of the best ship I have!" And in due time he sent him supercargo to the East, that he might learn all that a lad who had tumbled about among ropes and blocks and waves and rocks, ever since his birth, did not already know. But he forbade his wife to repeat to him the names of Rex and Max; nor would they ever again have been mentioned in his presence but for the report of a ship that had spoken the craft they took, and learned that it had been overhauled, and Max, of whom nothing more was ever heard, pressed into the British service, and Rex, ordered aloft on a stormy night, had fallen from the yard into the sea, and his grave was rolled between two waves.

As Elizabeth came home from the little church—the first time she went out after this—thinking, as she went, of the twilight when she found Champernoune, who had stolen from the lightsome scenes that greeted him and his young bride, to stand a little while beside the grave where his brother Chaslesmarie slept—she met old Ben Benvoisie.

"Well," he said, "you know how good it is yourself."

"Is not the curse fulfilled, Ben Benvoisie?" she demanded. "Are you going to spare me none?"

"None," said Ben Benvoisie.

The servants were running toward her when she reached the house. The master had a stroke. A stroke indeed. He sat in his chair a year, head and face white, speaking of nothing but his children's graves, they thought. "Too cold—too damp. Why did I bury there?" he murmured. "I will go have them up," he said. "Oh, why did I bury so deep—cold—cold—Elizabeth!" But when Elizabeth answered him, the thing he would say had gone, and when he died at last, for all his struggle for speech, it was still unspoken.

Ah, what a year was that when the long strain was over, and she placed him where she was to lie herself, at her father's feet! Things went on as they would that year. Wrapped in an ashen apathy, Elizabeth hardly knew she breathed, and living less at that time in this world than the other, the things of this world had small concern for her. Born, too, and reared in wealth, she could as easily have understood that there was any other atmosphere about her as any other condition; and the rogues, then, had it all their own way. Suits for western lands that were the territorial possessions of princes were compromised for sums she never saw; blocks of city houses were sold for taxes; heaven knows what else was done, what rights were signed away on papers brought for her name as administratrix. And when St. Jean came home from sea, where were the various moneys that his father had been calling in for so long a time? There was not a penny of them accounted for.

St. Jean was a man before his time. He looked about him. The great business had gone to the dogs, and some of the clerks and factors had gone with it; at least, they too had disappeared. Other men, in other places, had taken advantage of the lapse, established other houses, opened other fisheries, stolen their markets. There was not enough of either fleet left in condition to weather a gale. "It has all been at the top of the wave," said St. Jean, "and now we are in the trough of the sea." But he had his ship, the "Great-heart," and with that he set about redeeming his fortunes. And his first step was to bring home to his mother a daughter-in-law as proud as she—Hope, the orphan of a West Indian prelate, with no fortune but her face, and with manners that Elizabeth thought unbecoming so penniless a woman.

When St. Jean went away to sea again, he established his wife— Little Madame, the people had styled her—in a home of her own. For large as the Mansion was, it was not large enough to hold those two women: a home in a long low stone house that belonged to the estate and had once been two or three houses together,—at which one looked twice, you might say, to see if it were dwelling or bowlder,—and which he renovated and then filled with some of the spare pictures and furnishings of the Mansion-house. And there Hope lived, cheered Elizabeth as she could, and cared for the children that came to her. And how many came! And Elizabeth, who could never feel that Hope had quite the right to a place as her rival in St. Jean's affections, took these little children to her heart, if she could not yet altogether take their mother; and they filled for her many a weary hour of St. Jean's absences on his long voyages,—St. Jean who, in some miraculous way, now represented to her father and husband and son.

Elizabeth had time enough for the little people; for friends did not disturb her much after the first visits of condolence. Trouble had come to many of them, as well. Dorothy and Margaret and Belle and Jean, and their compeers, were scattered and dead and absorbed and forgetful, and she summoned none of them about her any more with music and feasting. Of all her wealth now nothing remained but a part of the land on the island and the adjoining main, with its slight and fickle revenue. Of all her concourse of servants there were only Phillis and Scip, who would have thought themselves transferred to some other world had they left Old Madame.

But the Mansion of Chaslesmarie was a place of pleasure to the children still, at any rate; and the little swarm spent many an hour in the old box-bordered garden, where the stately lady walked on Phillis's arm, and in the great hall where she told them the history of each of the personages of the tall portraits, from that of the fierce old Chaslesmarie of all down to the angel-faced child St. Jean; told them, not as firing pride with memories of ancient pride, but as storied incidents of family life; and as she told them she lived over her share in them, and place and race and memories seemed only a part of herself.

"Madame," said St. Jean once, when at home,—no child of hers had often called her mother,—"I think if we sold the place and moved away we would do well. The soil is used up, the race is run out—if we transplanted and made new stock? Here is no chance to educate the children or to rebuild our fortunes now. Somewhere else, it may be, I could put myself in better business connection—"

The gaze of his mother's burning black eyes bade him to silence. She felt as if in that moment he had forsworn his ancestors.

"Leave this place of whose dust we are made!" she cried. "Or is it made of the dust of the Chaslesmaries? And how short-sighted—here, where, at least, we reign! Never shall we leave it! See, St. Jean, it is all yours,"—and from command her voice took on entreaty, and how could St. Jean resist the pleading mother! He went away to sea again, and left all as before.

But the earth had moved to Elizabeth with just one thrill and tremor. The idea, the possibility, of leaving the place into which every fibre of her being was wrought had shaken her. It was a sort of conscious death into whose blackness she looked for one moment—so one might feel about to lose identity. She walked through the rooms with their quaint and rich furnishing, sombre and heavy, their gilded panels, their carved wainscot, the old French portraits of her people that looked down on her and seemed to claim her; she paused in the oriel of the yellow drawing-room, where it always seemed like a sunshiny afternoon in an October beech-wood—paused, and looked across the bay.

There gleamed the battlements of the fort that her grandfather, the baron, had built; there was the church below, there was the tomb, among the graves of those whose powers had come to their flower in him; the grassy knoll, beyond, gleamed in the gold of the slant sun and reminded her of the days when, a child, she used to watch the last glint of the low swells of the graves, across the blue waters of the bay whose rocky islets rose red with the rust of the tides. Far out, the seas were breaking in a white line over the low red ledge, and, farther still, the lighthouse on the dim old Wrecker's Reef was kindling its spark to answer the light on the head of Chaslesmarie that her grandfather had first hung in the air. Close at hand, a boat made in, piled high at either end with the brown sea-weed, the fishing-sails were flitting here and there, as there had never been a day when they were not; and the whole, bathed with the deepening sunset glow, glittered in peace and beauty. There had not been ten days in all her life when she had not looked upon the scene. No, no, no! As well give up life itself, for this was all there was of life to her. There was the shore where, when a child, she found the bed of garnets that the next tide washed away. Here could she just remember having seen the glorious old Baron Chaslesmarie, with his men-at-arms about him. Here had her dear father proudly walked, with his air of inflexible justice, and the wind had seized his black robes and swept them about her, running at his side. Here had her mother died. Here had she first seen the superb patrician beauty of her husband's face when he came from France, with his head full of Jean Jacques and the rights of man. Here was the little chapel where they married, the linden avenue up which they strolled, with the branches shaking out fragrance and star-beams together above them—the first hour, the first delightful hour, they ever were alone together, she and her cousin Louis. Oh, here had been her life with him—a husband tenderer than a lover, a man whose loftiness lifted his race and taught her how upright other men might be, a soul so pure that the light of God seemed to shine through it upon her! Here had been her joys, here had been her sorrows; here had she put her love away and heard the moulds ring down on that dear head; here had the world darkened to her, here should it darken to her forever when all the shadows of the grave lengthened around her. Father and mother, husband and child, race and land, they were all in this spot. These people, all of whom she knew by name, were they not like her own? Could the warmth of the blood bring much nearer to her these faces that had surrounded her since time begun—these men and women whose lives she had ordered, whose children had been fostered with her children, who half-worshipped her in her girlhood, who half-worshipped her still as Old Madame? Could she leave them? Not though St. Jean's "Great-heart" went down,—St. Jean's ship for which Hope on her house-top sat so long watching. "I refuse to think of it," she said. "It is infinitely tiresome." And then the children trooped in and stopped further soliloquy; and she let them dress themselves out in her stiff old brocades that had been sent for just after she married and had never needed to be renewed,—the cloth-of-silver and peach-bloom, the flowered Venetian, the gold-shot white paduasoy; she liked to see the pretty Barbara and Helena and Bess prancing about the shining floors, holding up the long draperies, and she would have decked them out in her old silver-set jewels, too, had they not been parted with long since when Cousin Louis was calling in their moneys. It all renewed her youth so sweetly, if so sadly, and the mimic play in some obscure way making her feel they only played at life, relieved her of a sense of responsibility regarding their real life. When they tired of their finery, she led them down, as usual, before the portrait of this one and of that, and told over the old stories they liked to hear.

"Madame," said little Barbara, lifting her stiff peach-blossom draperies, "why is it always 'then,'—why is it never 'now'?"

But the old dame's heart did not once cry Ichabod. To her the glory never had departed. It was as imperishable as sky and air.

It was the threatened war-time again at last; and Hope, with her sweet soft eyes watching from the house-top, saw her husband's ship come in, and with it its consort—just a day too late. The embargo had been declared, and he hailed from a forbidden port. Other sailors touched other ports and took out false papers for protection. St. Jean scorned the act. He relied on public justice: he relied on a reed. His cargoes were confiscated, and his ships were left at the wharf to rot before he could get hearing. In those two vessels was the result of his years of storm and calm, nights when the ship was heavy by the head with ice, days when her seamy sides were scorched and blistered by the sun, the best part of his life. And gone because he preferred poverty to perjury.

"Better so," said Old Madame. "I am prouder of my penniless son than of any merchant prince with a false oath on his soul." And her own contentment seemed to her all that could be asked. She never thought of regretting the matter; but she despised the General Government more than ever, and would have shown blue-lights to the enemy, had he been near and wanted a channel, were it not that he was Cousin Louis' enemy as well.

Alas! a bitterer enemy was near. One tempestuous winter's night the minute-guns were heard off Wrecker's Reef,—and who but St. Jean must lead the rescue? Hope, cloaked and on her house-top, with the glass saw it all; saw St. Jean climb the reef as the moon ran out on the end of a flying scud of cloud to glance on the foam-edged roll of the black wild seas; saw the others following along the sides of the ice-sheathed rock to carry succor to the freezing castaways, and saw, too, a plunging portion of the wreck strike one form, and hurl it headlong. It was her husband. And although he was brought back alive, yet the blow upon his breast, and the night's exposure in the icy waters, in his disheartened state, did deathly work upon St. Jean, and he was laid low and helpless long before his release.

Then Elizabeth sold the hay-fields along the main-land to pay the bills of the doctor, who was also the druggist, to try softer air for the prostrated man, to bring him home again. She had loved to see the sun ripening the long stretch of their rich grasses with reds and purples, with russets and fresh-bursting green again, as far as eye could see. But she forgot she had ever owned them, or owning them had lost them. They were there still when she gazed that way. Then the Thierry place followed, and the little Hasard houses,—they had not yet learned how to be poor.

"There is the quarry," said St. Jean, his heart sore as his hand was feeble. "We cannot work it now."

"The grocer took it long ago," said Elizabeth.

"And the Podarzhon orchard?"

"Oh, the Podarzhon orchard! Yes, your great-grandsire used to call it his pot of money. Well, the trees were old and ran to wood,—your father renewed so many! But the apples had lost their flavor,—what apples they used to be! Oh, yes, we ate up the Podarzhon orchard some time since. And the lamb-pasture brought the children their great-coats and shoes last year. And the barley-field—How lucky that we happened to have them, my dear!"

"And I dying," groaned St. Jean. "What, what is to become of them!"

"To become of them!" said the unfaltering spirit. "Is there question what will become of any of the blood of Chaslesmarie?"

A night came, at length, when Hope fainted in her arms—Elizabeth's last child was dead. "A white name and a white soul," said Elizabeth. "I thank God I knew him!" And the Geoffrey field went to bury him. "I shall be with him soon," she said, smiling, not weeping. "Heaven can hardly be more holy than he made earth seem, he was so like a saint!" After that, she felt as if he had no more than gone on one of his long voyages. She sold the few acres of the Millet farm in a month or two; they had nothing else to live on now but such small sales; and from a portion of the proceeds she put aside, in a little hair-covered coffer, her grave-clothes, with the money, in crisp bank-notes, that should one day suffice to lay her away decently between her graves. And then she and Hope sat down and spent their days telling over the virtues of their dead.

It was a summer day, when the late wildroses were just drooping on their stems and the wanton blackberry vines were everywhere putting out their arms, and all things hung a little heavily in the still air before the thunder-storm, that Elizabeth climbed alone, with her staff, to the dimple among the rocks where her dear ones lay. She paused at the top to look around her. Here swept the encircling river, with the red rocks rising from its azure; beyond it the mainland lifted softly swelling fields that had once belonged to her ancestors of glorious memory; far away to the south and east, over its ledges and reefs mounting purple to the bending sky, stretched the sea, its foaming fields also once theirs and yielding them its revenues. Now,—nothing but these graves, she said; the graves of renown, of honor, of lofty purity. "No, no," said Elizabeth aloud. "Renown, honor, purity are not buried here. St. Jean's children cannot be robbed of that inheritance. Fire that still burns must burst through the ashes. It is fallen indeed; but with these children it shall begin its upward way again!"

"Its upward way again," said a deep voice. And, half-starting, she turned to see old Ben Benvoisie sitting on one of the graves below her.

"So you are satisfied at last, Ben Benvoisie," said Elizabeth, after a moment's gazing.

"Satisfied with what?"

"Satisfied that not one child is left to my arms, and that, when the mortgage on the Mansion falls due, not one acre of my birthright is left to my name."

"Do you think I did it, then, Old Madame?" asked the man, pulling his cloak about him. "Am I one of the forces of nature? You flatter me! Am I the pride, the waste, the love of pleasure, the heedlessness of the morrow, the self-confidence of your race, that forgot there was a world outside the sound of the name Chaslesmarie? Did I take one life away from you?" he cried, as he tottered to his stick. "Nay, once I would have given you my own! Did I take a penny of your wealth? I am as poor to-day as I was seventy years ago when I laid my life at your feet, and you laughed and scorned and spurned it, and thought so lightly of it you forgot it!"

Elizabeth was silent a little. Her hood fell back, and there streamed out a long lock of her silver hair in which still burned a gleam of gold. Her black eyes, softer than once they were, met quietly the gaze that was reading the writing of the lines cut in her face, like the lines whipped into stone by the sharp sands of the desert.

"It was not these levelling days," she said. "I was the child of nobles—"

"And I was a worm at your feet. A worm with a sting, you found. But it was not you I cursed," he cried in a hoarse passion,—"not you, Elizabeth Champernoune! It was the master—"

"Louis and I were one," she answered him. "We are one still. A part of him is here above the sod; a part of me is there below it. We shall rest beside each other soon, as we did every night of forty years. Soon you, too, Ben Benvoisie, will go to your long sleep, and neither your banning nor your blessing will help or hurt the generation that is to come."

"Will it not?" he said. And he laughed a low laugh half under his breath. "Yet the generations repeat themselves. Look there!" And he wheeled about suddenly and pointed with his stick, as if it had been an old wizard's wand. "Look yonder at the beach," he said. "On the flat bowlder by which we found the bed of garnets when you and I were too young— eighty years ago, is it?—to know that you were the child of nobles, and I a worm!"

And there, on the low, flat rock, distinct against the turbid darkness of the sky, sat the pretty Barbara, a brown-eyed lass of sixteen, and the arm about her shoulder was the arm of young Ben Benvoisie, the old man's grandson, and his face, a handsome tawny face with the blue fire of its eyes, was bent toward hers—and hers was lifted.

"Leave them to their dream a little while, Old Madame, before you wake them," said the old man, in a strangely altered voice.

"I shall not wake them," said Elizabeth.

And they were silent a moment again, looking down at the figures on the rocks. And the two faces that had bent together there, had clung together in their first long sweet kiss of love, parted, with the redness of innocent blushes on them, and were raised toward the distant sea, now dimly streaked with foam and wind.

"I have seen ninety years," said old Ben Benvoisie. "And you, Old Madame?"

"I have lived eighty-five," she answered, absently.

"Long years, long years," he said. "But, at last," he said, "at last, Dame Elizabeth, my flesh and blood and yours are one!"

Elizabeth turned to move away, but his voice again arrested her. "Look ye!" he said. "When those two are one, once and forever, when Chaslesmarie is sunk in Benvoisie, when you are conquered at last, I shall tell them where Master Louis buried his moneys, Old Madame!"

She had been going on without a word; but she stopped and looked back over her shoulder. "Only they are conquered, Ben Benvoisie, who contend," she said. "And I have never contended. Perhaps I had rather see her dead. I do not know. But Barbara has her own life to live in these changed times. She is too young, I am too old, to make her live mine. And were I conquered," she cried in a great voice, "it is not by you, but by age and the slow years and death! I defy you, as I have defied Fate! For, take the bread from my mouth, the mantle from my back, yet while I live the current in my veins remains," cried the old Titaness, "and while I live that current will always run with the courage and the honor of the Chaslesmaries and Champernounes!"

"Not so," said the other. "Conquered you are. Conquered because your race ceases. Because Chaslesmarie is swallowed up in Benvoisie as death is swallowed up in victory!"

But she had gone on into the gathering darkness of the storm, from which the young people fled up the shore, and heard no more. And the storm burst about the island, and the old Chaslesmarie Mansion answered it in roof and rafter, trembling as if to the buffets of striving elemental foes. And all at once the flames wrapped it; and gilded wainscot, Dutch carving, ancestral portraits, were only a pile of hissing cinders when the morning sun glittered on raindrops, rocks, and river. And Elizabeth, with her little hair-coffer of cere-clothes and money, had gone to Hope's cottage, and old Ben Benvoisie was found stretched upon the grave where she had seen him sitting. And they never knew where Cousin Louis had buried his money.

"Miss Barbara! Barbara, honey!" called old Phillis, again, a little before noon. "Where's this you's hiding at? Old Madame wants ye. Don't ye hear me tell?"

And pretty Barbara came hesitatingly up the rocks that made each dwelling in the place look as if it were a part of the island itself, tearful and rosy and sparkling, And by her side, grave as became him that day, and erect and proud as his grand-parent, was old Ben Benvoisie's grandson.

"Barbara," said the Old Madame presently, breaking through the reverie caused by their first few words, "did my eyes deceive me yesterday? Have you cut adrift? Have you made up your mind that you can do without fine dresses and silver dishes and—"

"Why, I always have," said Barbara, looking up simply.

"That is true," said Elizabeth. "And so they do not count for much. And you think you know what love is—you baby? You really think you love this sailor-lad? Tell me, how much do you love him, child?"

"As much, Madame dear," said Barbara, shyly, dimpling, glancing half askance, "perhaps as much, grandmamma, as you loved Cousin Louis."

"Say you so? Then it were enough to carry its light through life and throw it far across the dark shadows of death, my child! And you," she said, turning suddenly and severely to young Ben. "Is it for life, or for a holiday, a pleasuring, a pastime?"

He looked at her as if, in spite of the claims of parentage and her all but century of reign, he examined her right to ask. "Since Barbara promised me," said he at last, "I have felt, Old Madame, like one inside a church."

"Something in him," said Elizabeth. "Not altogether the sweetness of the senses, but rather the sacredness of the sacrament."

And although they were not married for twice a twelvemonth, Elizabeth considered that she had married them that morning. And the reddest bonnet-rouge among the fishermen had a thrill as if all thrones were levelled when, at old Ben Benvoisie's funeral,—in the simple procession where none rode,—after young Ben and Barbara, they saw Hope and Old Madame walk, as became the next of kin.

And so one year and another crept into the past. And at length Old Madame fell ill.

"I am going now, Hope," she said. "I should like to see Barbara's baby before I go. But remember that there is money for my burial in the little coffer. And there is still the Dernier's wood-land to sell—"

"Do not think of such things now," said Hope. "God will take care of us in some way. He always has. We are as much a part of the universe as the rest of it."

"We are put in this world to think of such things," said Elizabeth. "We are put in this world to live in it, not to live in another. Now I am going to another. We shall see what that will be. From this I have had all it had to give. I came into it with the reverence and revenue of princes. I go out of it a beggar," she cried, in a tone that tore Hope's heart. "I came into it in purple—I go out of it in rags—"

Rags. Before they laid her away with those who had made part of her career of splendor and of sorrow, they opened the little hair-coffer,— moths had eaten the grave-clothes and a mouse had made its nest in the bank-notes. And to-day nothing is left of Chaslesmarie or Champernoune—not even a name and hardly a memory. And the blood ennobled by the King of France is the common blood of the fishers of the island given once with all its serfs and vassals—the island-fishers who sell you a string of herring for a shilling.

THE GODMOTHERS

THEY were all bidden to the christening, all the godmothers—if by good hap none had been forgotten.

And of course, they came. The christening of a L'Aiglenoir Franche du Roy [1] was no mean occasion, under the circumstances, but one to which the family must do honor, if they hastened from the ends of the earth—and beyond.

They did not arrive with the stir befitting L'Aiglenoir Franche du Roys. But that might be because of the inborn gentilesse which taught them the proprieties of the sick-room. The young mother, as she lay in the dim vast chamber of the old castle, hearing the cry of the wind over the cold Atlantic, saw them come in singly, and in groups, and at intervals. Very faint and weak, and with some awe in her soul before the new being she had evoked, perhaps she dropped asleep in the space of time between their coming; for when she opened her startled eyes another was appearing.

At first Rosomond did not comprehend it. She felt annoyed at the intrusion. She turned her eyes to the place where the bassinet swung under its laces, the pair of candles in the wall-sconce behind it making that the sole spot of light in the long room full of shadows, where lay the little morsel of life for which she had so nearly surrendered her own, and toward which her heart swelled with a sense of infinite dearness. "Do not, do not touch him!" she murmured apprehensively to the woman bending there with her purples sweeping about her, and the glitter of her diamonds like daggerpoints.

And then the plumed and coroneted woman had disappeared behind a curtain into the recesses of the deep casements perhaps; and the young countess closed her eyes forgetfully.

"Yes," she was saying to herself, when with a little flutter her lids opened again, some time afterwards, "that is the old countess who brought the Franche du Roy lands to the L'Aiglenoirs. It is her portrait that hangs high next the oriel in the sea-gallery. I could never satisfy myself, as I walked there in the late afternoons, if it were a shadow of the carved ceiling on her forehead, or a stain that had come out. The stain is there now. She was a king's favorite.

"Do not touch my little innocent child!" she cried suddenly, rising on one arm. Did her senses deceive her? Did she hear the woman answer, "But it is my child, too!"

And a shudder seized her as suddenly—that woman's blood ran in her child's veins! Ah, if she knew just where, she would let it out this minute! And then she fell back laughing at herself.

There were others in the room when her gaze again wandered down its length. Oh, yes, she had seen them all before. Had they stepped from their frames in the long sea-gallery?

The beautiful young being in the white brocade sown with violets, the band of brilliants in her red-gold hair, mother of the count's father, she who later had rivaled Eugénie in Eugénie's court,—Eugénie, who had the resources of an empire,—and the L'Aiglenoirs had nothing,—yet, ah, no, it was empty sound, the scandal that those resplendent toilets were a part of the bribes of senators! She who was a Bourbon D'Archambeau! Nor would Rosomond believe the rumor concerning moneys obtained by the dexterous writing of great officials' names, forgery, counterfeit, what you will, by that other laughing lovely thing, a wife out of the convent, a mother at sixteen, the last countess, launched upon life without a scruple or a sou, who loved pleasure so passionately that she came to live at last upon chloral and opium, and died dancing.

She had often silently made friends with these captivating young women, when unable to go out, and during her lonely pacing up and down the length of the sea-gallery, with the low roar of the surge in her ears, while her husband, who had brought her down here with a loving fancy that his child might be born in the ancestral stronghold which some of her own millions were restoring to its ancient grandeur, was away on the water, or in the hunt, or perhaps at the races.

She would not think ill of them now; they alone of all the women on the wall had not seemed to think ill of her, to look at her as a parvenu and an interloper, had seemed to have about them something of the spirit of the century, to have breathed air she breathed herself.

It was natural that the last countess, the pretty piquant creature, should have loved splendid gowns, kept in homespun all the earlier days by her father's mother, the old marchioness, the miser whose hands grew yellow counting her gold. Tante Alixe had told Rosomond of it. There she was now, the old marchioness, gasping for more air, but just as she was painted in her dusky robes, with the long ivory hands like the talons of a bird of prey,—the talons of a L'Aiglenoir,—mumbling of the revenue she had wrung from her peasants who starved on black bread to buy of her the privilege of living.

Perhaps it was thought she had that privilege too long herself. She had died suddenly—very suddenly. Her son, the marquis, was a partisan and a man of power; a great deal of gold was needed in the intrigues concerning the two kings.

And here was another who had died suddenly—but in the open air. There was a red line round her slender throat, too dull for the ruby necklace she wore in the portrait in the panel—the tall, fair aristocrat whose long white throat, alas! had felt the swift kiss of the guillotine's blade. There was not the look of hate and horror in the portrait that was on her face now; only the languor of many pleasures there, the proud and insolent indifference to the pain, the want, the suffering, from which those pleasures had been pressed like wine that left the must.

"The canaille," she seemed to say, "they die? So much the less vermin. They suffer? And what of it?"

Her husband had told Rosomond when he first led her down the long sea-gallery, the story of this proud lady who thought the world made only for her class. It had passed the idle hour; Rosomond had not thought of it again. He had told her all the stories,—that of the strangely wrinkled old baroness, with her eyes like sparks of fire in the midst of ashes, once herself blooming and fair to see, who had kept the keys of the king's hunting lodge and provided for his pleasures there. "Well, yes," the young count had said, "but what will you have? She was no worse than her time. They were infamous times." He had told her of that blue-eyed waxen woman painted in the Sir Peter Lely, a beauty who had followed the fortunes of Charles Stuart into France, very like, but who had come into the L'Aiglenoir family later by the church door; of the Vandyke, the blonde devotee, who went over with la reine Henriette, and came to a madhouse at last; of the Antonio Moro, vanishing in her golden-brown shadows, an attendant of the English Mary, a confidante of Philip of Spain, who had read her missal at an auto da fe; of the Rubens, the half-clad woman like an overblown rose, a great red rose with the sun on its velvet and dewy petals,—if face and frame spoke for her a woman who was only an embodied sin; of the Holbein, a creature whose appetites had devoured her and left themselves only on the canvas; of the possible Titian. "See the gold of her hair," said the count. "It was dyed. But all the same, Titian—it must have been Titian—knew how to hide the sun in every strand. What a luster of skin! What a bloom on the cheek—it never blushed with shame. What a luscious lip—it knew forbidden kisses, it denounced a brother to the Ten. What a glory in the eye—yet if all traditions are true that eye saw a lover disappear as the gondola touched the deep water that tells no tales. See the hand, what contour, what fineness, what delicacy—and the life in it! But it knew how to play with a poniard whose tip was touched with poison. She did her little best to betray Venice for a price, and she had to leave with the French army, of course." [2]

"I should think you would be glad it is all only tradition," Rosomond had said.

"I don't know. You see the king gave her a duchy, and she brought it into the family. The title lapsed, to be sure, and the revenues went long ago in gaming debts. Do you note that damsel in the white satin,—the Geraart Terburg,—her face is like a live pearl. Well, she was the stake once in some high play."

"That would have been dreadful if it were true."

"As you please," said the count with a shrug.

"And were there no good women, no honorable men?"

"Oh, but plenty! But, ma chérie, happiness has no history, virtue has few adventures. Their portraits fade out on the wall as they themselves do in the line. It is the big wills, the big passions, that are memorable, that drown out those others, the weak, that have made the L'Aiglenoirs what they are. Those imbeciles, they are like René's father the day of his burial, 'comme s'il n'avait jamais été.'"[3] And he went on with his narrative.

"But it is a gallery! If we had it at home and—pardon—reckoned its commercial value—"

"Alas! The pictures are no more certified than the traditions! And then one does not willingly part with one's people. Yet—if that were indeed a Titian—"

"You would not have gone over to America to marry me."

"I should not perhaps have gone over to America to marry the heiress of the new world, repeating the adventures of the knights of long ago, but in modern dress. I should have had no need. But I would have married you, Rosomond, had I met you on the dark side of the moon, or else have flung myself headlong into space!"

"You forget the attraction of gravitation."

"Your attraction is the greater."

"Now I do not believe you. The language of hyperbole is not the language of truth."

"Pleasantry aside, you must always believe I speak truth, my wife, when I say that whatever led me in the beginning, it is love that overcame me in the end. I could not perhaps have married,—I who love pleasure, too,—if you had not been the daughter of Dives. For we were beggared, we poor L'Aiglenoir Franche du Roys. But the thing being made possible, I simply entered heaven, Rosomond!"

"And I," said Rosomond, as she stood in the deep window-place, looking up at him a moment, and back again swiftly to the sea.

"And if it were a title against a fortune, as Newport said, and as the Faubourg held a matter of course, although heaven knows a title means nothing now and will not till the king—the good God have his majesty in keeping! is at home again—"

"Oh, let us forget all that, fortune or title!" Rosomond had said.

"No, no. For if the fortune arrive to repair the fortunes of the house of L'Aiglenoir, why not? It is your house, Rosomond. It is the house of your child. And we will make a new house of it. The L'Aiglenoir of the twentieth century shall again be the prime minister of the King of France. The new blood, the new gold, shall make new fortunes, shall bring back the old force, and will, and power, and we will leave these dusty memories behind and ask no one of them to the christening!"

"Perhaps so," Rosomond had said, half under her breath. "But you have been a self-indulgent, pleasure-loving people," she added presently. "And with rank, and wealth, with opportunity—it does not tend to bring back the old brute strength."

"Well, then," the count lightly answered her, "let us take some of the pleasure! See, how purple is the water beyond the white lip of the reefs. We will go try the outer sea, and drift an hour or two in the soft wind. And I will tell you how beautiful you are, ma belle Américaine, and you shall tell me what a sailor I am. It is not the sailing of the old sea-robber who came down here to assault the castle in the days of that grandmother of mine twenty times removed, in the days of La Dame Blanche, to take her with her belongings and marry her by storm—but it is pleasanter, my sweet."

*   *   *

That had been in the bright spring months. Now autumn winds swept the Atlantic and cried in the tops of the ragged pines below the castle's cliff. Many a day had Rosomond sat there, listening for the sea-measures, and fancying the beat of the surf was the washing of the wave under the keel that carried Tristan and Isolde a thousand years ago and more on the waters just beyond, heard the very music of Isolde's wild lament, watched for the white sail across the reef as if the sick knight lay in the courtyard within under the linden-tree, in all the pathos of song, and beauty, and tragic fate, felt herself taken into a world of romance where the murmuring of the breeze in the bough was the murmur of the skirts of the great forest of Broceliande.

But this had nothing to do with romance now. She lay in bed, with her little child near at hand, the attendants just without, in the tower-chamber where for generations the L'Aiglenoirs had been born.

Through the deep windows she saw the swift flying moon touch the clouds sweeping in the wind, and light the swale on the dark and lifted sea beyond, look in and now and again silver the faces of the paladins and maidens in the pale blue-green forest of the old tapestry that slightly rippled, and rose, and fell, as if with a consciousness of the windy gust that sung outside the tower. It was that old paladin with the truncheon, a paladin of Charlemagne's, from whom the Franche du Roys counted. It was the chatelaine with the flagon that gave him his quietus.

What did it all mean, though, at this moment? With the heavy swaying of the tapestry had these people by any chance left their silken shroud and come out into the room to look at the child?

Not the twelve white-faced nuns; not the featureless young squires and dames; but that old chatelaine of whose needle-wrought semblance she had always been half afraid, who carried the golden flagon and gave the knight to drink, perhaps for sleep, perhaps for death. Yes, that was she; but she had left her majesty in the hangings with her veil and horned head-piece, her trailing samite and cloth of gold of cramoisie. Here, with her thin, gray, tattered locks, pallid, pinched, and shrunken, white as some reptile blanched beneath a stone, what was she to be afraid of now? But this other— "Once the place was mine, mine and my love's!" she was exclaiming. "Till the sea darkened with their gilded prows, the sky darkened with their bitter arrows!" Ah, yes, how many hundreds of years ago it was since she defended the castle after a lance-head laid her lord low; and the sea-rover had scaled the heights and taken her, loathing and hating him, to wife. And from them had been born the line of the L'Aiglenoirs!

And what was she doing here? What were they all doing here, these women? What right had they in her room? Why were they looking with such ardent and eager eyes, murmuring among themselves, hurrying past one another toward the child?

"Give way!" was La Dame Blanche exclaiming. "I was the first."

"Après moi," said the laughing lady, flittering along in her butterfly gauzes, the diamonds in her tiara flashing out and reluming again. "I am the last."

"If so false a thing ever existed at all," said the woman with the mass-book,—or was it a book of jests,—the Flemish woman who sold her daughter for a tulip.

"I give you my word I existed!" was the gay reply.

"Under your own signature?" asked the pretty patched and powdered Watteau.

"Never mind whose signature."

"Worthless," murmured a lady lifting her black lace mask from features sharp as a death's head, and of a tint as wan as the tints of a Boucher design, "worthless in any event."

"Ah, madame, from you to me? I was but your natural consequence, you Voltairiennes, as you were all born on the night of St. Bartholomew!"

"Its tocsin still rings in the air! I am condemned ever to hear the boom of the bell," complained the dark person with the rosary.

And then the laughing lady twitched her beads, and there fell out from her sleeve the perfumed fan whose breath was fever, the gloves whose palms were deadly, brought with her Medicean mistress from Italy.

"A truce!" cried the gay lady. "The birth of an heir to the L'Aiglenoir Franche du Roys, with wealth to restore the ancient splendor, is an event for due ceremony and precedence. I am the child's grandmother, his very next of kin among us. And you know the rights of the grandmother in France."

"They are our rights!" came a shrill multitudinous murmur. "We all are grandmothers!"

"Are we all here?" came a hollow whisper from the chatelaine, the candlelight flickering in her flagon.

"All the fairy godmothers?" cried the gay lady.

"No, no," said La Dame Blanche, "there is one who has been forgotten."

"The wicked fairy," said the gay lady. "The rest of us are of such a virtue. He will value us like his other objets de vertu."

*   *   *

A cold shiver coursed over Rosomond, but her eyes burned with the intensity of her gaze. She understood it now. He was the child of their blood. That was why they were here, why they intruded themselves into her room. They had a right. It had been their own room. For how many generations had the L'Aiglenoirs been born in this room! She had never thought of this when she sailed so gaily out of harbor, a bride with her bridegroom, wearing his title, protected by his arm, so proud, so glad, so happy that she had the wealth he needed—all that so trifling beside the fact that they loved each other. She had never dreamed of the little child to come, who would be dearer than her life to her, and in whose veins must run a black drop of the blood of all these creatures.

And now— Oh, was there no remedy? Was there nothing to counteract it, nothing to dissipate that black drop, to make it colorless, powerless, harmless, a thing of air? Were there no sweet, good people among all those dead and gone women?

Ah, yes, indeed, there they were! Far off, by the curtain of the doorway, huddled together like a flock of frightened doves—gentle ladies, quiet, timid, humble before heaven, ladies of placid lives, no opportunities, small emotions, narrow routine, praying by form, acting by precedent, without individuality, whose goodness was negative, whose doings were paltry, their poor drab beings swamped, and drowned, and extinguished in the purples and scarlets of these women of great passions, of scope, of daring and deed and electric force, mates of men of force, whose position had called crime to its aid, whose very crimes had enlarged them, whose sins were things of power, strengthening their personality if but for evil, transmitting their potentiality—oh, no, these gentle ladies signified nothing here!

A cold dew bathed Rosomond and beaded her brow. But were the L'Aiglenoirs and their order all there were? Where were her own people? Had they no right in the child? Could they not cross the seas? Was there no requiting strength among them? None in the mother of her father, king of railroads, and mines, and vast southwestern territory, that stern, repressed woman who had spared, and starved, and saved to start her son in life? "Come!" cried Rosomond. "Come, my own people! Oh, I need you now, I and my child!"

But among all these splendid dames of quality, accustomed to wide outlook on the world, and a part of the events of nations, what had these village people to do,—these with their petty concerns, the hatching of chickens, the counting of eggs, the quilting of stitches; these perhaps more prosperous, with interests never going outside the burgh, whose virtues were passive, whose highest dream was of a heaven like their own parlors, a God in their own image, whose lives were eventless, whose memories were pallid, laid aside in the sweep of the great drama and without a part, whose slighter nature was swollen, and whose larger nature was shriveled from disuse? This colonial dame, her father the distilled essence of old Madeira and oily Jamaica, her heart in her lace, her china, and her sweetmeat closet, her scrofulous and scorbutic son lixiviated by indulgence—had she much counteracting force to give? Or had this one, in whom quarreled forever the mingled blood of persecuted Quaker and persecuting Puritan? Or this pale wife of the settler, haunted by fear of the Indian, the apparitions of the forest, and the terrors of her faith; or this other, the red-cloaked matron, fighting fire with fire, the familiar of witches? Was there help to be hoped for from this bland Pilgrim woman who, through force of circumstances, was married with her nursling in her arms while her husband was but three months dead? And did this downcast-eyed, white-kerchiefed mistress whose steadfastness her hardness countervailed, daughter of the Mayflower—the new sea-rover coming out of the East, whose Norse fathers had come out of the East before—do more than carry her back to the old Danes and Vikings ambushed in their creeks? Her people, indeed! Returning on the source—Oh, it was all one and the same! It was all misery!

What gifts were these grandmothers going to give the child then? she asked. Pride and lust and cruelty, mocking impiety and falsehood, bigotry that belied heaven as bitterly as unbelief, vanity and selfishness and hate, theft and avarice and murder? In the wild and wicked current of their blood the tide was hopelessly against him—his bones would be poured out like water! Her pulse bounded, her brain was on fire—Oh, no, no, the little child—the new-born—some one must come—some one must help—some one!

Some one was coming. There was a stir without; the wind was singing round the buttress as if it brought on its wings the cry of the bright sea, the murmur of the wide wood; the moonlight streamed in full and free.

"It is she," said La Dame Blanche.

"The wicked fairy—the unbidden godmother," said the gay lady with a warning gesture.

"The one whom civilization has forgotten," said the Voltairienne, readjusting her mask, "and whom culture has ignored."

How sweet were the thunders of the sea sifted through distance, the whispers of the wave creaming up the shingle, that crept into the room like the supporting harmony of the wind's song! There was a rustle as if of all the leaves of the forest, a quiver of reeds over blue water reflecting blue heaven, a sighing of long grass above the nests of wild bees in the sunshine. And who was this swift and supple creature with her free and fearless foot, large-limbed and lofty as Thusnelda, clad in her white wolfskin, with the cloud of her yellow hair fallen about her, carrying her green bough, strong, calm, sure, but with no smile upon her radiant face?

"The original savage," whispered the gay lady, as sovereign and serene the unbidden godmother moved up the room, and the others seemed to dissolve before her coming—to waver away and to vanish.

She parted the hangings of the bassinet, and rested her hand upon the sleeper of his first sleep, bending and gazing long.

"Waken," she said then, as she lifted and laid him at her breast. "Drink of thy first mother's life, a balsam for every ill, mother's milk that shall unpoison thy blood, and bring the thick, black drops to naught. Child of the weather and all out-doors, latest child of mine, draw from me will, and might, and the love of the undefiled, acquaintance with the rune that shall destroy the venom that taints you, shall blast the wrong done you! Draw large, free draughts! Return to me, thou man-child! I give thee the strength of my forest, my rivers, my sea, my sunshine, my starshine, my own right arm, my heart! I cleanse thee. The slime of the long years shall not cling to thee. I start thee afresh, newborn. By night in my star-hung tent the gods shall visit thee, by day thou shalt walk in the way of becoming a god thyself. I give thee scorn for the ignoble, trust in thy fellow, dependence on thine own lusty sinew and unconquerable will,—familiar friend of hardship and content, spare, and pure, and strong,—joy in the earth, the sun, the wind, faith in the unseen. This is thy birthright. Whatever else the years may bring, see that thou do it no wrong. I, the unpolluted, strong wild strain in thy blood, the vital savage, save thee from thyself. Sleep, now, sweet hope. The winds sing to thee, the waves lull thee, the stars affright thee not! Dear son of thy mother, sleep!"

And then a shiver ran through the long, moon-lighted tapestry, as the gust rose and fell, and the sea sighed up the reef, and there was only silence and slumber in the room.

But Rosomond's women, when they came again, wondered and were wise concerning a green bough that lay across the child.

EXPLANATORY NOTES

IN A CELLAR

1. *spirituelle:* witty and clever.
2. Fourier's fables refer to the writings of Charles Fourier (1772–1837), an early French socialist who developed an elaborate theory of a natural social order and advocated the formation of cooperative societies. Fourier's ideas were well known in the United States, where they influenced several experiments in social reform, most notably Brook Farm.
3. *point d'appui:* literally, basis or point of support; here a prop or fulcrum.
4. Gironde: a *département* in southwestern France known for its vineyards.
5. The phrase "in the city" probably refers to the Île de la Cité in Paris.
6. *marchand des armures:* armor merchant.
7. *flèche:* arrow.
8. *en gros:* wholesale.
9. *coûteau-de-chasse:* hunting knife.
10. crime of *lèse-majesté:* act of treason.
11. *Reine du Ciel:* an oath meaning Queen of Heaven and referring to the Virgin Mary.
12. shagreen: made of an untanned leather and dyed green.
13. Both Jacobins and Marianne refer to political extremists willing to use terrorism in the cause of egalitarian democracy. The Jacobins were among the most violent left-wing factions during the French Revolution. Marianne is the personification of the French republic; Spofford is referring to secret French societies known as the Mary Anne associations.

14. *Des babioles:* baubles or trinkets.

15. Benvenuto Cellini (1500–71) was a Florentine sculptor and goldsmith whose most famous work was a gold salt cellar made for Francis I of France.

16. *À gauche,—quelquefois c'est justement à droite:* literally, to the left—sometimes it is exactly to the right. In discussing whether to toss the spilled salt over the right or left shoulder, the narrator and the Baron are playing on the double meanings of *gauche* (left or clumsy) and *droite* (right or virtuous).

17. *boule blanche:* white ball used in balloting. A white ball is a vote in favor; a black ball is a vote against.

THE AMBER GODS

1. I wouldn't give a *fico:* literally, I wouldn't give a fig; *fico,* from the Italian, sometimes refers to an obscene gesture of contempt.

2. From the seventh stanza of "The Witch of Atlas" (1820) by Percy Bysshe Shelley, one of Spofford's favorite poems. Like Yone, Shelley's witch is a beautiful creature with no sympathy for the problems of others.

3. "An Elegie, or Friends Passion, For His Astrophill" (ll. 103—105) by Matthew Roydon (fl. 1580–1622), one of the poems commemorating Sir Philip Sidney included in the "Astrophel" section of Edmund Spenser's *Colin Clouts Come Home Again* (1595).

4. A novel in German by Wilhelm Meinhold, *The Amber Witch* achieved widespread popularity in the English translation (1844) of Lady Lucy Duff Gordon. It is available in the Dover Press collection, *Five Victorian Ghost Novels,* edited by E. F. Bleiler, who regards it as the best nineteenth-century novel about witchcraft.

5. The poetry in this scene is from Robert Browning's "Pippa Passes" (1841) and functions on several complex levels. The poem is about a girl who spends one day passing by the four people she considers the happiest in her town. As she passes, she sings a song that, unknown to her, has an important redemptive effect on their lives. This complex poem suggests both that art can be redemptive and that the artist can be unaware of the real effect of his work. The lines quoted are drawn from the second section of the poem, "Noon," in which Jules, a sculptor, has been tricked into marrying Phene, a woman of the lowest class. At first, he plans to give her money and separate from her, but Pippa's song convinces him that Phene has a moral sense that he can awaken and cultivate. The allusions thus ironically extend Spofford's treatment of art, morality, and sexuality.

Explanatory Notes

Spofford often enjoyed telling the story of Robert Browning's discovery of these lines in her work. She wrote to Pattee: "The story was printed in the first number of the Atlantic after its purchase by Messrs. Ticknor and Fields, and the magazine was sent to Mr. Fields in Florence. He lent it to Robert Browning, who was enthusiastic in praise of the story. When the next number came, (the story had been divided into two parts) that also was lent to Mr. Browning. The next morning, before breakfast, he came running to Mr. Fields, crying 'Oh, Fields, Fields, I hope you didn't think I knew what was coming when I praised this story!' What was coming was the quotation of passages from his own work" (unpublished letter, 11 Nov. 1914, Penn State).

6. The significance of the peculiar Latin phrase, *Astra Castra, Numen Lumen,* remains puzzling. Barton Levi St. Armand translates it as "cut star, numinous light," but it could also be translated as "the star is cut, the power is the light." It appears to be a medieval motto that points to some kind of fading or blocked light. The lines may have had a clearer meaning to nineteenth-century readers. Higginson, who was an important mentor to both Spofford and Dickinson, used "Astra Castra" as the title of Dickinson's "Departed-to the Judgment" and "Numen Lumen" as the title of her "I live with Him—I see His face—" (St. Armand, *Haunted Dusk* 118).

CIRCUMSTANCE

1. Lady Margaret is the heroine of "Lay of the Last Minstrel" (1805) by Sir Walter Scott.

2. Spofford's extensive use of old Methodist hymns and Biblical references in this story implies an affirmation of Christian principles which is not characteristic of her other major works at this time. Although she knew the Bible extremely well, the limited biographical information we possess suggests that she was not a particularly devout or fervent Christian during this part of her life.

3. Spofford's final line alludes to the departure of Adam and Eve from Eden at the end of Milton's *Paradise Lost:*

> They looking back, all th'Eastern side beheld
> Of Paradise, so late their happy seat,
> Wav'd over by that Flaming Brand, the Gate
> With Dreadful Faces throng'd and fierie Arms:
> Some natural tears they drop'd, but wip'd them soon;

Explanatory Notes

The World was all before them, where to choose
Their place of rest, and Providence their guide:
They hand in hand with wandering steps and slow,
Through Eden took their solitary way.

IN THE MAGUERRIWOCK

1. The Maguerriwock district is located near Calais, Maine, where Spofford was born and spent her childhood. The mountain referred to in the story is now called Magurrewock Mountain.

THE MOONSTONE MASS

1. The imagery and ideas of the story draw from several famous Romantic poems, most notably S. T. Coleridge's "Rime of the Ancient Mariner" (1798) and "Kubla Khan" (1816). The name of the ship, the *Albatross,* alludes to the bird shot in the "Ancient Mariner" and the curse that results from this act.

2. Linnaea: a slender flowering evergreen plant.

3. When the Israelites first came to Canaan, they are intimidated by the Anakim, the sons of Anak, who are referred to in the Old Testament as giants or "men of great stature": "And there we saw the giants, the sons of Anak, which come of the giants: and we were in our own sight as grasshoppers, and so we were in their sight (Num. 13:33).

4. Jemschid (usually spelled Jamshid) is an important figure in Persian mythology. During the first three hundred years of his seven-hundred-year reign, Jamshid was a happy and beneficent ruler whose achievements included the invention of weaving, iron-smelting, navigation, and medicine as well as the discovery of precious gems and minerals. Jamshid was eventually punished and killed after he became overly proud and boastful.

5. According to legend, when forced by the Inquisition to publicly recant his assertion that the earth moved around the sun, Galileo reluctantly agreed, but whispered softly "*Eppur si muove*" ("And yet it moves").

Explanatory Notes

THE BLACK BESS

1. St. Elmo's fire: a flame-shaped electrical discharge that sometimes appeared on the masts and riggings of ships on stormy nights.

HER STORY

1. St Cecilia is the patron saint of musicians. According to legend, she once charmed an angel with her music. Moreover, she is sometimes called the inventor of the organ.

2. The instrument being tuned and played is a violin made by the Amati family, seventeenth-century Cremona violin makers. One member of the family trained Stradivari.

3. Bayadere: a dancing girl dressed in eastern costume. The *bajaderes* of India danced before images of the gods.

4. Antinous, page of the Roman emperor Hadrian, is a model of masculine beauty.

MISS SUSAN'S LOVE AFFAIR

1. *espièglerie:* mischievousness or roguishness.

OLD MADAME

1. Spofford took many liberties with historical fact, but the story was inspired by her knowledge of the family of Captain Francis Champernowne (1614–87). Spofford's primary source of information was probably Charles Wesley Tuttle, her husband's law partner, who wrote a historial essay about Champernowne (Halbeisen 128).

Explanatory Notes

THE GODMOTHERS

1. The name may be significant. "L'Aiglenoir" means the black eagle; "Franche," frank, candid, natural; "du Roy," of the king.

2. The painters mentioned were all famous for their portraits: Sir Peter Lely (Dutch, 1618–80), Sir Anthony Vandyke (Flemish, 1599–1641), Antonio Moro (Dutch, 1525?–75), Peter Paul Rubens (Flemish, 1577–1640), Hans Holbein (German, 1497?–1543), Titian (Italian, 1477–1576); Geraart Terburg (usually spelled Gerard Terborch) could refer to either the father (Dutch, 1584–1662) or son (Dutch, 1617–81).

3. *comme s'il n'avait jamais été:* as if he had never existed.